"We were at the top of a mountain in north Georgia just after daylight and a long night patrol and raid. Here we were with a group of young Rangers conducting an after action review, all listening intensely to our Ranger mentor. No, it was not Ranger School but it could have been. It was a group of young Ranger Captains from the 75th Ranger Regiment who were participating in the Regiment's 'Mongaday' exercise and our Honorary Colonel of the Regiment, COL (Ret.) Ralph Puckett, was sharing his observations from the patrol. This was not unusual as he routinely participated on these and many other exercises and live-fire training events. His remarks always came at the end of our After Action Reviews and were always the most useful to every Ranger present. I heard more times than I can remember, 'he should write a book.'

Words for Warriors is a must read for every leader from platoon level to General Officer. A legend among Infantrymen and Rangers, COL (Ret.) Ralph Puckett elegantly shares lessons and wisdom from 56 years of leading, teaching, training, and mentoring Warriors in combat and peace from his experiences in such diverse environments as Korea, Colombia, Vietnam, Puerto Rico, Panama, and Europe. Throughout his Army career and years as the Honorary Colonel of the 75th Ranger Regiment, COL (Ret.) Puckett selflessly gave his time and dedicated himself to preparing Warriors, their families, and units for combat. Thanks to this book, generations of Soldiers will benefit from one of our Army's most respected Warriors."

—Purl K. Keen, Brigadier General, U.S. Army

"I have had the privilege of reading Ralph Puckett's *Words for Warriors*. It is an extraordinary book written by an extraordinary man. It is a compilation of essays and think pieces written over a period of time by Colonel Puckett. They focus on the essentials of the trade of the warrior in a way unlike the field manual or the 'I was there' books available today. If Gaius Hardnosius, Centurion of the IX 'Spanish' Legion in Britain in the time of Boadiccea, could read this book he would recognize the ideas and suggestions as a most valuable tool in the management of his Century. That is just the point. The problems faced by today's combat leaders are little different from those faced by the Roman Legions. The technology has changed, but the hearts and minds of Soldiers are little different today than they have been since time immemorial. Puckett focuses on the care and training of Soldiers to bring them to the highest state of mastery of the profession of arms. He looks at the Soldier's needs and motivations in a variety of situations. He calls on his own extensive combat experience and his experience as a teacher of men to provide boiled down wisdom that leaders can use. It would be fair to say that a great deal of it will not be the thunderclap of revealed wisdom to a student of leadership. It would also be fair to say that the information here presented has seldom been put together in such a practical form and expressed so well by a man who is a superb combat Soldier rather than a school room thinker. Every combat officer and non-commissioned officer should read this book."

—Donald C. Bowman, Lieutenant Colonel, U.S. Army Retired

"Ralph Puckett is the Ranger's Ranger, toughminded, intense, Spartan, always right on point. He delivers his views the same way he would fire a rifle.

Puckett's lifelong love is Soldiering and the Soldier, and especially the Infantryman. For him the epitome is the Ranger.

Like so many, I'm proud to say I served under Ralph Puckett—and there I learned what discipline really is, what most Soldiers and Soldiering really are. It's all in this book.

Puckett knows firsthand that war is hell, and his thoughts are always of the Soldier who faces that inferno. The covers of this book could be made of steel, but when you open them, you find the story of deep respect and affection for the Soldier and a gripping personal commentary on battle.

The aim of the book is the motivation and celebration of the warrior spirit that sustains the fighter in battle. In this regard,

Puckett has the authority of a Soldier wounded five times in two wars.

Puckett has a strong conviction that backs up everything he says. In this book of words, there is no mincing. Not for Ralph Puckett."

—John R. Galvin, General, U.S. Army Retired

"*Words for Warriors*, mentoring at its best, is Ralph Puckett's 'After Action Review' of over sixty years of practicing, observing, inquiring, thinking and always learning about leading America's great Soldiers. No theoretical 'construct' or 'paradigm' here, just lots of experience based, insightful and, most of all, pragmatic ideas. Use them as catalysts for your own or your subordinates' leadership skill and style development."

—Ronald G. Odom, Colonel, U.S. Army Retired

"Ralph Puckett is a Warrior and Ranger legend. This book captures the essence of the tools all combat leaders need on today's battlefield to fight, win and bring their Soldiers home alive. *Words for Warriors* provides the military leader a ready-made professional notebook that should be reviewed quarterly so we do not forget why we serve and how we should serve. Why learn the hard way? Ralph Puckett provides invaluable insights for all combat leaders on Soldiering."

—Clarence K. K. Chinn, Colonel, U.S. Army Retired

"Throughout history it has been the warrior at the critical place and time that has made the difference between success and failure, between victory and defeat, between freedom and servility. Those of us that have had the privilege to observe warriors always wonder how those wonderful humans are created. The qualities of a warrior are always the same, be it Horatius at the bridge, Cortez confronting an empire, a teenager charging with Pickett at Gettysburg, an official pressing the harder right even when it is a career ender, or a Ranger running to the side of a fallen brother. Ralph Puckett has repeatedly demonstrated those qualities and now in *Words for Warriors* he clearly describes them for us. It is not the art of grand strategy that Sun Tzu gave us, but it is the art of making a difference."

—Dr. Sam Holliday, Director Armiger Cromwell Center

"It would be folly not to read this book. COL Puckett is one of the most highly regarded Soldiers and leader of Soldiers in our time. His example and experiences have molded many excellent combat leaders and will do the same for you. Any Soldier will become a better warrior by reading and listening to *Words for Warriors*."

—A current Special Forces Detachment Commander who asked to remain anonymous for Operational Security

"Colonel Puckett's *Words for Warriors* is a timely and informative book. He continues to mentor us in all aspects of the profession of arms. His service from Korea, to Vietnam to visiting with Rangers in Afghanistan and Iraq (in his late 70's when most men of his age are on the golf course or in a retirement home) testifies to his caring nature and prowess as a Warrior. Leaders would do well to heed his sage advice as it comes from years of experience, study and thought. Here is advice from an experienced Warrior with decades on the battlefield as opposed to the advice we usually get from an experienced academic with years of schooling working in a think tank."

—Greg Birch, Command Sergeant Major, U.S. Army

"With an insight as sharp and pointed as the tip of a bayonet, Colonel Ralph Puckett's *Words for Warriors* is a compilation of combat and leadership experience from one of the U.S. Army's most decorated and venerable Soldiers. Whether Infantryman, engineer, clerk or cook, each and every American Soldier is first and foremost a warrior. As such, this work should be required reading for all who aspire to be true members of the Profession of Arms."

—JD Lock, Lieutenant Colonel, U.S. Army Retired
Author of *The Coveted Black and Gold* and *Rangers in Combat*

PRAISE FOR *WORDS FOR WARRIORS*

"*Words for Warriors* is truly a one of a kind resource with tremendous application for leaders of all ranks. Colonel Puckett's common sense approach and professional insights make this a reference you absolutely want on your book shelf so you can refer to it often."

—William J. Leszczynski, Jr., Brigadier General,
U.S. Army Retired

"In *Words for Warriors* COL Ralph Puckett draws from almost sixty years of personal experience and observation to capture the essence of what it takes to prepare and lead Soldiers in combat. Absolute must read for leaders preparing to deploy to combat on your first or fourth rotation and for anyone else that wants a glimpse into the art of combat leadership."

—James "Craig" Nixon, Brigadier General, U.S. Army

WORDS FOR WARRIORS

A Professional Soldier's Notebook

COLONEL RALPH PUCKETT

U.S. Army Retired

Words for Warriors: A Professional Soldier's Notebook

Copyright © 2007 Ralph Puckett. All rights reserved. No part of this book may be reproduced or retransmitted in any form or by any means without the written permission of the publisher.

Published by Wheatmark™
610 East Delano Street, Suite 104
Tucson, Arizona 85705 U.S.A.
www.wheatmark.com

Publisher's Cataloging-In-Publication Data
(Prepared by The Donohue Group, Inc.)

Puckett, Ralph.
Words for warriors : a professional soldier's notebook / Ralph Puckett.

p. ; cm.

Includes bibliographical references and index.
ISBN: 978-1-58736-805-9

1. Military art and science--United States--Handbooks, manuals, etc. 2. Command of troops. 3. Leadership. 4. United States--Armed Forces--Officers. 5. United States--Armed Forces--Military life. 6. Soldiers--United States. I. Title.

UB210 .P83 2007
355.3/3041   2007922669

CONTENTS

Disclaimer xiii
Dedication. xv
Acknowledgments xvii
Foreword xxi
Introduction xxiii

Section I: Honorary Colonel of the Regiment
Honorary Colonel of the Regiment 3

Section II: Leadership
Be There 15
Chewing Gum Can Be a Combat Multiplier 21
Commitment to Country 23
Give Credit Where Credit Is Due 26
Delinquent Soldiers Appreciate Being Appreciated 29
Developing Junior Leaders 31
Motivating Soldiers 35
Set the Example: The Most Important Leadership Principle . . 42

Section III: Command and Staff
Murphy's Laws Are Always in Effect 47
Object to the Brink of Insubordination 51
Roles and Missions and How to Train for Them 55
Safety Is No Accident. 59
What Do You Do When You Have More Than You Can Do? . 62
Find a "Golden Voice" for Your Ceremonies 65

What I Want My Chaplain to Be. 67
Commanders and Staff Can Learn from Each Other. 71
Beware of Experts 73
Surround Yourself with Capable Subordinates. 75
Tactical Operations Center 77
Take Your Medicine. 81

Section IV: Warriors

The Warrior Ethos 85
Warriors: Chief Nana 88
Warriors: King Henry V and a Band of Brothers 90
Warriors: The Spartans. 94
Warriors: Task Force Ranger, Mogadishu October 3–4, 1993. .97
Why Men Fight. 100

Section V: Training

Part I: Individual Training

AARs Are a Valuable Teaching Tool 105
Instilling Army Values Can Help Prevent Atrocities 109
Army Values and a Warrior Who Lived Them 117
Basic Training. 125
To Develop Combat-Ready Soldiers You Must Have
    Battle-Focused Training 130
Boots on the Ground: Man Is the Ultimate Weapon 133
Discipline Takes over When Your Body and Mind Tell
    You to Quit. 138
Educate the Military. 140
Calling for and Adjusting Supporting Fires 142
Overcoming the Reluctance to Kill 145

Part II: Unit Training

Casualty Play in FTXs. 149
Chain of Command 152
Chemical Warfare Is a Threat 154
Dade's Monument. 157

Prepare for a Disaster 160
Expect the Unexpected 165
Leave No Man Behind 170
Long Range Surveillance Units 173
Good Marksmanship and Fire Superiority 176
Master the Fundamentals and Win 181
Tough Training Saves Lives 184
Veterans Can Be Great Trainers 188

Section VI: Taking Care of Soldiers

Hurry Up and Wait 193
Lightening a Soldier's Load Is a High and
   Continuing Priority 195
Really Listen to Your Soldiers 197
Make Care of the Feet High Priority 200
Mentoring 202
Misfits May Have a Place 205
Send Your Soldiers to School 208
Thank the Cooks and KPs 210
You Never Know the Impact You Are Having 212

Section VII: Personal Development

Be All You Can Be 217
Become the Leader You Want to Be 220
How Can We Develop Courage? 223
Learn from Your Mistakes and Those of Others 231
You're a Problem if You're Not Physically Fit 234
Reducing Stress 239
Strive for Excellence (Excellence Is Its Own Reward) 244
Your Word Is Your Bond 247

Section VIII: Home Front

Army Wives 253
Educate the Public 257
Developing Better Relations with the Media 260
Honoring Veterans 265

Section IX: Race and Gender

Blood's Common Color 273
Fraternization Hurts Combat Effectiveness 275
Gender Integration of the Army 277

Section X: Tactics and Strategy

Are We Ready? 287
The Clock Is Ticking 292
Our Enemies Are Willing to Accept Tremendous
    Casualties 296
Never Go Administrative. 298
Operations Other Than War 301
Operation Bushmaster 307
Terrorism. 311
Transformation 318
Will We Ever Learn? The Most Important Lesson from
    Vietnam 322
Worth Dying For. 328
You Can't Defend a Position by Sitting on It! 331

Section XI: The Goal

The Greatest Compliment 335

Bibliography 337
Endnotes 349
Index 373

DISCLAIMER

The views expressed in this book are those of the author and do not reflect the official policy or position of the Department of the Army, Department of Defense, or the United States government.

DEDICATION

Words for Warriors: A Professional Soldier's Notebook is dedicated to all those people, both military and civilian, who, by their words and deeds taught me lessons that, although very valuable, are not contained in any military program of instruction.

And to my wife, Jeannie, whose assistance and support made this task possible.

ACKNOWLEDGMENTS

As in every other task that I have accomplished, *Words for Warriors: A Professional Soldier's Notebook*'s completion and success were achieved only because I was helped and encouraged by many individuals. They gave their time, suggestions, and moral support to me when I needed it most—at those times when I began to think that I would never be finished.

Most of all, I appreciate my wife Jeannie's continual urging and encouraging me to "get on with it" as she tried to convince me that the results would be worth the effort.

There are many people who have reviewed and commented on the manuscript in various stages of its being written and rewritten. Many of them have experienced the challenges that I have described in the book and spoke from experience. Lieutenant Colonel John Lock, U.S. Army Retired, a U.S. Army Ranger and published author of several books, was a mentor throughout the lengthy process of writing the manuscript and having it published. He advised me on a format that would bring coherence and readability to the essays. Lieutenant Colonel Don Bowman, U.S. Army Retired, another U.S. Army Ranger and long-term friend, was also very helpful, reading carefully and commenting extensively on two different drafts of the manuscript. I incorporated several of his comments into the essays and they are the better for it.

There are many others who reviewed various drafts and provided helpful suggestions. Among these are Command Sergeant Major Greg Birch, an admired Soldier and former command sergeant major of the 75th Ranger Regiment; Colonel K.K Chinn, former commander of the Ranger Training Brigade; General John G. Galvin, U.S. Army Retired, whom I first met when he and I served together in the 65th Regimental Combat Team in Puerto Rico. He later replaced me as the Advisor to the *Escuela de Lanceros*, the Colombian Army's Ranger School, where he made many improvements of what I had accomplished and moved the *Escuela* on the road to the great institution that it has become. Dr. Sam Holliday, the director of the Armiger Cromwell Center, whose writing and intellect I greatly admire; Dr. Douglas Johnson, a professor at the U.S. Army War College, whom I met when he was a cadet candidate for West Point, and I was the Training Officer at the USMA Preparatory School; Brigadier General Ken Keen, the 11th Colonel of the 75th Ranger Regiment; Brigadier General William J. Leszczynski, Jr., U.S. Army Retired, the 9th Colonel of the 75th Ranger Regiment, who selected me to be the Honorary Colonel of the Regiment for which I will always be grateful; Major General Ken Leuer, U.S. Army Retired, the first commander of the 1st Battalion, 75th Infantry (Ranger) that later grew to be the 75th Ranger Regiment; Lieutenant General Hal Moore, U.S. Army Retired, a great battlefield commander and the co-author with Joe Galloway of *We Were Soldiers Once ... and Young*; Brigadier General Craig Nixon, the 13th Colonel of the 75th Ranger Regiment; Colonel Ronald Odom, U.S. Army Retired, who, as a company commander serving with me in the 2-502nd Regiment (Airborne) in Vietnam, did a magnificent job in the many tight situations that he faced; and a Special Forces Commander, who, for reasons of operational security, asked to remain anonymous. A special thanks to my USMA classmate, Dolphin Overton, a jet ace during the Korean War, who urged me to continue after he had read the first draft.

I am especially grateful to my good friend, Lieutenant General R. L. "Sam" Wetzel, U.S. Army Retired, a plebe in my squad at West Point who has risen far above his squad leader, for his very complimentary Foreword.

I appreciate the assistance that I received from my publisher,

Wheatmark, Inc., and its staff. They were very helpful in assisting me along the way to publication.

I can never thank enough those Soldiers and others who throughout my life have been my mentors, sometimes unbeknownst to them. These "Words" are based in many cases on what they taught me. Just as I benefited from their advice while I was on active duty, I have continued to be helped by their assistance while I labored to write *Words for Warriors: A Professional Soldier's Notebook*. To those whom have gone unmentioned, I can only say an inadequate "Thank you!"

FOREWORD

On July 1, 1948, I walked through the sally port of the Central Area at West Point, New York, as a skinny, unworldly young man fresh from the hills of West Virginia. After the abrupt greeting by a cadet upperclassman, I was turned over to Cadet Ralph Puckett, my squad leader. Ralph Puckett then proceeded to turn me from a young high school kid into a man and a Soldier. He was my first mentor. To this day he tells people that "Sam Wetzel succeeded because I taught him to spit shine shoes!" I have never forgotten this launch of a military career that culminated when I retired forty years later from the V U.S. Corps Parade Field in Frankfurt, Germany, and moved to Columbus, Georgia, to once again be reunited with my good friend Colonel Ralph Puckett.

Colonel (Retired) Ralph Puckett is one of our nation's finest combat warriors, highly decorated for gallantry and heroism in the Korea and Vietnam Wars. He has blessed us by sharing his experiences and those of other outstanding leaders with this book: *Words for Warriors*.

Colonel Puckett put together an outstanding series of his well-documented leadership essays into one volume that should be required reading for every new officer in every service. It should be on the shelf of any leader, military or civilian. This volume is replete with his personal examples and also examples of other former Soldiers and leaders depicting situations regarding training of leaders and units, mentoring, strategy and tactics, personal development, and many other items. He even includes a section on the home front involving wives, the media, educating the public, and honoring veterans.

Words for Warriors is well-written and easy to read with a Table of Contents that takes you to your current problems or situations with examples and ideas of how others in the past have approached them. As I read this book, I thought back on some of my own situations from when I was a lieutenant to my commanding general days and thought, "Gee, why didn't I think of that?"

Warriors today have possibly the greatest challenge facing them since WWII in the form of the Islamic Radical movement that is rolling like a plague throughout the world. All warriors would do well to read and follow the advice in this book of one of our nation's finest combat warriors, Colonel Ralph Puckett. I commend it to you to include in your required reading.

—R. L. "Sam" Wetzel, Lieutenant General, U.S. Army Retired.

INTRODUCTION

[T]here is more to be learned about men against fire than has ever appeared between the covers of books.[1]
—Brigadier General S. L. A. Marshall

I believe that success on the battlefield comes primarily from what we do in preparation for the day that the battle is joined. I believe that everything we do—not just that activity that we call training—affects how successful we will be. Administration, recognizing commendable performance, discipline, the example we set, and many other things contribute to that success.

Field manuals and courses of instruction at service schools are beneficial sources of information. They were invaluable to me. What I learned from the sometimes-casual comments of others was often related specifically to a problem I faced and, in some cases, was more beneficial. The fact that I did not come up with the thoughts on my own never caused me any concern. I wanted to learn from others rather than to learn the hard way from my own actions.

Participants in the War Fighting Seminars of the Infantry Pre-Command Courses repeatedly expressed many of the questions and comments in *Words for Warriors: A Professional Soldier's Notebook*. The groups included experienced officers and noncommissioned officers (NCO) from WWII, Korea, Vietnam, Grenada, Panama, and Desert Shield/Desert Storm. The essay, "Veterans as Trainers," suggests ways in which we may tap this valuable resource.

This reservoir of untapped knowledge from fellow Soldiers is often overlooked. *Words for Warriors* makes much of it easily available.

Some people say that they only learn from their mistakes. That is costly education. Learning from other people's successes and failures is a better way. If perusing the suggestions contained in *Words for Warriors* results in one American Soldier's life being saved, the book will have been worthwhile.

The suggestions are not limited to combat, however. Much is accomplished in the everyday activities—training, administration, logistics, and personnel management—that occupy so much of a commander's time and effort. Anything that improves these vital functions contributes to increased combat effectiveness.

Words for Warriors addresses tactics, training, administration, special staff, public relations, self-development, and a myriad of other subjects that are the responsibilities of commanders. (Civilian leaders face similar problems. Change the military context to that of the civilian world and *Words for Warriors* would be of benefit to those individuals.) "Operation Bushmaster" discusses a technique used effectively in Vietnam to ambush an enemy. "Find a 'Golden Voice' for Your Ceremonies" stresses the importance of selecting announcers carefully because how well they perform affects the entire ceremony. "Discipline Takes Over When Your Body and Mind Tell You to Quit" describes the importance of performing the "little things" correctly again and again until they are ingrained habits. "Become the Leader You Want to Be" discusses how our daily decisions and actions determine what we will become and suggests a concept for improving oneself. Following the suggestions in "How Can We Develop Courage?" can help prepare one for the inevitable time when he confronts his own fear.

Soldiers today know that tomorrow they may face some intractable challenges. Junior officers, in particular, have framed many questions as I talked to them in the Infantry Officer Basic Course (IOBC) and Infantry Captains Career Course (ICCC). Candidates in Officer Candidate School (OCS) raised similar concerns. Questions include: "What did you do when everything began to go wrong? How do you prepare for that?" (See "Prepare for a Disaster.") "Did you ever have a Soldier who was reluctant to kill the enemy?" (See "Overcoming the Reluctance to Kill.")

The questions and comments were not always related to training and combat. "How do we improve our relationships with the media?" (See "Developing Better Relations with the Media.") "How do we find the time to do all that must be done?" (See "What Do You Do When You Have More Than You Can Do?")

Both the battalion and regimental commanders in their student orientations given on the first day of BOLC II (Basic Officer Leaders Course II) at Fort Benning urged the students to develop an organized approach to improving their leadership style and ability. "Become the Leader You Want to Be" and "Be All You Can Be" provide suggestions that may assist individuals at all levels in their quests for self-improvement.

While at a much lower level, Soldiers undergoing Basic Combat Training programs for either the Infantry or one of the non-combat arms also are concerned and in conversations with me spoke freely about some of the problems they expect.

These questioners know that there is no hard and fast solution, that an appropriate response is affected by "the situation."

These problems have confronted most of us and will face others—particularly commanders at the battalion level and below—in the future. *Words for Warriors* describes what others have done when faced with similar challenges. The problems themselves and suggested courses of action came from superiors, peers, and subordinates. Enlisted men, particularly noncommissioned officers, were a valuable source. These essays are an attempt to provide leaders the benefit of that collective experience. Those of us who have gone before owe those who follow that much. The suggested approaches in all the essays have been tried and found effective. You may be able to improve your performance by adapting the suggestions to your specific situation. While not foolproof—nothing is—the comments can serve as a guide or a "heads up" to commanders.

There are goals that are appropriate for your organization and are appropriate for your training program regardless of the roles and missions of your unit—whether combat, combat support, or combat service support. There are fundamental principles that, if implemented in your training program, will bring success. These goals and principles are discussed in the *Words for Warriors* essay entitled, "Roles and Missions and How to Train for Them."

As you read these essays, I hope that the ideas will be as helpful to you as they were to me. I hope that, like me, you can learn from others and by so doing avoid some problems and solve those you cannot.

The ideas contained in *Words for Warriors* are fundamental; they are basic. There is nothing new. They contain suggestions that may be appropriate to any unit. You may not agree with all of them. Do not accept any without thinking or analyzing them thoroughly. Mao Tse-Tung advised us:

> We should carefully study the lessons which were learned in past wars at the cost of blood and which have been bequeathed to us .... We must put conclusions thus reached to the test of our own experiences and absorb what is useful, reject what is useless and add what is specifically our own.[2]

Quotes from people—mostly military leaders—throughout history set the tone at the beginning of each essay. Other comments are sprinkled throughout the essays giving support to the discussion and adding interest. They also help to connect today's Soldier with the past, illustrating that what he faces today is nothing new. The same problems have confronted Soldiers in the past.

As a matter of form, I have capitalized the word Soldier. I did that out of respect for his noble calling and to honor a word—a name—that has meant so much throughout our history. When I see Soldier with the capital "S" he or she is a real person to me. The term with the small "s" is generic and does not elicit the respect that the individual deserves.

I will welcome your comments both favorable and critical. Please send them using the address below. Thank you!

Colonel Ralph Puckett
U.S. Army Retired
2024 Country Club Rd
Columbus, GA 31906-1013
TEL: 706 324 3436
FAX: 706 324 3436
E-MAIL: ralphpuckett@mindspring.com

Section I

HONORARY COLONEL OF THE REGIMENT

HONORARY COLONEL OF THE REGIMENT

If I can keep one Ranger from dying, my "tour of duty"
as Honorary Colonel will have been worthwhile.

—Colonel Ralph Puckett, U.S. Army Retired

The activities of HCOR ... [are] designed to promote
and enhance the history and traditions of the regi-
ment..., promote the war fighting ethos among Sol-
diers, and create cohesion among the members of the
regiment. Examples of activities are as follows: (1)
Attending command ceremonies. (2) Participating in
award ceremonies. (3) Speaking on regimental ... his-
tory and traditions at dinings-in or other similar func-
tions. (4) Maintaining contact between CONUS or
OCONUS battalions or elements of the regiment. (5)
Assisting in historical professional development pro-
grams for officers and NCOs.

—AR 600-82

In 1996, Colonel William J. Leszczynski, Jr., Commander, 75th Ranger Regiment selected me to be the Honorary Colonel of the Regiment (HCOR). The secretary of the Army appoints the HCOR. To be eligible, the nominee must have been a colonel or general officer and have served in the regiment at one time. This latter prerequisite caused some delay in my appointment, because I had never served in the regiment. It did not exist during my active duty. However, Colonel Leszczynski believed that my having commanded the Eighth Army Ranger Company during the Korean War and my other Ranger/special operations experiences should be sufficient grounds for the appointment. Although the action officer at the Department of the Army objected initially, Colonel Leszczynski prevailed.

I was very flattered and pleased. I would follow in the footsteps of my friend, Colonel Frank Dawson. He had led the 5th Battalion Rangers off Omaha Beach. His heroic action was instrumental in establishing the Ranger motto: "Rangers lead the way!"

Colonel Leszczynski wanted me to spend as much time with the Rangers as I could—to have a sense for their states of mind—about what they were thinking. In addition, he wanted me to observe and comment on as much training as I could. I was in total agreement.

I was not "up" on weapons and equipment or doctrine, but I could still be of benefit to the Rangers. I knew that fundamentals—those individual and small unit skills that must be mastered for a unit to be combat ready—made the difference in success or failure. (I am convinced that if you accomplish the fundamentals better than the enemy you're fighting, you will win.) I would focus on fundamentals whenever I observed training.

Although a new second lieutenant without one day of troop duty, I had been selected to form, train, and command the Eighth Army Ranger Company, the first Ranger unit established after World War II (WWII). Later, I had served in various capacities for twenty-six months in the Ranger Department, U.S. Army Infantry School; I had formed and commanded the Orientation School and the Noncommissioned Officer Academy in the 65th Regimental Combat Team (RCT) in Puerto Rico. I had also been a company commander in that RCT. I had been the first Ranger advisor to the Colombian Army with the mission of establishing its Ranger School, the *Escuela de Lanceros*. I had spent three years in the 10th Special Forces Group in Germany commanding "B" and "C" Teams for 30 months and serving as Group S2 for six.

Much of my experience in the Army had focused on developing and training small unit leaders. They are at the cutting edge and have to be successful for the unit to succeed. Concentrating on the development and training of small unit leaders is what interested me the most. I believed that my experience had prepared me to be the Honorary Colonel and that I could contribute to the combat readiness of the 75th Ranger Regiment.

Regimental commanders suggested activities that would interest me and that they wanted me to observe. They gave me a free hand to go wherever I wished and told me that I would be welcome everywhere. Subordinate commanders and their staffs were just as open to my visits. It was helpful when some staff officer was given primary responsibility for keeping me informed about significant activities in which the regiment was involved.

I made a trip to Afghanistan in 2004. I will always be indebted to Colonel Craig Nixon, the commander of the 75th Ranger Regiment, and to Major General Stanley McChrystal, who supported Colonel Nixon's request. I also went to Iraq in 2006. This time, Colonel Paul LaCamera, the regimental commander, and then Lieutenant General Stan McChrystal agreed to my visit.

I also made two trips to Korea, went to Alaska, attended live-fire exercises in New Mexico, at Fort Knox and Fort Campbell, Kentucky, and at Fort Benning, Georgia, and observed special testing and evaluation exercises conducted at the Florida and Mountain Ranger training camps. I attended the 3rd Battalion's three-day Team Leader Course; participated in D-Day celebrations in Normandy; served on the Ranger Assessment and Selection Program (RASP) Board when commissioned and noncommissioned officers were evaluated for possible assignment to the regiment; attended predeployment planning sessions; and participated in changes of command for the regimental and battalion commanders. During one battalion change of command, I served in place of Regimental Commander Colonel Nixon, who was with his wife as she gave birth to their fourth child. I served as the promoting or reenlistment officer on several occasions. I attended dozens of company changes of command, promotion ceremonies, and social functions. I was pleased to be included.

One of the most interesting activities in which I was involved was the periodic commanders training conferences. At these meetings, regimental and battalion commanders discussed upcoming activities. The conferences were sometimes dubbed "The Road Ahead." At one meeting, Colonel Nixon, shortly before he was reassigned, briefed the commanders on what he saw the Regiment doing perhaps ten years in the future. This briefing was important as it focused attention on the future that, as Colonel Nixon saw it, would be significantly different from what the regiment was doing at the present. Colonel Nixon's previous assignment to the Joint Special Operations Command gave him an insight that the battalion commanders did not have.

I remember observing a Mangoday at the Ranger Mountain Camp in North Georgia. The name, Mangoday, comes from a fierce warrior group of Genghis Khan. Although small, the group contributed significantly to the Mongolian commander's conquest of much of the world.[1] The exercise is a physically and professionally demanding Ranger training mission conducted by a group of captains. The regimental commander selected from across the Regiment the officers who were to take part; they were not limited to the combat arms. He accompanied the patrols so that he personally could observe and evaluate his officers.

On one Mangoday, I was at an exercise control point around midnight somewhere in the mountains. The exercise controller and Deputy Regimental Commander, Lieutenant Colonel Luke Green, was forming an "enemy" patrol from the OPFOR (opposing force) that would be the ambush target for the Rangers. Lieutenant Colonel Green suggested that I join the eight-man patrol. He put a white band around my arm and another around my helmet so that the Rangers would recognize that I was administrative. He radioed the observer controller (OC) with the patrol and told him, "Colonel Puckett is the last man in the patrol," expecting the OC to inform the Rangers.

Our (enemy) patrol proceeded about a mile up a mountain trail. Suddenly, there were bursts of machine gun and rifle fire and hand grenade simulators! The OPFOR, as they had been instructed, fired one complete twenty-round magazine and then fell "dead." The Rangers ran to them and took anything that might be of intelligence value.

Knowing that I would be expected to comment on the Rangers' performance, I did not lie down as the OPFOR had done. I walked around when the ambush was sprung and the initial fires took place. I wanted to see what was happening. I then went down on my knees as one Ranger captain came running over to where I was. He yelled at me, "Get down!" I went down further but still kept my head up so I could observe the action. He yelled at me again, "Get down!" When I made no move, he yelled to his leader, "Hey, Joe, this guy won't get down!" Joe yelled back, "Put your knee in his back and make him go down!" As my attacker put his knee in my back, I turned to him and very quietly said, "I'm administrative." With that, he yelled, "Who are you?" I responded, "I'm Colonel Puckett." My adversary jumped up and ran away, yelling, "Oh, my God! It's Colonel Puckett!" I never asked who the Ranger was as I was afraid he might be embarrassed. I thought the whole affair very humorous.

The next night, as Regimental Commander Colonel Stan McChrystal (now lieutenant general), and I entered the room where he was to speak to the Rangers, all came to attention. As soon as Colonel McChrystal said, "Be seated, gentlemen," all the captains turned around and yelled "Colonel Puckett, it was Captain Gray!" pointing at him as they did. Everyone had a big laugh. I have often heard the story repeated generally with embellishments.

Jim Gray was the intelligence officer (S2) for the 3rd Battalion. Each time I came into the battalion's headquarters, some Ranger would sneak around to Jim's office and tell him that there was someone in the front office who wanted to see him. Jim was always taken aback when he saw that the "someone" was Colonel Puckett. I often joked that when I got in shape I was going to challenge him to a showdown fight in front of the regiment. Both he and I shared a lot of laughs. I think I cemented our friendship when I asked him to be my guest at a formal Ranger dinner. At my table were Phil Piazza, president of the Merrill's Marauders Association, and the presidents of two Ranger associations. Jim was with a lot of living history.

On my first trip to the Joint Readiness Training Center (JRTC) at Fort Polk, Louisiana, I visited one of the platoons in a "hide" position that was waiting for a nighttime pickup by helicopters. As I went to each of the Rangers on alert, I lay down beside him and discussed his specific task. I asked him what his sector of fire was, who was on each side of him, where his squad leader was, and other related questions. We also talked about his Army experience and his family. In one of these conversations, the young Ranger said, "Sir, it's really great you being out here with us as old as you are!" He immediately realized what he said, blushed, and blurted out, "Sir, you're not really old but you know what I mean!" We both had a good laugh.

I remember a Mangoday in the swamps near the Florida Ranger Camp. The Rangers had just taken an objective after making a night parachute assault into the exercise and wading and boating an extended distance in the swamp. I visited each of the security positions to talk with the Rangers. They were a bedraggled bunch. I told one of them how I admired his physical fitness—his ability to do what he was doing while carrying such a heavy pack. I remarked, "I bet I can't even pick up your pack, let alone carry it." He looked at me and said, "Sir, I bet you could before you got so old." I'm sure that he meant to assuage any feelings of inadequacy that I might have. His remarks gave me a good chuckle.

Whenever I visited training, the commander always assigned an escort officer or NCO to "look after" me. They were always well informed about the training, helpful, and courteous. I enjoyed them all and marveled at the caliber of young Rangers in the regiment.

The Rangers at all levels always treated me with deference and respect. They seemed genuinely glad to see me, and my admiration of them was obvious. Their comments got back to me one way or the other. "The colonel pulled a poncho over his head and went to sleep in the snow!" "The colonel lay down in the sand besides us for about twenty minutes. I never knew a colonel to do that!" "The HCOR put that Ranger's cold feet against the colonel's chest to warm them!"

Because I had been a Ranger company commander during the Korean War and a battalion commander in Vietnam, I was able to inject my personal experiences when describing the Army's performance against fanatical enemies over extremely difficult terrain and under punishing weather conditions. The Rangers were curious about what had occurred, how we had fought, and the effectiveness of our weapons and equipment. In particular, they wanted to know how we had fared with an inadequate amount of clothing, when they were experiencing discomfort with the most modern and efficient clothing available.

I believe that the greatest improvement in combat readiness can come from attention to fundamentals. Improving them will do more to diminish casualties than any other step we can take. We must focus on our most junior leaders: the team and squad leaders. They are in direct command of the Rangers and "make it happen." They are also our least experienced leaders. They give 110 percent and only need to be taught.

An after action review (AAR) always followed a training exercise. When appropriate, I compared my combat experience to what the regiment was doing. I suggested improvements and used combat examples where violations of fundamentals had resulted in unnecessary casualties. I hoped that something that I would say or do would save the life of at least one Ranger. If I accomplished that much, I would consider myself successful. (A regimental command sergeant major and others have told me that incorporating some of my suggestions had resulted in fewer casualties. What a great feeling!)

Safety was always important, especially during a night live-fire, so I gave safety a lot of attention. We did not want a single Ranger hurt, and we did not want to lose the special dispensations that we have for our training.

In the tactical training that I have observed over the years—not just in the Ranger regiment, but in units I have commanded or whose training I have observed—there are some basic skills that were inadequately performed and not corrected. The unit's most junior members make these mistakes. That is not surprising; they are the least experienced. They want to do what is expected. However, they don't know how. Corrective action requires a lot of supervised training. Leaders—particularly squad and team leaders—must correct every mistake and shortcoming until correct actions become habitual. Because these first line supervisors are themselves inexperienced, they can benefit by close observation by their superiors.

I often encouraged the regiment to "move to a higher level of training." I believe strongly in making the training exercises tougher and causing unit commanders and their Rangers to react to unforeseen events. I sometimes recounted historical examples where those situations occurred. Some are from my own experience. I want the Rangers to face disaster and react to it. And I want them to learn from the experiences of others.

Training should push the Rangers (and all Soldiers) to the limit of their physical and professional capabilities. Stress and overcoming it has to become part of their lives. When it becomes a life-or-death matter in combat they will be as prepared as they can be. Succeeding when everything is in your favor and goes as planned is not a good test of your training status. Reacting to the unforeseen can be.

Scenarios for moving to a "higher level of training" include overwhelming enemy force, high casualties, and exercises that last longer than the unit commander suspected. What happens if a company is facing annihilation? Suppose the company commander and other leaders are killed or seriously wounded; there are many casualties among the troops; or the company is surrounded and being pounded? What does the company commander (or whoever takes over) do? What does the battalion commander do? If there is no reaction force ready to go we may lose a company. Incidentally, the North Koreans and Chinese in Korea often prepared an ambush for the reaction or reinforcing element that then found itself facing destruction.

Another scenario that is easy to imagine is the last chopper being shot down as it exfiltrates a load of Rangers. One minimally trained insurgent can do the job with one rifle-propelled grenade (RPG) put into a chopper's turbine as it lifts off. With a chopper down and many Rangers and the aircrew dead or wounded, what do we do? It can happen. I remember an occasion in Vietnam when a guerrilla knocked a fully loaded C130 out the sky with one round. There were no survivors.

Injecting the unexpected into play adds interest, challenge, and training value. A unit that performs well when everything goes bad can consider itself well trained. To this end, I often spoke to the regimental commander and his S3 (operations officer) and other officers at battalion level recommending a "higher level" of training.

A "tour" as Honorary Colonel is for two years. As I write this, I have been the HCOR for more than eleven years! About six months before each change of command for the regiment, I always wrote the commander-to-be to tell him that he should consider whom he would like to have as the HCOR. There might be someone he knew better, someone with whom he might be more comfortable. I expressed my appreciation for having been the HCOR, and how much I enjoyed the honor. I told him that I would be proud to continue to serve in that capacity if he wanted me but that my feelings would not be hurt if he chose someone else. So far, each has kept me.

I have served with great regimental commanders. Colonel Bill Leszczynski, the 9th Colonel of the Regiment, retired as a brigadier general (promotable), selected me and had me appointed. Colonel Stan McChrystal, the 10th Colonel of the Regiment, succeeded him. The next were Colonel Ken Keen, the 11th Colonel and Colonel Joe Votel, the 12th Colonel, now both brigadiers. Colonel Craig Nixon became the 13th Colonel of the Regiment in the summer of 2003. He is now a brigadier general. Colonel Paul LaCamera, the 14th Colonel, followed Colonel Nixon in 2005. I have no doubt that he will be selected for promotion to general.

Any success that I have had as the Honorary Colonel is based on several factors. First, I am really excited and honored to be the

HCOR, and it shows. I often express these feelings to the commanders and Rangers because I want them to know how I feel. When complimenting them, as I often do, I usually conclude my remarks with, "Be proud, but don't be satisfied." I work hard at establishing a good working and personal relationship with each regimental commander, his staff, and subordinate commanders. There is usually someone designated to keep me informed. How well he accomplishes this task directly affects how well I can do my job. In addition, the commanders are personally involved. Colonel Paul LaCamera, who is the current commander, scheduled an appointment with me during his first week of command and has followed up with several other informal chats. His predecessors did similarly. These early conferences aided me to become more helpful to him almost immediately.

I am careful never to intrude. I always couch my suggestions in the most diplomatic terms. I am not the commander. I recognize and always keep foremost in my mind that the commander is far more qualified than I. I see myself as being another pair of eyes that might be of assistance to him. I try to spend as much time as I can with the Rangers, and I prefer that the time be during training. Living in Columbus, GA, a short distance from Fort Benning where the headquarters for the 75th Ranger Regiment, and the 3rd Battalion are located, is a major advantage because it is easy for me to participate in those units' activities.

Being the Honorary Colonel of the 75th Ranger Regiment, the best light Infantry unit in the world, is a privilege and honor. Every time I am with the great Rangers who comprise that fine unit, I recognize that I am walking with giants; I am with heroes. They are a national treasure. They are our finest warriors. America is fortunate to have them. I am fortunate to have served with them.

Section II

LEADERSHIP

BE THERE

One of the most valuable qualities of a commander is a flair for putting himself in the right place at the vital time.[1]

—Field Marshall Viscount Slim

Alexander the Great was an inspirational warrior who "led from the front." He could truthfully state:

> I have no part of my body, in front at least, that is left without scars; there is no weapon, used at close quarters, or hurled from afar, of which I do not carry the mark. I have been wounded by the sword, shot with arrows, struck from a catapult, smitten many times with stones and clubs—for you, for your glory, for your wealth.[2]

Alexander's men knew that he had been and would always be with them. "He lived no better than they did, woke earlier, worried worse, and suffered wounds more frequently than any of them." He had been and always would "be there" no matter what the situation.[3]

He became more and more reckless in each subsequent battle. During one assault he climbed a ladder leaning against the fortress wall and leaped to the ground landing in the midst of the enemy. His men had to follow to prevent him from being killed. That may have been Alexander's goal. He was, however, grievously wounded and was never the same thereafter.[4] Most, if not all of us do not want to be able to say what Alexander said. We should not totally disregard our safety as Alexander did.

In *The Mask of Command*, author John Keegan describes three other military leaders in addition to Alexander. He comments on each of the leader's exposure to enemy fire. "Wellington also commanded from close at hand. In this, he was perhaps exceeding contemporary expectations of risk-taking."[5]

Grant felt that a "commander's place was out of range of fire which, since the introduction of the rifle, swept the field in a density and to a range which would have made Wellington's habits of exposure suicidal."[6] However, Grant did not always keep out of danger, sometimes inadvertently coming under fire from Confederate riflemen. His composure under fire earned the admiration of his Soldiers. One private remarked, "'Ulysses don't scare worth a damn' ... Nor did he. His physical no more than his moral courage was never in doubt."[7]

For a fourth example, Keegan could have picked someone like Joshua Lawrence Chamberlain, Mathew B. Ridgway, James Van Fleet, or many others who led from the front. Instead Keegan uses Hitler as an example of a leader who did not lead from the front; he was not "there" with the troops. Keegan impugns Hitler's courage because he commanded so far from the front.

I strongly agree that Hitler's micro-control contributed to the downfall of the German Army. However, he should not have been at the front. Fighting the war should have been left in the hands of his army commanders. As far as his personal courage, Hitler had proved himself in WWI, where he performed heroically as a messenger. He was wounded three times, including being temporarily blinded by gas. He was distinguished or decorated five times, once with the Iron Cross First Class.[8]

A leader should not risk his life foolishly. His men do not expect it; they do not want to lose the leadership on which their success and lives may depend. While they do not expect foolhardy action, they do expect that their leaders share reasonable risks.

On August 13, 1967, Company B, 2nd Battalion (Airborne),

502nd Infantry as part of a battalion assault, landed on a "hot" landing zone (LZ). The LZ was literally "hot" in that it had been set ablaze by the preparatory artillery fires. The paratroopers came under enemy mortar, automatic weapons, and rifle-propelled grenade (RPG) fire. One platoon leader, Second Lieutenant Thomas Petramalo, was hit by an RPG and died from the wound the following day. Other men were wounded. Company commander, Captain Ronald G. Odom, reported the situation to me as I flew over in my Charlie Charlie (command and control helicopter). I decided to land and see it for myself.

As my radio operator, Private First Class James L. Spears, and I debarked from the chopper and it lifted off, Ron ran to meet me. He repeated what he had told me over the radio. It was obvious that the company's situation left much to be desired.

I said to Ron, "I am going to stay on the ground with you. I want to see that you get all the support you can possibly use. I have complete confidence in you. You know your company and more about commanding it than I do. You are in command. I just want to ensure that you have all the help you can use. Get your company into a well-dug-in defensive perimeter and get prepared for a fight." I knew that I could depend on Ron; he was solid.

I radioed the chopper circling overhead and told the pilot, Major Payne, to return to base. I radioed my Tactical Operations Center (TOC) and directed that artillery— Dustoff (casualty evacuation choppers), flare ships, and Puff the Magic Dragon (C130 with Gatling gun)—be alerted as I expected all would be needed before the night was over. While I could have marshaled the support just as well from my TOC, I felt that my presence on the ground would be beneficial.

Spears began to dig us a foxhole about ten yards from where Ron was locating his. We would be close by but not in his way. He busied himself with the preparation of the defensive position while I checked with my TOC. As the company prepared, the enemy continued with sporadic fire.

As darkness fell, the enemy fire became heavier. Ron and his artillery forward observer, First Lieutenant Donald A. Nemetz, were calling in fires. It was effective, causing the enemy to regroup before another assault. The first few times that Ron called for support, I followed on my command net with a "Do it!" It really was not necessary, but I thought that my emphasis would be a steadying influence.

The fight waxed and waned. During lulls, we supplied the Rangers with ammunition and other necessary items and evacuated the wounded and killed. I moved about the battlefield helping with casualties and supplies and gave a lot of "atta boys." First Lieutenant Dave Campbell, the Company XO, deserves praise for the superb job he did "pushing" ammunition and other supplies to the company. It was a tough battle, but the great support from the artillery and aviation enabled Ron and his Company "B" Rangers to prevail against a major threat. When dawn came, the battlefield was once again calm as the enemy broke contact.

I called for my Charlie Charlie and withdrew after walking the perimeter and congratulating the troops. They had done a marvelous job.

Ron was due for rotation in two days. I spoke with the brigade commander, Brigadier General Salve Matheson, and asked him to expedite a Silver Star for Ron; I wanted to present it at the change of command. General Matheson went to bat for me so I was able to pin the medal on a very surprised Ron Odom the next day. I made a few remarks congratulating a representative from each platoon (we were still in the jungle so we had to be in a defensive posture) on the fine job that they had done. I also said that there would be a "helmet full" of medals for them as soon as we could process the recommendations that their executive officer (XO) was preparing. It was a great day.

I hated to say good-bye to Ron. Not only had we gone through a trying battle together, I had great respect for the outstanding leader that he was. He had always come through when the chips were down. I would miss him. Captain Dick Boyd, another outstanding and courageous leader, took command from Ron. Unfortunately, sadly, Dick was killed in action shortly thereafter.

Our brigade deputy commander told me later that Ron had

remarked in his farewell conference, "I never would have made it if the Ranger had not been with us." One of Ron's platoon leaders, First Lieutenant Tom Courtney, said, "Having the Ranger on the hill that night was the same as having another rifle company with us in the fight."

In a letter many years later, Colonel Ron Odom wrote:

> I think it is not possible to elaborate too much about how positively I was affected, as a commander, nor how my leaders and Soldiers were affected by the above actions and words of our battalion commander. His presence and actions during the battle were a constant source of confidence and a reminder that we would get all the support we needed, that all we had to do was our job. After all, that's what Colonel Puckett was doing. If he were going to "stay with us till (sic) it's over," then we knew we would be successful.[9]

That's heady praise, but I put it in proper perspective. I gave only one order to Ron during the fight. That was to get into a dug-in defensive perimeter position. I never fired a shot. He ran the show. He and his Company "B" troopers did the fighting.

Leadership classes and lectures often place great emphasis on the decisions and actions of commanders on the field of battle. They are analyzed and critiqued from a Monday morning quarterback viewpoint or with an open-minded analytical examination of what was decided and done and the results of those decisions. Seldom is the aspect of the commander's presence described in great depth. What impact did his presence have on the morale and confidence of his Soldiers? How did that affect the outcome of the battle?

When General Matthew Ridgway took command of the Eighth Army in Korea in December 1950, it was a dispirited, beaten force that had been bloodied by massive Chinese attacks. He visited lower units, talked to commanders, relieved those in whom he had no confidence, and listened to the Soldiers. General Omar N. Bradley, chairman of the Joint Chiefs of Staff, described Ridgway's actions thusly:

> It is not often that a single battlefield commander can make a decisive difference. But in Korea Ridgway would prove to be that exception. His brilliant, driving, uncompromising leadership would turn the tide of battle like no other general's in our military history.[10]

By "being there" General Ridgway's assurance—his command presence—imbued in his Soldiers the confidence and fighting spirit that they needed to attack and win.

In writing about General U. S. Grant, J. F. C. Fuller said:

> Grant is at his best when tumult surrounds him, because he is unaffected by it, and though he may issue no single order, his presence at once counteracts panic, it allays fear, it induces confidence. His imperturbable appearance and his inevitable cigar restore a broken line more firmly than a fresh division.[11]

I believe that in many cases Grant's presence was of greater significance than any decision that he made or any order that he gave. My being there with Captain Ron Odom and Company B/2-502nd was more important than any order I gave. The troops had never had a battalion commander stay with them through the night. I was a steadying influence. I was there.

CHEWING GUM CAN BE A COMBAT MULTIPLIER

Do what you can with what you have, where you are.[12]

—Theodore Roosevelt

We were on the side of Mt. Olympus in Greece on a very hot, dusty day. Our group consisted of the "C" Team of Charlie Company, 10th Special Forces Group, and one of its "A" Teams. We were on a theater-wide unconventional warfare maneuver after having entered the country clandestinely from a U.S. Navy submarine. We were moving cross-country en route to linking with units of the Greek Raiding Force. The countryside over which we had been moving the previous day and today was rugged, steep, and extremely dry. We had found no water during the entire time and had exhausted all that we carried. Not only was the dearth of water affecting us negatively, the 70–100 pound rucksacks were also exacting a toll on our bodies and morale.

When my troopers stopped to rest, I could tell they were extremely tired. So was I. They had "dry mouth," and their lips were flecked with white sputum. Morale was very low. Getting these dispirited Soldiers moving again would be difficult. What was I to do?

Suddenly, I remembered that I had two packs of Wrigley's Spearmint Chewing Gum in my pack. That meant that I had a total of ten sticks for the twenty of us! I broke each stick in half and gave a piece to each Soldier, who immediately put it into his mouth and began to chew. Chewing the gum stimulated saliva flow and satiated some of the thirst!

As I handed each trooper his "ration" of gum, I made light of our situation and bragged about his perseverance during a very trying time. After a moment or two, we "saddled up" and moved on, reaching our linkup in a few hours.

Later during the after action review, many of my troopers said that the gum had been a lifesaver. It lifted morale and helped quench their debilitating thirst; they proclaimed that it would have been hard to continue without that needed boost. (I, of course, knew that they would not have quit no matter what the difficulty, but I did acknowledge that the boost to morale had been a combat multiplier.)

The lesson is not that every leader should pack extra chewing gum in his rucksack. However, the lesson is that little things, coupled with leader confidence, enthusiasm, and encouragement—a "We can do it!" attitude—can make a difference. When things look the worst, the commander must exhibit the most confidence and a positive attitude.

COMMITMENT TO COUNTRY

---

*There must be within our Army a sense of purpose,
and a dedication to that purpose. There must be a willingness to march a little further, to carry a heavier load,
to step into the dark and unknown for the safety and
well being of others.*

—General Creighton Abrams

The need to encourage our junior commissioned and noncommissioned officers to remain in the service of their country is
a never-ending task. It begins the day they "report in" and continues until they depart. As the Global War on Terrorism (GWOT)
grinds inexorably onward with no end in sight, this need for
encouragement has never been greater. Many Soldiers have experienced multiple deployments and see more just ahead. Only
those who have endured an extended absence from home with the
concomitant missed birthdays, ball games, first proms, and graduations can understand and empathize with the emotional strain
that these deployments bring. Add to that the danger of serious
injury or death and we have all the ingredients for a decision to
leave the Army.

Soldiers who continue to serve despite these drawbacks "put
the welfare of the nation, the Army, and subordinates before their
own."[13]

I used those words of General Creighton Abrams, former
Army chief of staff, to introduce my remarks to the officers of the

1-502nd Battalion, one of the units of the 101st Division (Air Assault). The occasion was a two-day leadership seminar in 2004.

The battalion commander, Lieutenant Colonel Kent Schweikert, an old friend from the 75th Ranger Regiment, had invited me to participate. Kent is truly a "quiet professional" and was in his second year of battalion command. The primary purpose of the seminar was to "pump up" and motivate the officers for continuing commitment to the Army and to our country. I had served with the 101st in Vietnam; it was good to "come home."

I began: "The message I want to bring to you can be simply stated. You are vital to the security of this great nation in which we live. We appreciate what you do for our country. If you remember nothing else of what I say never forget this: 'You are vital; you are appreciated.'"

I continued: "We are going through some trying times in our Army today. Some of our young leaders—perhaps some of you in this seminar—are dissatisfied and are leaving our Army. You know the sources of disillusionment better than I so I will not dwell on them."

I have listened to many of our junior leaders as they recounted wistfully and almost apologetically their reasons for leaving. The burdens of the many separations fall disproportionately on the wives who must carry on in the absence of the other half of the marriage. While these women are magnificent in their steadfastness, their frustration and loneliness are understandable. Their influence on their husbands is major and, in many cases, the most significant. Nothing expresses this pressure better than, "If mama ain't happy, ain't nobody happy."

We need to pay more attention to and give more recognition to the wives. Although they do not wear the uniform, they truly are part of our strength. As the lyrics of a popular ballad state, they are "the wind beneath our wings." We cannot do without them. They deserve all that we can do to let them know how important they are to our Army.

What can we do to alleviate or minimize this problem? As long as there are deployments and wars, the quandary will not disappear. The personnel policies that govern everything that we do are determined at a much higher level than what most of us will ever attain. We are not helpless, however. There are things that we can do. Although sounding simplistic, those things boil down to convincing our Soldiers: "You are vital to our country. We appreciate you." How do we do that? Here are some things that we can say.

There are great intrinsic rewards in serving in our Army. First comes the satisfaction of knowing that you are necessary to the continued existence of a free America. You are needed.

You are part of an organization that is held in high regard by your countrymen. The military is an honorable profession. Recent polls have shown that our citizens rate the military as the organization with the highest integrity in our country. It will continue to receive that approbation as long as we have Soldiers like you.

You are setting an example of patriotism and dedication to duty for your Soldiers, your children, and the citizens of this country.

You are part of an organization that demands all that you can give it, that requires you to be all that you can be. Furthermore, you have the satisfaction of knowing that only a very few Americans—Soldiers like you—can meet the standards of integrity, professionalism, and physical fitness that your Army demands.

You know that America has entrusted you with the lives of our Soldiers. They are our nation's most precious resource.

Our arguments will only be as persuasive as our concern for the welfare of our Soldiers and families. Actions speak louder than words. We must convince them by everything that we do that we value them, that they are important to us, and that we will do what we can to make the hardships easier to bear. We need to begin accomplishing that mission the day they report in and continue until the day they depart. It is an awesome responsibility, and one that we must not shirk.

GIVE CREDIT WHERE CREDIT IS DUE

Humility must always be the portion of any man who receives acclaim earned in the blood of his followers and the sacrifices of his friends.[14]

—General of the Army Dwight D. Eisenhower

At one time or another, most of us find ourselves in a position where we receive praise for some success. The achievement may be a job well done, an inspection in which our unit was rated exceptionally high, or an award for some act of heroism or service.

In all of these circumstances, the master of ceremonies or the commander presenting the award may describe our accomplishments and assignments with great enthusiasm. He may enumerate the decorations and awards that we have received. He describes us as if we can walk on water. In fact, the speaker may imply that we have accomplished that feat in the past! This bountiful praise is expected and generally accepted by the audience as the introducer's way of recognizing and showing appreciation for our modest accomplishments. The audience may be impressed and, if we have any humility, we will be embarrassed. However, we can easily put the more than generous compliments in perspective. We can give credit where credit is due.

Our leadership manual states "leaders who demonstrate selfless service give credit for success to others and accept responsibility for failure themselves."[15]

Whatever success we may have achieved undoubtedly had

to come about because of the prodigious efforts of our subordinates—by those sometimes faceless and ignored individuals who toil on what may be mundane tasks to bolster the team's efforts. We can demonstrate a gracious humility, win the appreciation of our subordinates, and deflect the lavish praise to where it belongs by saying something like this: "Whatever I have accomplished is a result of the support that I received from the many outstanding Soldiers who helped me along the way. Without their help I would have accomplished little. I would be nothing. I know who did the work; I know who did the heavy lifting. I would be remiss if I did not give credit where credit is due." That is not only accurate but also fitting. The troops will recognize and appreciate this probably unexpected recognition.

Of course, giving credit where credit is due—even lavishly—is appropriate, and generally pays great dividends by increased effort on the parts of our subordinates. All of us like our efforts to be recognized, particularly by our boss.

There are many ways that we can recognize the contributions of our Soldiers and civilians. They include awards, passes, public praise, and unit newsletters. Brigadier General Willard Pearson, commander of the 1st Brigade (Separate), 101st Airborne Division in Vietnam initiated the policy of citing in brigade general orders heroic combat actions. A common practice during the Civil War, citing individuals assures both immediate recognition and provides support for formal awards.[16]

Recognition does not always have to be limited to individuals. The Turning Blue ceremony for Infantry Soldiers who have completed basic training and the senior status review for OCS provide an opportunity to recognize a unit or groups of individuals. Banner Days or Family Days, while focusing on the unit or teams, provide another opportunity to acknowledge achievement.

When Major General Courtney Whitney was asked why General MacArthur was great, the former answered, "It was because he made his men feel that their contribution was an important one—that they were somebody."[17] One of the better ways to give credit is to write thank-you notes. Personalizing your expressions of appreciation pays great dividends because they are both justified and usually unexpected.

Sherman's march through the South had been strongly opposed by the leadership in Washington. Grant, however, defended Sherman's daring gambit. When it proved successful, it was widely acclaimed. Since he had approved the strategy, Grant would have been blamed if Sherman had failed. However, Grant magnanimously gave "the credit to Sherman saying, 'the question of who devised the plan of march from Atlanta to Savannah is easily answered: it was clearly Sherman, and to him also belongs the credit of its brilliant execution.'"[18] While Coach Bear Bryant came on the scene many years after Grant, Bryant acted in accordance with Grant's advice. "There's just three things I ever say. If anything goes bad, then I did it. If anything goes semi-good, then we did it. If anything goes really good, then you did it. That's all it takes."[19]

If Grant could give credit where credit is due, so can we. We will never regret it.

DELINQUENT SOLDIERS APPRECIATE BEING APPRECIATED

Human nature is eternally hungry for recognition. The perfect food for this hunger is credit, written or spoken, acknowledgment of service rendered. Give the credit— all the credit—to the other person—when giving credit is second nature, you will take your place among the world's bigger people, for that is the way of bigness the world over.[20]

—James T. Mangan

Every Soldier wants to believe that his work is worthwhile, recognized, and appreciated. "In the Army, respect means recognizing and appreciating the inherent dignity and worth of all people."[21]

I was working in my office one night after all the headquarters personnel had gone home. I had returned after supper to do some paperwork. As I sat at my desk I heard a tentative knock on the door. When I looked up, there was a Soldier pulling a vacuum after him. He asked, "Sir, may I vacuum your office?" I replied, "Certainly, go right ahead."

I returned to my papers as he went about the office with the vacuum. When he came to my desk, I rose and moved away so that he could finish the job.

When he finished and prepared to leave, I asked him his name and then said, "Private White, I appreciate your cleaning my office."

That seemed to puzzle him. He hesitated a moment and then, obviously embarrassed, said, "Sir, this is company punishment for something I did. I have to do it. You don't need to thank me."

I responded, "I know you're on a punishment tour, but I appreciate what you did anyway. You've done a good job cleaning my office. If you didn't do it for me, I might have to do it myself."

That seemed to amuse him. He smiled and then said, "Sir, you're the first one who ever thanked me for something I did!"

I smiled and thanked him again as he left. I don't know if my "thank you," which was nothing more than common courtesy, had any lasting effect on White. It was the courteous thing to do. More important, I hope that it conveyed in some small way that I recognized him as an individual of value to our brigade.

I believe that commanders can over time have a significant impact on their Soldiers if they show the common courtesy of recognizing and thanking their Soldiers for what they do, even if what they do is a punishment for some minor misdeed. These recalcitrant Soldiers feel bad—perhaps even ashamed for what they have done. A simple "thank you" is recognition from above that they are not considered incorrigible.

Try it. You'll be glad you did, and you'll benefit from it.

Developing Junior Leaders

Battles are fought by platoons and squads. Place emphasis on small unit combat instruction so that it is conducted with the same precision as close-order drill.[22]

—General George S. Patton, Jr.

When General William F. "Buck" Kernan talked to members of the 75th Ranger Regiment about the invasion of Panama, he spoke from his perspective as the regimental commander at the time. He said, "When the battle was joined—when the first shot was fired—success or failure of the attack was in the hands of my team leaders." There can be no stronger endorsement of the value and importance of training junior leaders than that statement.

Colonel Kernan had to depend on the most junior leaders in the chain of command to do the right thing, because they were the ones closest to the action. They were at the cutting age—at the point of the bayonet. He could affect the battle at the macro level by using supporting fires, maneuvering subordinate units, and by personal example, but ultimately the troops would perform only as well as they had been trained. What had been learned and become second nature to them because of the rigorous, repetitive, battle-focused training would be what the troops would do when the chips were down. Training makes the difference

I believe that the squad leader deserves the same importance that General Kernan placed on the team leaders. While one may argue about the relative significance of team and squad leaders, none is more important than these junior leaders. They are at the cutting edge. Our focus as leaders should be on developing them. They need the initiative, knowledge, and self-confidence to meet this responsibility. They develop these characteristics in training before the battle is joined.

As a Ranger company commander in Korea and later, as a battalion commander in Vietnam, I saw that the greatest shortcoming was in our junior leaders, and this was to be expected because they have the least experience. Although my observations since retirement have been more limited, they support my active duty experience. I see the same situation in the 75th Ranger Regiment, our premier light Infantry unit. I saw it in the 25th Infantry Division several years ago while observing some live-fire exercises. Major General Bob Clark, Commanding General, 101st Airborne Division (Air Assault), made the same observation about his division at a commanders and staff combat leadership seminar in which I participated.

When the Eighth Army Ranger Company was training and, later, after combat contacts, we conducted brief, informal critiques. The focus was on "How can we do better next time?" Leaders and individual Rangers described what they had done and suggested improvement. In this way, mistakes or, more often, actions that could have been accomplished better were enumerated without concern for any condemnation because it was not forthcoming. Improvement was the goal.

We used a similar approach in training instructors in Discovery, the outdoor experiential education program I established and led after leaving the Army. Trainees critiqued their own performance and described what they could have done that might have been better. When critiquing others, trainees began with positive comments before turning to areas needing correction or improvement. The focus was always on safety because much of what we did was potentially dangerous.

We need competent leaders, especially when things go wrong. When communication fails, leaders become casualties, reinforcements don't materialize, relief does not occur, and resupply is impossible, the small unit is on its own.

Developing those leaders is a tough challenge. Rigorous training in a supportive environment develops leaders with the initiative, knowledge, and self-confidence to make those decisions. Through repetitive drills these leaders and their Soldiers master skills necessary for combat readiness. Fundamentals become second nature, a matter of discipline and habit. Commanders must allow these junior leaders to make mistakes as they train. By doing so we can prepare them to take more responsibility. We set them up for success as we give them more responsibility and require more from them while allowing them to make mistakes. A "Zero Defects" mentality results in overcontrol. We must avoid that cancer.

Dispersion affects leadership. Low-ranking enlisted men and junior officers are making decisions formerly made by senior NCOs and officers.

Discipline is the glue that makes individual Soldiers remain on the field of battle no matter how debilitating the fear of death and mutilation might be.[23] Discipline is essential to esprit de corps. As units train to standard—as they do things right—they become disciplined and combat ready. They are imbued with confidence in themselves and their leaders, their training, and equipment.

Whether the unit succeeds or fails, lives or dies, depends on the training level and toughness of the individuals and the competence of their junior leaders. There's nothing new there. The question we as leaders should be asking ourselves is, "Are we developing the junior leaders and Soldiers that the modern battlefield requires?"

The American GI is smart. He knows when he is well-trained and well-led. You can't fool him. He recognizes good, tough, battle-focused training. He'll accept the hardships that go with that training because he understands the purpose. It's to help him stay alive while he does the toughest, most dangerous job in the world.

Our Army must be prepared to fight and win our country's wars. In the Global War on Terrorism, just as in previous wars, victory or defeat will be affected significantly by how well small units perform. We must prepare the leaders of those units. If we fail, this negligence will cause America to waste some of her most valuable assets, the sons and daughters that fight our wars.

MOTIVATING SOLDIERS

People tend to repeat behavior they are rewarded for. *(Emphasis in the original.) That statement initially appears to be too simplistic, too direct, too naïve. To put all the motivation theory into one tiny encapsulated statement may seem ludicrous. Yet, it turns out to be the only sane statement to make about motivation. Simply reward what you want to see repeated. Establish the kind of work environment that literally compels spirited performance. Motivation is an inside job; it comes from a person's desire to accomplish something important, something that person wants to do. Anytime a leader attempts to motivate someone to do something the leader wants done (and experiences resistance from that someone), the result is manipulation—not motivation.*[24]

—Bil Holton, PhD

Task Force Soldier, an initiative by Army Chief of Staff Peter J. Schoomaker, was (and is) directed at developing the warrior ethos and combat effectiveness of every Soldier regardless of branch or duty. I was fortunate enough to be involved with one of the teams located at Fort Benning, Georgia, when this vital program was being developed. The team members agreed that there were several basic skills and tasks that every Soldier needed to master in order to succeed and survive on the battlefields on which our Soldiers find themselves in Iraq and Afghanistan and any other in the future. There are basic skills that each Soldier has to possess; there are several tasks that every Soldier has to be able to perform. These requirements were forced on the Army in Afghanistan and Iraq because every Soldier, regardless of branch and assignment was vulnerable. One example—the ambush of the 507th Ordnance Maintenance Company (the Jessica Lynch story)—hit the headlines and emphasized the obvious. Every Soldier must be prepared always to fight and defend his unit and himself. Otherwise he could become a casualty. The Warrior Ethos is expressed in the Soldier's Creed that begins and ends with the words, "I am an American Soldier." Developing that willingness— even desire—to close with and destroy the enemy, if necessary, is vital. It is the foundation of becoming a warrior.

Lieutenant General William Wallace, commander (at the time), Combined Arms Center, Fort Leavenworth, Kansas, said:

> To be a warrior, you've got to be able to use your individual weapon. You've got to be able to operate in small, lethal teams if called upon to do so. You've got to have that mental and physical capability to deal with the enemy regardless of whether you're a frontline Soldier or you're someone fixing helicopters for a living, because you are a Soldier first and a mechanic second.[25]

General Peter J. Schoomaker summed it up when he said "Everybody's a rifleman first."[26] The Chief's emphasis on individual combat skills is part of a larger program to infuse the "warrior ethos" into the entire Army. The focus on technical skills in the past has caused achieving and maintaining basic combat skills to be neglected.[27]

The tasks and skills were codified in what became known as the "40 & 9"—40 skills and 9 battle drills—and disseminated throughout the Army. Basic training programs were expanded and revamped to train to these tasks. They apply to all male and female Soldiers regardless of branch or duty assignment. Although my contacts with the male and female officer students in BOLC II (Basic Officer Leadership Course II) were somewhat limited, I found all of them to be very enthusiastic about mastering combat skills. Seeing females who weighed less than one hundred pounds carrying their machine gun with great pride was particularly impressive to me. They asked for no special consideration because of gender or size.

Soldiers in the Basic Combat Training Brigade (BCTB), which provides initial entry training to some noncombat arms Soldiers at Fort Benning, were enthusiastic about the new responsibilities being placed on them. While one may argue (and I agree) that there probably is a basic difference in the mental and emotional outlook of a Soldier in, say, a combat service support branch (CSS) and an Infantryman, those CSS Soldiers were motivated to accept the challenge placed on them to be a warrior.

> Motivation grows out of people's confidence in themselves, their unit, and their leaders. This confidence is born in hard, realistic training; it's nurtured by constant reinforcement and through the kind of leadership—consistent, hard, and fair—that promotes trust. Remember that trust, like loyalty, is a gift your Soldiers give you only when you demonstrate that you deserve it. Motivation also springs from the person's faith in the larger mission of the organization—a sense of being a part of the big picture.[28]

Pride and esprit come from within oneself. They are based on several beliefs—that I have a tough, important mission; that I am well trained and capable of accomplishing that mission; that I have competent leaders; that I belong to an outstanding unit; that I had to meet high standards (the rites of passage) to be accepted into that unit; and that others recognize these facts about me.

Certainly, there is no tougher, more dangerous, or more important job than that of the Soldier. We would be hard-pressed to find anyone who disagrees with that statement! Convincing the Soldier that he is well trained will not be hard if we train him well. He knows when he is good at his job. Train him to be all he can be. There is no reason—there can be no excuse—for settling for anything less.

Getting competent leaders is the next criterion. From what I have seen in the last ten to fifteen years, I am very favorably impressed. Contacts with brigade and regimental commanders convince me that they are very capable. Most of the drill sergeants conducting training in our centers are combat veterans. They know their stuff. They are impressive, and their trainees listen to them. The Army is certainly focusing on the task of developing competent leaders.

The fact that we are at war in Afghanistan and Iraq is certainly an influence that trainers can use to motivate our Soldiers. When trainers who are combat veterans connect their personal experiences with training goals, it focuses the attention of the trainees and enhances motivation.

We can do a better job in preparing Soldiers to be drill sergeants by selecting more who have earned the coveted Ranger Tab. There can be little doubt that the Ranger School graduate has improved his knowledge of small unit tactics because of the emphasis on tactical problems. During the course, he was required to get people to perform difficult tasks under sometimes extreme conditions of fatigue, emotional stress, sleep and food deprivation, and physical and weather hardships.

However, almost every Ranger School graduate will state that what he has learned about himself is the most valuable outcome. Because of the huge demands placed on him, he knows that he has great, although not unlimited, potential within himself if he is just willing to pay the price. That is an invaluable core belief of a warrior. Drill sergeants who are Ranger grads will be better prepared to instill that belief in their trainees.

How do we convince the Soldier that he is in an outstanding unit? That's not as easy as the previous tasks. First, of course, the unit must be outstanding.

Our commanders recognize the importance of unit pride. For example, visit any training unit at Fort Benning, and you will be impressed with the effort to connect today's Soldiers with the unit's history. As you enter the battalion area, signs proclaiming the glorious combat history of that battalion and its parent regiment greet you. You see more of the same when you enter the battalion headquarters. The emphasis on tradition is so impressive that you might initially be mistaken about the mission of that battalion: is it to train individual Soldiers, or is this the headquarters of a combat-ready Infantry battalion? The leaders are using this positive influence to motivate their trainees. You will be impressed, and, yes, you can feel the sense of pride that permeates that headquarters and the Soldiers you will meet.

We can have esprit and it can/should be based on a valid appraisal of the unit's capability. You cannot fool Soldiers; they know whether they are in a combat-ready organization. You do not have to tell them they are good (although it helps). They will know that.

What about the rites of passage? Basic training and advanced individual training are the first steps. Task Force Soldier has done and is doing much to enhance the prestige of basic training. Certainly enlightened leaders can elicit the last ounce of effort from young men wanting to prove themselves men! The same applies to females. As I said about my observation of the females in BOLC II, they were not hesitant in stepping forward and giving all that they had. Any person who successfully completes this training has reason to be proud. His leaders ensure that he is reminded often of his success. When he reports to his unit, the process continues.

Every unit commander should aspire to the highest standards. Why not be all that you can be? Why not aim for having every Infantryman qualify for the Expert Infantryman Badge (EIB).

That aspiration is not a manifestation of "badge disease." It is a very high, yet attainable, goal. The badge is a concrete, visible symbol of excellence. Ask anyone who has the EIB if he is proud of it. You had better believe it! The same goes for the Expert Field

Medic Badge (EFMB). There is no badge similar to the EIB or EFMB for other branches.

The Army has authorized the Army Combat Action Badge (CAB) to be awarded to non-Infantrymen who have met certain criteria in combat. Commanders should ensure that all those who have earned the CAB have it awarded to them at an appropriate ceremony. Savvy commanders take advantage of other means to recognize commendable performance. These include something as simple as a word of encouragement, announcements at formations, articles in the unit or post newspaper, and other similar approaches.

The last criterion is getting others to recognize the importance of the Soldier's job and the high standards required of him. We can do better. Banner days, unit activation ceremonies, intracompany competition, picnics, and unit newsletters help spread the word. Maybe we ought to look at the Marines. No matter how much one may criticize them for their emphasis on public relations there can be no doubt that they are masters at convincing every Marine of his importance and the importance of the Marine Corps.

The line Infantry is the backbone of our Army. It has the toughest, most dangerous mission. The Infantryman has to be in outstanding physical condition. He has to be highly skilled in the tactics and techniques of the individual Soldier. His squad, platoon, company, battalion, and brigade must be smoothly functioning, highly efficient fighting machines. He must believe that he and his unit are the best that our Army can produce. Moreover, he has to know that others recognize his accomplishments.

Those requirements don't just exist for the Infantrymen; they apply to every Soldier. The Army Chief of Staff has emphasized the necessity for all Soldiers to be warriors—to have that pride and confidence that comes from knowing that they individually and their units are combat-ready and can successfully meet any requirement that they may face.

We can achieve all those goals. We do it by a battle-focused training program based on the mastery of basic skills by all in the unit. When we do, we will have individual Soldiers, both male and female, who can accomplish any appropriate mission no matter how tough. We will also have Soldiers who are proud of themselves and their job. They will be "fully trained and ready to go into battle with all flags flying and guns at the ready."[29] They will know that they do not have to take a backseat to anybody—no, not to any Marine nor any paratrooper nor any Ranger!

SET THE EXAMPLE: THE MOST IMPORTANT LEADERSHIP PRINCIPLE

All these Soldiers have their eyes on you. If they see you are discouraged they will all be cowards; but if you show them you are making preparations against the enemy, and if you call on them, you may be sure they will follow you to try to imitate you. Perhaps it is fair to expect you to be a bit better than they are. You are a captain, you see, and you are in command of troops and companies, and while there was peace, you had more wealth and honor; then now when war has come, we must ask you to be better than the mob, and to plan and labor on their behalf, if necessary.[30]

—Xenophon, Athenian Historian, mercenary Soldier, and Disciple of Socrates

I will not send troops to danger which I will not myself encounter.[31]

—The Duke of Marlborough

FM 22-100, *Army Leadership*, tells us that "BE, KNOW, DO (emphasis in the original) clearly and concisely states the characteristics of an Army leader."[32] Army Chief of Staff General Eric K. Shinseki stated in his foreword to the FM, "Whether supporting, training, or fighting, America looks to you to BE, KNOW, and DO what is right"[33] (emphasis in the original).

When we were being trained and prepared for leadership, setting the example was always stressed. Command Sergeant Major Greg Birch, the regimental sergeant major (RSM), 75th Ranger Regiment, wrote in his RSM Note #3, "Leaders must live the standard every day."[34] The regimental commander, Colonel Craig Nixon, emphasized the RSM's words: "All Rangers are expected to know, live, and enforce the standards—every day."[35]

Innumerable commanders, historians, and others have proclaimed the importance of leading the way. Although setting the example applies to all circumstances, we most often use combat examples when we want to illustrate this principle. There is no question that a leader's example is most important when the situation is deteriorating. Brigadier General S. L. A. Marshall wrote that "spectacular intervention" might be required "in extreme emergencies, when the stakes are high and the failure of others to act has made the need imperative." However, he added, some leaders may "practice self-exposure to danger in hope of having a good moral effect on men."[36]

Setting the example is not limited to combat. It applies to everything that we do. Some of my best role models, teachers, and mentors were noncommissioned officers with whom I served or came in contact after I retired. Most of that mentoring came about by the way they performed or by what they said in informal conversations with me. Regardless, I was astute enough to give credence to what I was observing. If it can be said about anyone that they have "been there, done that" it applies to our senior noncommissioned officers.

One of the best noncommissioned officers I had the privilege of getting to know was Command Sergeant Major Jimmy Pickering. One day when I was visiting him, I posed a theoretical question. "Suppose the chief of staff of the Army asked you what he could do to improve the combat effectiveness of the Army without requiring more money or more Soldiers, what would you say?" The sergeant major replied quickly as a flash, "Know the standard. Enforce the standard. Be the standard." He gave me a copy of a letter that he distributed to his NCOs whenever he was assigned to a different unit. The letter expanded on this theme while maintaining its brevity.

"The Army has established standards for all activities. Standards are formal, detailed instructions that can be stated, measured, and achieved. They provide a baseline to evaluate how well a specific task has been achieved. You must know, communicate, and enforce standards."

The phrase "Set the example, and be the standard," in Command Sergeant Major Pickering's words, is the most important leadership principle. According to him, "If you know the standard and enforce the standard, you will be the standard by which other Soldiers are judged. You <u>will</u> (the Sergeant Major Pickering's emphasis) change the Army every time you interact with a Soldier; change it for the better."[37] I agree with Command Sergeant Major Pickering that nothing would improve our Army more. We would do well to follow his advice.

Section III

COMMAND AND STAFF

MURPHY'S LAWS ARE
ALWAYS IN EFFECT

Everything is tougher in combat. Things go wrong. Confusion is normal. Nothing ever happens the way it was planned. The Normandy invasion had many examples. (The scattering of the paratroopers is mentioned several times in *Saving Private Ryan* and is described vividly in Clay Blair's *Ridgway's Paratroopers*.) Everything takes longer than expected. Train for it. Think of things that can go wrong, such as losing several key leaders, receiving high casualties, landing on hot landing zones (LZ), encountering unexpected minefields, and meeting much stronger enemy resistance than expected. You, yourself, can become a casualty.

Murphy's War Laws reign supreme. Here are some other things that can "go wrong."[1]

- Friendly fire—isn't.

- Recoilless rifles—aren't.

- Suppressive fires—won't.

- You are not Superman; Marines and fighter pilots take note.

- A sucking chest wound is Nature's way of telling you to slow down.

- If it's stupid but it works, it isn't stupid.

- Try to look unimportant; the enemy may be low on ammo and not want to waste a bullet on you.

- If at first you don't succeed, call in an air strike.

- If you are forward of your position, your artillery will fall short.

- Never share a foxhole with anyone braver than yourself.

- Never go to bed with anyone crazier than yourself.

- Never forget that your weapon was made by the lowest bidder.

- If your attack is going really well, it's an ambush.

- The enemy diversion you're ignoring is their main attack.

- The enemy invariably attacks on two occasions: when they're ready. When you're not.

- No OPLAN ever survives initial contact.

- There is no such thing as a perfect plan.

- Five-second fuses always burn three seconds.

- There is no such thing as an atheist in a foxhole.

- A retreating enemy is probably just falling back and regrouping. The Ol' Ranger's Addendum, or else they're trying to suck you into a serious ambush.

- The important things are always simple; the simple are always hard.

- The easy way is always mined.

- Teamwork is essential; it gives the enemy other people to shoot at.

- Don't look conspicuous; it draws fire. For this reason, it is not at all uncommon for aircraft carriers to be known as bomb magnets.

- Never draw fire; it irritates everyone around you.

- If you are short of everything but the enemy, you are in the combat zone.

- When you have secured the area, make sure the enemy knows it too.

- Incoming fire has the right of way.

- No combat-ready unit has ever passed inspection.

- No inspection-ready unit has ever passed combat.

- If the enemy is within range, so are you.

- The only thing more accurate than incoming enemy fire is incoming friendly fire.

- Things which must be shipped together as a set, aren't.

- Things that must work together can't be carried to the field that way.

- Radios will fail as soon as you need fire support.

- Radar tends to fail at night and in bad weather, and especially during both.

- Anything you do can get you killed, including nothing.

- Make it too tough for the enemy to get in, and you won't be able to get out.

- Tracers work both ways.

- If you take more than your fair share of objectives, you will get more than your fair share of objectives to take.

- When both sides are convinced they're about to lose, they're both right.

- Professional Soldiers are predictable; the world is full of dangerous amateurs.

- Military intelligence is a contradiction.

- Fortify your front; you'll get your rear shot up.
- Weather ain't neutral.
- If you can't remember, the Claymore is pointed toward you.

OBJECT TO THE BRINK OF INSUBORDINATION

Physical courage is never in short supply in a fighting Army. Moral courage sometimes is.[2]

—General Matthew B. Ridgway

A strong man that wields power and influence can often be dangerous. Because of his strength he may appear invincible and always correct (or think that he is). A strong commander must have a staff (including subordinate commanders) composed of men with backbones. If they are "yes men," the commander will only hear what his subordinates think he wants to hear. He will not have the benefit of reasoned opinions that though differing with his own provide him valuable insight into ramifications of what he is planning. Commanders, particularly strong commanders, have difficulty in knowing the real state of their commands because they have the difficult, sometimes impossible task of seeing through the façade presented by subordinates.

Army General Omar N. Bradley said, "A good leader must sometimes be stubborn. Armed with the courage of his convictions, he must often fight to defend them. When he has come to a decision after thorough analysis—and when he is sure he is right—he must stick to it even to the point of stubbornness."[3]

One of the most valuable lessons proffered to me while I was a first classman (senior) at West Point was expressed simply as:

> If you believe that your commander is about to
> make a serious mistake with the action he is con-
> templating, it is your duty to object to the point
> of insubordination. To do otherwise would be dis-
> loyal. When he (your commander) has listened
> to your arguments and says, "That's my decision!"
> your job then is to salute, say, "Yes, sir!" and move
> out. You are then to work extra hard to do what
> your commander wants.

A significant disagreement, albeit friendly, occurred in 1954 during and after the battle of Dien Bien Phu in Vietnam. The French were urging the United States to commit ground forces in the fight against the Viet Minh. General Matthew B. Ridgway, through his strong arguments, convinced President Eisenhower not to become engaged "in a land war in Southeast Asia."[4] Another famous disagreement, much less friendly, was between General Douglas MacArthur and President Truman concerning the conduct of the Korean War. President Truman relieved General MacArthur because of insubordination when he publicly criticized the President's decision not to bomb mainland China.

There may be occasions, particularly in combat, when there is no time to express disagreement. However, when the situation permits, it is the subordinate's duty to present opposing views when he feels strongly about the commander's decision.

I remember one example, in particular, from my own personal experience. I was a company commander in the 65th Infantry Regimental Combat Team in Puerto Rico in 1954. While home on Christmas leave, my executive officer (XO) wrote me some disquieting news. He said that I had been selected by the regimental commander to form a noncommissioned officer academy when I returned. The XO said that my replacement had been selected and was already in command!

When I returned to Puerto Rico, I immediately tried to learn more about the change. The regimental S3 and each of the three battalion commanders urged me to fight the establishment of the

Academy with all my ability. From their comments to me, I knew that they would not support the Academy and probably would resist cooperating with me.

The regimental commander called a meeting attended by the three battalion commanders, his principal staff, and me. At this meeting, no one spoke except the commander and me. I objected strenuously to the commander's plan. I stated unhesitatingly that the battalion commanders were against the idea and would not support the Academy. I also stated that if the commander stuck with his decision, then I expected his staff (who also had expressed to me their lack of support) to check in with my orderly room both when they came and left the area. I was on very thin ice. I received not one word of support from anyone although all had expressed to me their objection to the Academy. Finally, the commander let me know in no uncertain terms that his decision was final. I stood at attention and said, "I will do my best to make the Academy something of which you will be proud!" I saluted and left when dismissed. Unfortunately, my commander made very critical references to the argument in my next three efficiency reports (ER)! While his comments were against regulations—commenting on events that had not happened during the rating period—the ERs stuck.

I, of course, was upset when I read the reports many years later. Back then, raters were not required to show reports to rated officers. However, I felt that I had done the honorable thing.

With hindsight, I know I could have presented my objections in a more respectful although just as forceful manner. I had been disrespectful and belligerent. I had resolved before the meeting that I would not give an inch and that I would fight the commander's desire with every ounce of my being. I view my entire "performance" as unprofessional. What was unprofessional was not my expressing disagreement—that was my duty—but the manner in which I did it.

Decisions can be of much greater import, say, in combat or when pertaining to something of great importance. The principle is the same. The loyal subordinate, when appropriate, will let his commander know of the subordinate's disagreements. As I said above, to do otherwise is disloyal.

I remembered that injunction and tried to live by it. I hope that my troops felt that I would listen to them with an open mind and not hold it against them if they objected strenuously to what I contemplated.

If you disagree with your boss' decision, it is your professional duty to object strenuously "almost to the point of insubordination" until the boss says that there is to be no more discussion; you have your orders. Not many officers will do that. Some seniors cannot accept strong objection. Those in high command who cannot are dangerous; they have surrounded themselves with "yes men."

Roles and Missions and How to Train for Them

One of the most important psychological principles of objective setting is that the objective must be believable, reachable, and specific. Part of the believability is the legitimacy of the objective-giver. Is the leader believable? Are objectives doable? Reachable? They are if discriminating leaders know how to torque objectives just enough to elevate the standard of excellence to a level that exceeds the team's initial reach but not their grasp. When leaders push their people to meet a particularly challenging objective and succeed after concerted effort, they will feel a sense of satisfaction and "a degree of relief scarcely ... equaled."[5]

—Bil Holton, PhD

Commanders establish training goals, giving careful consideration to the roles and missions assigned to their units. These goals vary widely. However, some training goals are appropriate all the time for any unit regardless of its branch and the mission assigned by higher headquarters. These are:

1. Every Soldier will be in the best physical condition possible; every Soldier will be a tiger.

2. Every Soldier will be highly skilled in the tactics and techniques of the individual Soldier; every Soldier should know

his stuff. There are basic Soldier skills taught in basic and advanced individual training that every Soldier must know. There are others that apply specifically to the function of the Soldier's unit or section.

3. Every fire team, squad, platoon, and company will be a highly effective combat machine. If the section is Combat Support (CS) or Combat Service Support (CSS), the functions of the small teams will differ from that of Infantry. However, that fact does not negate the requirement for each section to be an effective team capable of supporting the combat arms. BOLC II (Basic Officer Leadership Course II), a program for all newly commissioned second lieutenants regardless of their branch and gender, has as its mission: "To develop competent, confident and adaptable lieutenants, grounded in warrior tasks, able to lead Soldiers in the contemporary operational environment."[6]

4. Every Soldier will have the confidence and esprit that make him believe that he and his unit are the best that the United States can produce.

To develop a training program that accomplishes these goals, there are fundamental principles that, if implemented, result in success. They include the following:

1. A demanding, progressive, well-organized, battle- and mission-focused training program that requires adherence to high standards can turn ordinary people into outstanding Soldiers.

2. Since you never know when you will be required to put everything on the line in combat, you must always be ready. For combat support and combat service support, being ready includes not only the skills required to accomplish the unit's responsibilities but also the requirement to be ready to fight as Infantrymen if the need arises. I have observed second lieutenants in BOLC II as they trained in live-fire convoy operations, in MOUT (military operations in urban terrain), and in night

tactical exercises. After BOLC II training is over, the expected end result is "an officer who is trained in warrior tasks and warrior battle drills, who is self-aware and adaptable ... and who embodies the warrior ethos."[7] If you are a headquarters or a CS or CSS unit, ask yourself when was the last time your unit exercised this responsibility. "If you have not practiced basic defensive drills in a variety of typical situations, you are not prepared."[8] It is doubtful that your section can perform adequately to defend itself if the need arises. Practice these tactical skills with the work unit—your CS or CSS section. Train to fight with the same people you work with every day.[9]

3. Outstanding physical fitness is vital; as a combat Infantryman, you're nothing if you're not in superb physical condition. Outstanding physical fitness helps every Soldier perform regardless of his job—whether in combat, combat support, or combat service support. Stamina is the most important facet of physical fitness.

4. Mastery of fundamentals is vital. Fundamentals are basic tasks such as fire and maneuver, camouflage, scouting and patrolling, care of equipment, immediate action drills, etc. This training can be accomplished during downsizing and restrictive budgets. CS and CSS units also have individual and small unit skills and capabilities that must be developed.

5. Strive for excellence in *every* activity. "Good enough" is never good enough until it is the best that you can do. Whenever you settle for anything less than your best, you're cheating yourself, your Soldiers, our Army, and this great country.

6. Integrity must be the core value in everything a Soldier does. Integrity is the unflinching adherence to high standards of duty and honor no matter what the physical risk, the emotional stress, or the ridicule of others. Integrity requires you to do your best, to do your duty. Remember: Winston Churchill once said that duty is the noblest word in the English language.

By establishing these goals and basing your training program on these principles, your unit will be successful in garrison and in combat.

SAFETY IS NO ACCIDENT

The principle is this: no safety check can ever be routine, no matter how often performed, when the lives of men are involved. It is an insidious temptation to slight checks on regulations when things have been going safely for days—but this is the danger, because it dulls alertness. [10]

—Major General Aubrey "Red" Newman

"We follow the Safety SOP (standing operating procedure) for two reasons. Firstly, we do not want to have a Ranger injured or killed because of human error, and secondly, if we have a Ranger seriously injured or killed because of a violation of SOP, changes to the way we train will be mandated. We will not be able to continue with our battle-focused training as we have done in the past. Our training for combat will not be as effective as it is today."[11]

As I listened to the words of Colonel Ken Keen, Commander, 75th Ranger Regiment, I remembered my experiences as the national safety coordinator for Outward Bound, Inc. I also recalled my business, Discovery, Inc. These two organizations rely heavily on physically rigorous and emotionally challenging outdoor activities to develop self-confidence and teamwork. At Discovery, compliance with the safety policy and procedures was a condition for employment. The insurance company that provided our liability and accident insurance was the insurer for more outdoor programs than any other. The vice president of that company said that Discovery was the safest of all the corporations that they insured. The reason was because of our emphasis on safety. Safety awareness permeated all that we did.

Attention to safety should be a disciplined response. This disciplined approach underlies everything that we do. Our training demands that safety awareness and following safety procedures become so ingrained in us that our actions are automatic. That does not mean that we are not thinking; it means that we do not deviate from the procedures without major extenuating circumstances and then only with approval of the appropriate authority.

The commander ensures that his unit always follows the safety procedures in every aspect of everything it does. It does not deviate. As a result, safety procedures become second nature; following them is the only way that the unit performs.

"Safety, risk management, and fratricide prevention are interrelated and do not differ in peacetime from combat."[12] General Wayne A. Downing emphasized this point, saying, "If your subordinates say, 'If this was combat, I would have done it another way,' then something is wrong with your training. Realistic training and safety are not incompatible; safety is an inherent part of all operations; the chain of command is responsible for safety; no one else."[13]

Colonel Paul LaCamera, Commander, 75th Ranger Regiment, stated in his Commander's Policy, " Off-duty safety is as important as on-duty safety." Many of his Rangers engage in high risk, potentially dangerous activities, such as hunting, boating, scuba diving, skydiving, motorcycle riding, and swimming. While more difficult to control because the Rangers are not under the Commander's direct supervision, he, nevertheless, emphasized the requirement for and benefits of following sound safety procedures.

Developing this conditioned or disciplined response in all subordinates is an aspect of all training. Safety is not considered as a separate item; it is part of performing to standard—of doing things correctly.[14]

By his every action and word, the commander conveys to subordinates the importance (or lack thereof) that the commander places on safety. The safety awareness—adherence to the safety standards of the command—is a direct reflection of how the subordinates perceive their commander.

The commander may promulgate a written statement describing his "Safety Philosophy." He might stress the reasons for and importance of following safety procedures. He might express his views verbally. No matter how he states his philosophy or how important he says safety is, what he *does* will be what his subordinates remember.

WHAT DO YOU DO WHEN YOU HAVE MORE THAN YOU CAN DO?

Do essential things first. There is not enough time for the commander to do everything. Each commander will have to determine wisely what is essential and assign responsibilities for accomplishment. He should spend the remaining time on near essentials. This is especially true of training. Nonessentials should not take up time for essentials.[15]

—General Bruce C. Clarke

Commanders complain, justifiably so, that they have more than they can accomplish. The Mission Essential Task List (METL) tells them what their senior commander has said is essential for the unit to be able to accomplish. "Essential" means that the task is vital. The unit must be able to accomplish the tasks to standard or the unit is not combat ready. Commanders who are truthful with themselves know that there is insufficient time to achieve the standard in all the METL. What do you do when you have more than you can do?

"Army leaders set priority and balance competing demands. They focus their organizations' efforts on short- and long-term goals while continuing to meet requirements that may or may not contribute directly to achieving those goals.... You must make the tough calls.[16] ... A highly developed system of time management may be the only way for organizational leaders to handle all the demands upon them."[17]

The METL for the 75th Ranger Regiment is over an inch thick. It contains hundreds of tasks. Recognizing that training to standard on all of those tasks was impossible, the regimental commander, then Colonel Stanley McChrystal, concluded that accomplishment of all of them rested on competence in four basic areas of expertise. These areas became known as the "Big Four" within the Regiment. They were 1. small unit drills, 2. marksmanship, 3. medical training, and 4. physical fitness. He reasoned that these skill areas had to be mastered for the Regiment to be capable of accomplishing its combat missions. He did not limit training to those areas. Joint training exercises were a significant part of the master training program. However, the Big Four were always emphasized. (When the Regiment's Table of Organization and Equipment (T/O&E) changed with the addition of numerous vehicles, a fifth skill, driving, was added.)

The Eighth Army Ranger Company, activated on August 25, 1950, was the first Ranger unit established after WWII. This very small company had a Table of Organization and Equipment (T/O&E) of three officers and seventy-four enlisted men. The volunteers consisted primarily of low-ranking Soldiers from service units in Japan. They were good Soldiers but were not Infantrymen. As a consequence, the training program focused on the basic skills that Rangers would need to be combat ready. There was no METL. Instead, as the company commander, I established four training goals. First, every Ranger would be a tiger; he would be in the best physical condition of his life. Second, every Ranger would know his stuff; he would be highly skilled in the tactics and techniques of the individual Soldier (TTIS). Third, each subordinate unit and the company as a whole would be a smoothly functioning, combat-ready, killing machine. Fourth, the Ranger would have confidence that he, his leaders, and the Eighth Army Ranger Company were the best that the United States of America could produce. The Big Four for us could be expressed as physical fitness, individual skills, small unit tactical proficiency, and esprit. These training goals can be closely aligned with Colonel Stan McChrystal's "Big Four." (These Ranger company goals are appropriate for any unit of every branch at every level.)

The 75th Ranger Regiment's "Big Four" and the Ranger company's training goals demonstrate how an insurmountable list of tasks can be concentrated into a reasonable list of requirements. You can answer the question, "What can I do when I have more than I can do?" by following a similar approach.

FIND A "GOLDEN VOICE"
FOR YOUR CEREMONIES

There are three things that ought to be considered be-fore some things are spoken—the manner, the place, and the time.[18]

—Robert Southey, English Poet and Scholar

How many times have you attended a ceremony—a change of command, presentation of awards, or graduation—when the announcer mumbled and mispronounced words? Probably too many to enumerate.

The announcer is really the MC—the master of ceremonies. In many respects, he sets the tone for the entire ceremony. If he speaks clearly and authoritatively while using correct English and pronouncing the words properly, the ceremony is off to a good start.

The "golden voice" cannot perform properly without thorough preparation. He needs to have in writing the sequence of events, and the names and titles of the "distinguished guests" in proper order who will be mentioned in the introduction. Written introductions and explanations are indispensable. If the ceremony is outdoors, the wind could cause a problem unless the notes are incased in plastic sheet protectors. Having each sheet tabbed in a loose-leaf notebook is helpful. Having "filler" material is also a good idea in the event that there is an unforeseen delay.

The commander, the officer in charge (OIC)—the individual

responsible for pulling the ceremony together—should choose his speaker carefully. The personnel officer (S1) is often selected because of his duty position. However, the responsibility should be assigned to him only if his speaking voice meets the highest standards. Once the speaker is chosen—and there may be several "tryouts"—the OIC should rehearse his speaker until the latter is comfortable with what he has to say. Do not slough off this important responsibility. A good announcer is one more sign of a well-led unit. Be sure you have the best. A properly prepared "golden voice" will do wonders for a ceremony.

WHAT I WANT MY CHAPLAIN TO BE

The Chaplain should be where the troops are most miserable![19]

—Colonel Dorian Anderson

There are no atheists in foxholes.[20]

—William Thomas Cummings, Priest

Chaplains have provided valuable assistance to me as a commander. I was able to call on them for advice on the myriad problems that I encountered. I looked on them as personal friends and special staff even though they did not "belong" to me. They gave me an insight into my command and my individual Soldiers that I could not get elsewhere. I am indebted to them.

One of these chaplains that greatly helped me was Chaplain (Captain) Francis Lewis, the 65th Regimental Combat Team chaplain, in Puerto Rico. I don't recall how we met but I know that we soon had a personal relationship that transcended the chaplain-church member context. We often saw each other socially. He often visited the company I commanded and, later, the Regimental Orientation School and the Noncommissioned Officer Academy, both of which I formed and commanded. He alerted me to possible complaints and morale problems and advised me as to corrective actions that I might consider. He also provided moral support to me as I faced the many difficulties associated with my responsibilities.

Chaplain (Captain) Jim Ammerman, the 10th Special Forces

Group chaplain in Germany, assisted me in the same way as Fran Lewis. Jim never hesitated to join me on the numerous field training exercises (FTX) that we had. Like Fran, Jim also offered valuable advice in meeting the pressures of this fast-paced assignment.

Chaplains Bud Connett and James J. Murphy in the 1st Brigade (Separate), 101st Airborne Division in Vietnam, were everything that I could hope for in a chaplain. They would spend time with the troopers while in the bush looking for Charlie.

During retirement, I became friends with Chaplain (Captain) Tom Wheatley, Ranger Training Brigade. Tom was personable and as physically tough as any of the Rangers. He went out of his way to meet and encourage the Rangers when they were training under the most miserable conditions.

The 75th Ranger Regiment chaplains, Chaplain (Lieutenant Colonel) Steve Berry and Chaplain (Major) Tom Soljeim were outstanding examples of Ranger chaplains. Like Wheatley, these two went wherever the Rangers went, including combat deployments. I also became acquainted with one of the battalion chaplains, Paul Lasley. He was my escort on a couple of live-fire exercises. He was thoroughly "tuned in" to the tactical situation and gave a running commentary as the exercise progressed. He called each Soldier by name and spoke to them as they went about their business.

These chaplains from the 1st Brigade, the Ranger Training Brigade, and 75th Ranger Regiment "spoiled" me. They were physically tough, tactically savvy, courageous, and respected and admired by the Soldiers. The Ranger chaplains had met the same standards as the Soldiers they served. They were paratroopers and Ranger qualified. They made the same road marches and met the same high physical standards. They asked for and received no special consideration. They were exactly what I wanted as my unit chaplain.

I want him to meet the same physical, tactical, and appearance standards as my Soldiers. Except for the cross on his collar, he should look like my Soldiers. If married, I expect him to be a true "family man." I expect him to be the epitome of integrity and decorum. I want him to have the courage of his convictions; I want him to be forthright in his dealings with my Soldiers and me. He must have the moral courage to state what he believes rather than what he thinks I want to hear. If he does the latter, he is being dishonest and may cause harm to my Soldiers and my command.

I have not said anything about his spiritual or professional qualifications. I turn to something that Chaplain Berry wrote. While he expressed the importance of meeting the same standards as his Soldiers, he puts "first and foremost" a dedication to an excellent ministry.

> First, no substitute exists for a sense of calling to the chaplaincy. (Emphasis in the original) I know of no civilian equivalent for the ministry roles which we fulfill, be it chaplain or chaplain assistant. As participants in a total institution, Ranger ministry team members wear the same clothes, conform to the same physical standards, and suffer the same privations, as do their parishioners. No other group of pastors or their helpers can make this claim. Thus, military ministry retains a unique texture, replicated nowhere else. Second, we must be able to demonstrate both technical and tactical expertise. Whether the task be preparing a sermon, safeguarding a chapel offering, preparing a religious support estimate for a contingency operation, completing a thirty-mile foot march, or moving to a grid location with map and compass, we cannot allow our ministry team to fall short. Remember: we will relentlessly pursue excellence in all things. Finally, we must retain a healthy balance between our dual roles as pastors and Rangers. Let there be no doubt that we are, first and foremost, a pastoral team, committed to excellence in ministry.

However, we are also Rangers who must be able to function alongside other Rangers in combat operations. We must be at once spiritually and physically fit and able to care for ourselves, as well as others, both in peace and war.[21]

My chaplain was a trusted member of my team. He provided great assistance to me in the exercise of my responsibilities. My command team would have been weaker without his support. Your chaplain can do the same for you if you make him a part of your team.

Commanders and Staff Can Learn from Each Other

The best teams were just the opposite [of the worst teams]. People shared a vision and were committed to both. They supported one another and took on responsibilities freely .... Communication flowed freely.[22]

—Anthony J. Le Storti, Ranger and Educator

One of the many beneficial things commanders and their staffs can do is meet periodically to discuss mutual problems. What causes difficulty for one usually affects the others. Most have similar problems. These discussions can be helpful.

FM 22-100 describes the benefits that can be gained when commanders and staff work together: "Organizational leaders must understand what's going on within their own and the next higher echelon staff. Networking allows them to improve communication and mission accomplishment by giving them a better understanding of the overall environment. Networking requires leaders to constantly interact and share thoughts, ideas, and priorities. Informed staffs can then turn policies, plans, and programs into realities."[23]

In Vietnam in the 1st Brigade (Separate), 101st Airborne Division, we three battalion commanders tried to get together at least once each week to discuss our mutual concerns. The discussion had no agenda. Each commander brought to the group his problems and shared with the others his approach to solving the problems bothering the other commanders.

When given a warning order or just a mention of a possible new orientation of our efforts, we would discuss the way in which we would like to see the areas of operations (AO) assigned, the general direction of our movements, and other facets of the pending operation. We usually agreed on how we would like to see the broad outline of the operation evolve in support of the brigade commander's intent. (Our term was "Concept of Operations.") We then expressed our views, individually or collectively, with the brigade commander, his deputy, and the S3. This obvious cooperation among the battalion commanders pleased the brigade commander and certainly made us feel greater "ownership" in the coming operation, since almost invariably the brigade concept had obviously incorporated much of what we had suggested.

Astute commanders require cooperation among their subordinate commanders and staffs.

Cooperation pays big dividends.

BEWARE OF EXPERTS

The real expert on this subject is a student in your class!

—Unnamed Consultant

Every commander has almost certainly been faced with a problem that he was unable to solve. On the surface, it might appear to be monumental. Yet, when a solution is found, it may seem so simple. The commander might ask himself, "Why didn't I think of that?" Maybe he was just too close to the problem. Maybe his experience did not provide him with the background for an answer. Maybe the answer just did not come to him. Whatever the reason, he needs a solution. Talking to other commanders may be helpful. They may have faced and solved the same difficulty.

You may have the "expert" in your unit. Discuss the problem with your subordinates particularly your noncommissioned officers (NCO). Your NCOs have a wealth of experience. There is often a noncom who has faced exactly the same problem you are facing. He will be able to say, "Now, when I was in the ..., we did ... when we faced that situation." There is your answer!

Your search for a better way is not limited to commissioned and noncommissioned officers. In the highly educated Army that we have today, there may be a wealth of knowledge in your lowest-ranking enlisted men or in the civilians that support your unit. If the problem is significant and particularly difficult, a group study approach may be helpful. If the group suggests a course of action they begin to feel ownership of it when it is implemented thus helping to ensure their support.

The Army often goes to an outside agency for research and a solution for a problem. While this approach has sometimes been appropriate, there are dangers. We (the Army) sometimes place unwarranted reliance on outside help.

Several of my Army War College classmates selected stability operations as the subject for an essay that each student was required to write. A group of them made a trip to a "think tank" that had an Army contract to research the problem. The "action officer" responsible for the research project, at the end of the conference with the students, said "You have the expert on this subject in your class. He is Lieutenant Colonel Ralph Puckett. He has written the only paper ever prepared on stability operations." The paper to which he referred was a twenty-page essay I had submitted in one of my graduate school classes! Since then, I have never looked at an "expert" with the same amount of awe.

SURROUND YOURSELF WITH CAPABLE SUBORDINATES

Surround yourself with the best people you can find, delegate authority, and don't interfere.[24]

—President Ronald Reagan

After commissioning in 1949, I attended the Branch Immaterial Course, the Ground General School, in Fort Riley, Kansas. All new second lieutenants except OCS graduates attended this three- to four-month course. The goal was to teach us the skills and knowledge all second lieutenants needed regardless of which branch they were in. As a consequence, the instruction was wide-ranging with sub-courses on a multitude of topics.

We were organized into platoons. The school staff assigned to a particular platoon presented almost all the instruction. I remember one officer in particular—Captain Jack Null, a combat veteran of WWII. He was an easygoing instructor with a great sense of humor. There was hardly a class in which he did not repeat his favorite "maxim"—"Surround yourself with capable subordinates." I remember him well.

The classes were taught mainly in discussion style. We, the students, would be queried concerning our "actions and orders" for a variety of leadership challenges—tactical, administrative, and logistical. Sometimes we were particularly challenged by a problem at which time we would ask, "Sir, what would you do?" If it were a particularly thorny issue, Captain Null might smile and respond, "That's when I would turn to one of my highly capable subordinates and ask him for his suggestions!" Captain Null made his point. We weren't expected to know everything. We shouldn't be hesitant in admitting that.

Few people, if any, who have achieved any measure of success, did it alone. They know that success in almost all circumstances is a team effort. In football, the running back makes a gain because the offensive line and the fullback helped clear the way. Just as in football, success in the Army depends on a team effort.

FM 22-100, *Army Leadership*, states rather simplistically, "Developing subordinates consists of observing the subordinate's performance, comparing it to the standard, and then providing feedback to the subordinate in the form of counseling."[25] While that is the gist of subordinate development, the FM goes to great lengths to explain how that task may be accomplished. Suffice it to say that leaders have this responsibility for developing their subordinates. Both they and their subordinates will benefit from the effort.

Developing subordinates is one way to surround ourselves with capable subordinates. We have an obligation to those who work for us to assist them in achieving their potential. As we assist in their development, we will benefit. The effort that we expend in developing them is returned to us with interest in the form of a higher level of performance.

Tactical Operations Center

The teams and staffs through which the modern commander absorbs information and exercises his authority must be a beautifully interlocked smooth-working mechanism. Ideally, the whole should be practically a single mind.[26]

—General Dwight D. Eisenhower

The Tactical Operations Center (TOC) is a vital element of combat command because it is the headquarters and nerve center within which the commander and his staff plan and conduct current and future combat operations. Consequently, its efficiency significantly influences the combat effectiveness of the unit.

Many things affect the TOC's efficiency. The following are some actions that can improve the functioning of this vital command and control center.

<u>Noise:</u> TOCs have a tendency to become noisy. I have been in Tactical Operations Centers where the noise level from straphangers and other off-duty personnel and visitors made concentration difficult. A calm, quiet TOC provides a less stressful atmosphere conducive to better performance. It is not an appropriate place for people to stand around shooting the breeze. Noise makes it difficult for people to concentrate. Radio operators have difficulty hearing. Battle captains must maintain control. Strong, immediate, and corrective action is required.

<u>Rest:</u> TOC personnel become fatigued; it's unavoidable. Commanders ensure that those off shift are out of the TOC and resting. This problem is difficult to control. Without command attention, the staff will not rest. While planning for the invasion of Afghanistan, General Tommy Franks, recognizing the need for sufficient rest, told his chief of staff: "The whole staff is going to be working long hours. I want to make sure people don't burn out. This isn't another passing crisis. We're in this for the long haul."[27]

On short two- to three-day exercises, some staff will decide to stay awake the entire time. But just because they are capable of keeping their eyes open for that long, does not mean that the staff members are alert. Shifts should be rotated as scheduled. The training is beneficial. In the real world, some conflicts may last for months or years as they have in Afghanistan and Iraq. Train for that eventuality.

Other Assets: LNOs (liaison officers) need to be proactive. The air, ANGLICO (Air/Naval Gunfire Liaison Company), civil affairs, and other representatives working with your unit either full-time or for the current training exercise or combat action need to ensure that their capabilities are recognized and used fully. These LNOs can give guidance and suggestions to the supported troops.

Communications Discipline: The Net Control Station (NCS) must be aggressive and strict. Radio discipline along with security deteriorates rapidly if violations are not prevented or corrected by the NCS and commanders. Those monitoring the net must pay attention. However, noise in the TOC can make this task difficult.

Meetings: Everybody complains about meetings. There are too many. Call only those absolutely necessary. Keep them short and to the point. Although easier said than done, the goal deserves your attention.

STAFF RELATIONS WITH:

Subordinate Units: Be proactive, not passive, with subordinate units. Go to them; ask questions. Ensure understanding. Be proactive without interfering. Proactive staff can help by assuring synchronization and coordination. There is a fine line between too much supervision and not enough. Staff must not permit something to fall through the cracks because they are fearful of over-supervision. With care, staff can check without interfering. Staff can be a help rather than a hindrance to subordinate units.

Higher Headquarters: Be proactive, not passive, with higher offices. Do not assume that each request or question will be acted upon. CHECK! Excuses like, "They told me ..." or, "They just don't understand," are not appropriate.

Subordinates at every level have a tendency to make disparaging remarks about higher headquarters. Such comments, especially when made by senior officers and noncommissioned officers in your unit, can be detrimental to morale and to the establishment of good working relationships. Stop the critical comments immediately or the discontent will feed on itself. When a situation with staff personnel at a higher level needs correction, your subordinates should speak to you. You can take the appropriate action.

When the 1st Brigade (Separate) 101st Airborne Division reverted to division control shortly after the division (minus) deployed to Vietnam, I was the brigade executive officer. No one in our brigade was happy with this new situation. We were used to "doing our own thing" with our own assets. Now, Division was in control and did not seem to be as cooperative and supportive as it should have been. As a result, there was a lot of grumbling and complaining by our staff. This unhealthy and disrespectful discontent permeated to the lowest levels in our headquarters. I had to take action.

At one of the briefings for our commanding general, I directed that all of those present (except the general) were to remain after the briefing. When the general had departed, I spoke briefly and directly. I reminded the staff that we were a part of the division. While we had enjoyed our most enviable position as a separate brigade, that situation no longer applied. I stated emphatically that the complaints and criticisms that I had been hearing were unprofessional and unacceptable. I directed in no uncertain terms

that they would be stopped immediately. Being the true professionals that they were, there was no more problem.

Support Units: Be proactive—not passive—when dealing
with support elements. Assure yourself by follow-up that your request is receiving the attention it deserves and that the support
element knows what you want. Ask support how it might do a
better job of supporting your unit.

A smoothly running TOC pays big dividends in combat effectiveness. These suggestions can help achieve that goal.

TAKE YOUR MEDICINE

Once each day every man of us, under close supervision, choked down a bitter, dime-sized yellow malaria pill. It was an automatic Article 15 offense—one subject to nonjudicial punishment—to be caught sleeping outside one's mosquito net, no matter how hot it was. Even so, we began losing men to malaria within two or three weeks. Within six weeks, fifty-six troopers from my battalion alone had been evacuated to hospitals, suffering serious cases of malaria.[28]

—Lieutenant General Hal Moore

Where our Soldiers fight and have fought are often some of the unhealthiest places on earth. We encounter diseases that are unknown to us or are unusual in the relatively healthy environment in which we spend most of our lives.

We may be particularly susceptible to some diseases because we have lived in relatively benign surroundings. However, many so-called "tropical diseases" affect the indigenous population as well. For example, the North Vietnamese Army (NVA) Soldier who walked from his training area over the Ho Chi Minh trail to South Vietnam carried fifty antimalaria pills, enough for one a day while on the march. He also carried one hundred vitamin B1 tablets to be taken three times a week. Despite these precautions and having lived under similar conditions all his life, almost all of the NVA Soldiers contracted malaria and an average of three or four in each 160-man company died while making the journey.[29]

Jungle fighting in WWII and Vietnam exposed Soldiers to malaria, hepatitis, and other diseases. While not unknown in our country, they are prevalent in the jungles of the Pacific, Southeast Asia, and much of the Southern Hemisphere. As a preventive measure, we took pills daily that were supposed to protect us from these diseases. If we were faithful in following the regimen, we were more likely to avoid falling prey to the sickness.

Some Soldiers refrained from taking the pills hoping that they would become ill and be taken to the hospital for a couple of weeks. To them, anything was better than facing the dangers of combat. Ensuring that all Soldiers took their daily medicine is a command responsibility—just like everything else.

A relatively effective way to enforce this—if any procedure could be called that—is for leaders to give each Soldier his daily ration of pills and have him swallow them in front of the leader. If the unit is in an area where there are chow lines, having the Soldier take his pills as he moves through the chow line is an easy way to accomplish the task. (While not "medicine," staying hydrated prevents heat injuries. In much of the training in our Army today, leaders require their Soldiers to drink a prescribed amount of water at specified times during the day.)

When I was commanding the Eighth Army Ranger Company in Korea, I remembered what one of my leadership instructors, a South Pacific veteran, had told us in a leadership class. Each Soldier was required to take his pills as he entered the chow line. I'm not sure why it made such an impression on me. Perhaps it was because it was such a simple and logical solution to a real-life problem that I thought I might—and eventually did—encounter one day. It works.

Section IV

WARRIORS

THE WARRIOR ETHOS

"The warrior ethos (emphasis in original) *refers to the professional attitudes and beliefs that characterize the American Soldier. At its core, the warrior ethos grounds itself on the refusal to accept failure."* [1]

—FM 22-100

We hear the words "warrior" and "warrior ethos" used almost every time someone speaks about our Soldiers who are fighting for our freedom today. What exactly is a warrior and what is the warrior ethos?

A warrior is a Soldier whose character is exemplified by a set of values. He is steeped in patriotism and tradition and exemplifies duty, honor, and country. He requires physical and moral courage. Selfless service is the core of his makeup. He unhesitatingly accepts his duty of looking after his buddy even at the risk of life.

He can rise to almost unbelievable feats of bravery and self-sacrifice and overcome the disadvantages of inferior numbers and technology. He never gives up. He will not accept failure. Warriors can be developed by rugged, progressive, realistic, high risk, battle-focused training.

He has practiced individual and small unit tasks so many times that he does them automatically. They become second nature, a matter of discipline and habit.

The warrior epitomizes the Soldier's Creed.

On December 24, 1944, during the "Battle of the Bulge," an entire U.S. Armored Division was retreating from the Germans in the Ardennes Forest. A tank destroyer commander spotted an American digging a foxhole. The GI, Private First Class Vernon L. Haught, 325th Glider Infantry Regiment, looked up and asked, "Are you looking for a safe place?" "Yeah," answered the tanker. "Well, buddy," Haught drawled, "just pull your vehicle behind me... I'm the 82nd Airborne, and this is as far as the bastards are going."[2] Haught was a warrior.

Discipline makes an individual Soldier remain on the field of battle no matter how terrible the conditions of fear, death, and mutilation might be.[3] Discipline is essential to esprit de corps. As units train to standard—as they do things right—they become disciplined and combat ready.

A Soldier is sustained by knowing that there are units with which he is physically joined on his right and left. Today and in the future, as was often the case in Korea and Vietnam, companies and smaller units may operate alone. This situation is certainly prevalent in Iraq and Afghanistan. As dispersal increases, psychological and real support slips away. Resisting a diminution of confidence requires physical, mental, and emotional toughness—characteristics that are developed through rigorous, realistic combat training.

Are we developing the warrior that the modern battlefield requires? "All Soldiers ... need to develop and display the will to win—the desire to do the job well—to persevere, no matter what the circumstances."[4]

Everything that the 75th Ranger Regiment does contributes to changing Soldiers into warriors. There is a culture of excellence that is almost palpable. The handpicked leaders at every level know and accept the responsibility placed on them by General Creighton Abrams, former Army chief of staff. When directing the formation of the 1st Battalion, General Abrams said, "Wherever the battalion goes it must be apparent that it is the best."[5] Being "the best" leaves no room for slack. The new privates are self-selected in that they volunteered for airborne and the Rangers. To be accepted by the regiment, they must meet the standards imposed by RIP (Ranger Indoctrination Program). These new Rangers are immediately influenced by this culture that declares that only their best is acceptable. They see their officers and noncommissioned officers "leading the way" and recognize that they must become highly skilled, physically tough, and thoroughly disciplined. They are willing to sacrifice to meet these standards. This culture is a positive influence that permeates the regiment.

Rangers are not the only warriors. Although other units in our Army are not governed by the special policies affecting the Ranger regiment, they contain outstanding Soldiers and officers. These units train hard to reach and maintain a high level of combat readiness.

Our Army's mission is to deter our enemies. If deterrence fails, our Army must be prepared to fight and win our country's wars. Properly trained, physically and emotionally conditioned Soldiers with competent junior leaders are vital to success in combat. Highly skilled warriors led by competent leaders can win and survive on today's more fluid, lethal, and unforgiving battlefield.

There is a greater need for warriors than ever before.

Warriors: Chief Nana

But the Apache was ever the great opponent[6]

—Paul Wellman, Author

"The ability to forge victory out of the chaos of battle includes overcoming fear, hunger, deprivation, and fatigue …. The warrior ethos is crucial."[7] Apaches set the example long ago.

In 1881, Nana, the last of the great Apache chiefs, although fat, wrinkled, suffering from rheumatism and eighty-one years old, determined to make one more stab at the hated U.S. Cavalry.

He was living in Mexico along with the other warriors driven there by the Cavalry. Nana gathered his warriors and found them beaten and hiding from the Long Knives (the name given to the cavalrymen because of the sabers they carried). Somehow he imbued in them the will to win and developed a fighting spirit fueled by a desire to kill the white man. When he crossed the border into the United States with fifteen warriors, twenty-five more joined him.[8]

Nana and that small band flamed across the desert of the Southwest and wrote a chapter of history that would live forever. In less than two months, they ranged over more than one thousand miles, living off the land as they fought. The Apaches rode their horses hard traveling as much as seventy-five miles in a day. They ate them when they could no longer go.[9] (The U.S. Cavalry considered a horse's maximum daily capability to be 25 miles.)[10]

The Apaches knew the land; they knew where every water hole was located. They had learned to stimulate saliva by holding a small pebble in their mouth.[11] Because of the way they had lived their entire lives, they had the confidence that made them believe that they were equal to any task and better than their enemy. Like the Spartans who fought and died at Thermopylae, the Apaches would never surrender. They were determined to prevail.

Nana and his small band of warriors fought eight pitched battles—winning them all. They killed thirty to fifty enemies and wounded many more. They captured more than two hundred horses and mules. They eluded capture by over one thousand Soldiers and three to four hundred civilians. Nana did it all with a force no greater than forty men.[12]

How did he do it? How did he overcome the vicissitudes of age and a crippling disease that would have incapacitated a lesser man? Nana had lived his whole life facing the greatest challenge of all: combat. He had fought the white man and other Indians all his life. He had survived in a most hostile environment. He was the epitome of that tribe whose warriors had become "lean, sun-baked, imbued with shocking cruelty and vitality, endowed with deadliness and malice beyond all other tribes of American Indians. After centuries of wandering, they were named from their one outstanding trait: *apache—enemy*."[13] Nana was an Apache.

The Apache warriors who comprised Nana's war party had, like Nana, lived the hard-bitten life of the Apache warrior. They were as physically tough as Nana. Like Nana, they hated the white man who had killed their wives and children, driven them from the land where they had once freely roamed, and violated every treaty to which the Apaches had agreed. They were ripe for a charismatic leader. Nana was that leader. His inspirational leadership imbued in them the self-confidence and fighting spirit that convinced them that they could kill the "Long Knives."

Thus, the warrior ethos is about more than persevering under the worst of conditions; it fuels the fire to fight through those conditions to victory no matter how long it takes, no matter how much effort is required."[14]

WARRIORS: KING HENRY V AND A BAND OF BROTHERS

From this day to the ending of the World ...
But we in it shall be remembered ...
We few, we happy few, we band of brothers.
For he today who sheds his blood with me
Shall be my brother.[15]

—Shakespeare

The Battle of Agincourt occurred on October 25, 1415. In a pitched battle that lasted little more than three hours, a depleted, exhausted army of 5,000 English archers and 900 men-at-arms led by King Henry V routed a freshly mounted and better-equipped French force numbering between 20,000 and 30,000.[16] (These figures are disputed by other studies.) Just over one hundred English lay dead. Between 7,000 and 10,000 French lost their lives, among them the flower of French chivalry.[17] (Some studies give the French an advantage of only three to two. If accurate, the number of French dead would be impossible.) In addition, the English took 1,500–1,600 prisoners.[18]

Henry V had invaded France for several reasons. By fighting a popular foreign war, he would strengthen his position at home; and he hoped that he could improve his financial position by either gaining lands in France, by ransoming noble prisoners, or by extorting money from the French King to get Henry to leave.

Henry's army landed in Northern France on August 13, 1415,

and besieged the port of Harfleur. The town surrendered on September 22; the English departed October 8. Because the campaign season was coming to an end and the English Army had suffered many casualties through disease, Henry decided to move his army to the port of Calais, the only English stronghold in northern France. He hoped to rest and reequip over winter for the campaign season of 1416.

During the siege, the French were able to call up a large feudal army which the commander of the French troops, Charles d'Albret, deployed skillfully between Harfleur and Calais, mirroring the British maneuvers along the Somme river, thus preventing them from reaching Calais without a major confrontation. D'Albret forced Henry into fighting a battle that, given the state of his army, he would have preferred to avoid.

Prior to the battle, King Henry spoke to his troops (reminiscent of the scene in the movie, *Henry V*). French accounts state that he told his men that if the French won, he and the English dukes, earls and other nobles had little to worry about because they would be captured and ransomed for a good price. The common Soldier on the other hand was worth little and so they had better fight hard. As FM 22-100 directs, the King was certainly inculcating in his Soldiers "the commitment to do their part to accomplish the mission, no matter when, no matter where, no matter what."[19]

The battle was fought in a defile formed by the wood of Agincourt where the French army had placed itself to block the English from reaching Calais. The English spent the night of October 24 on the ground with little shelter to protect them from the heavy rain that was falling. Early on the morning of October 25, St. Crispin's Day, Henry maneuvered his army consisting of about 1,000 men-at-arms and a few thousand footmen. He arrayed them in three lines each with archers on the flanks and dismounted men-at-arms in the center.

The French were also in three deep lines. That they outnumbered the English is not in dispute. What the actual figures were is open to question. Unfortunately the terrain restricted the French to the same frontage as the English. With the exception of a few knights, all the French were dismounted.

Henry's archers prepared fortifications of palings—pointed stakes—that were to protect the archers from the charge of the French knights. The English began the battle by firing a barrage of arrows at the French.[20]

The knights were nothing more than a rabble assembled at the request of King Charles VI. They evidently had not learned from the earlier battles of Crecy and Poitiers, both of which were disasters for the French.[21] When the mounted knights charged, they became even more disorganized and were repulsed. Some were so burdened by their armor that they became mired in the mud. Despite this difficulty, the French attackers reached the English who were being driven to the rear. At that instant, the English archers began using their hatchets and swords and moved into the gaps in the French lines overwhelming the French. The second and third lines of the French followed and met the same fate as the first.

A force from the castle appeared to protect their King's baggage. Henry, believing that his rear was under attack, ordered all the prisoners to be killed. Though savage, this act prevented the captives from arming themselves with the weapons that were strewn across the battlefield and, with the attacking French, may have been able to crush the English. The next morning, Henry returned to the battlefield and killed all the wounded French where they lay. Again, an act of savagery. However, it is doubtful that many, if any, would have survived, considering the very primitive medical care that was available.[22]

The catastrophic defeat that the French suffered at the Battle of Agincourt allowed Henry to fulfill all his campaign objectives. The French in the Treaty of Troyes (1420) recognized him as regent and heir to the French throne. The agreement was cemented by his marriage to Catherine of Valois, the daughter of King Charles VI.

What characteristics sustained the English? Courageous leadership and inspiration of King Henry V were key. Patriotism, better tactics (the employment of the weapons available and the long bow in the hands of expert archers), and the defensive works (the emplacement of the stakes) were key. The battle demonstrates the value of disciplined troops who used the terrain to advantage. It is also a classic example (by the French) of not learning from history.

WARRIORS: THE SPARTANS

---

*Knowing the likely outcome of the battle, Leonidas se-
lected his men on one simple criterion: he took only
men who had fathered sons that were old enough to take
over the family responsibilities of their fathers.*[23]

—Herodotus, Greek Historian

In 480 BC, King Leonidas, 300 handpicked Spartans, and other
Greeks fought the battle of Thermopylae. Their mission was to
delay the Persian Army long enough for the Spartan's families to
escape.

The Persians greatly outnumbered Leonidas and his small
force. When the Spartan warriors saw the enemy, they told their
king that the enemy was so numerous that their arrows would blot
out the sun.

The Spartan, Dienekes, who was described as the bravest of all
Spartans responded, "So much the better. We can fight better in
the shade."[24]

The Spartans accomplished their mission. The 300, including their king, died as they adhered to their creed that required
a Spartan warrior to be victorious in battle or his lifeless body to
be carried home on his shield. They were finally defeated through
treachery. Their courageous battle is memorialized in poetry: "Go
passerby to Sparta tell. Obedient to her law we fell."[25] (This trans-
lation was contained in my high school Latin textbook.)

The foundation of Spartan strength rested on reforms introduced around 600 BC. Before that time, life in Sparta was similar to that in other Greek cities. Art and poetry flourished. Beginning in the 6th century BC, however, the Spartans looked upon themselves as merely a military garrison in preparation for war. Their discipline pointed to war. Boys began military drill at the age of seven and entered the ranks at twenty. Men were permitted to marry, but they had to live in the barracks until thirty. From the ages of twenty to sixty, all Spartans were obliged to serve as *hoplites* (foot Soldiers) and to eat at the *phiditia* (public mess). Under their stern discipline, the Spartans became a race of resolute, ascetic warriors, capable of self-sacrificing patriotism, as demonstrated by the devoted three hundred heroes at Thermopylae.[26]

What characteristics sustained the Spartans? King Leonidas set the example by his courageous leadership. He truly led from the front and died with his Soldiers. Tough training that began when males were only boys and continued through adulthood prepared each male for his first responsibility: service to Sparta. He lived in a warrior culture. He knew what was expected of him. His creed required that he place his duty to his country and to his fellow Spartan above all else. He and his comrades knew what was required and what every Spartan would be. He would be a warrior.

The warrior culture, which developed in each Spartan a love for Sparta and the acceptance of the responsibility to die for his city-state if need be, made him a formidable foe on the battlefield. A commander today can adapt some of the Spartans' tough philosophy to his own training program. He begins by establishing a culture of excellence. Instituting a battle-focused training program that concentrates on and masters fundamentals is the first step. Perhaps the most important requirement for developing this culture is a leader who sets the example by everything that he does. He also requires all his leaders to meet those same standards. This environment develops in a Soldier the pride that comes only when he has confidence in himself, his comrades, his leaders, and his unit. When every Soldier believes that he and his unit are the best in the United States Army, the commander will have succeeded in establishing that culture of excellence. The results will be apparent on the field of battle.

"The warrior ethos concerns character, shaping who you are and what you do. In that sense, it's clearly linked to Army values such as *personal courage, loyalty to comrades, and dedication to duty.* (Emphasis in the original.) Both loyalty and duty involve putting your life on the line, even when there is little chance of survival, for the good of a cause larger than yourself. That's the clearest example of *selfless service.*"[27] (Emphasis in the original.)

WARRIORS: TASK FORCE RANGER, MOGADISHU OCTOBER 3–4, 1993

Surrender is not a Ranger word....I will never leave a fallen comrade....Readily will I display the intestinal fortitude required to fight on to the Ranger objective and complete the mission, though I be the lone survivor.[28]

—Ranger Creed

On October 3–4, 1993, in Mogadishu, Somalia, Task Force Ranger succeeded in accomplishing its mission of capturing key members of warlord Aideed's staff. As the Rangers began their withdrawal, they were surrounded and came under extremely heavy fire from hundreds of Aideed's Soldiers. In a fifteen-hour battle, the most intense land combat since Vietnam, men were killing each other at a distance of ten yards. Courageous action by Rangers and airmen was the norm. Before the Rangers could be extricated, six were killed. Twelve other Soldiers in the quick reaction force were lost. "The Somali death toll was catastrophic. Conservative counts numbered five hundred dead among more than a thousand casualties."[29]

"The ability to forge victory out of the chaos of battle includes overcoming fear, hunger, deprivation, and fatigue."[30] TF Ranger succeeded because it was composed of warriors. They were Rangers.

A Ranger is a Soldier with a special attitude: self-assured, determined, demanding of himself and of those with whom he soldiers, a person for whom only his best is acceptable, a person who strives to be all he can be.

A Ranger is a product of hard, demanding, realistic training in a unit led by aggressive, motivated, example-setting leaders who will not accept anything but the best. "The Army wins because it fights hard; it fights hard because it trains hard; and it trains hard because that's the way to *win*."[31] (Emphasis in the original.) He has learned the most important lesson that anyone can ever learn, and that is that how far he can push himself is limited only by his determination.

A Ranger is justifiably proud of his accomplishments. He has the pride that comes from doing well a tough and dangerous job.

A Ranger's pride and self-confidence are reinforced by being a member of a unit with great *esprit* based on the confidence that can come only through the knowledge that he, his leaders, and his unit are superbly competent.

Today the American Ranger epitomizes the American fighting man. He is the most superbly trained, the most aggressive, the most highly skilled, and the most dedicated Soldier. As General Creighton Abrams, former army chief of staff, expressed it, "Wherever the Ranger goes he is recognized as the best." Being the best requires total dedication. Rangers strive for excellence in everything that they do. They are never satisfied with their performance. They know that "good enough" is not good enough until it is the best that they can do. They continue to push themselves. They give 100 percent and then some to every task. "Rangers lead the way!"

No statement is more inspiring or sets higher standards than the Ranger Creed. That article of faith states explicitly and simply how Rangers define themselves. The words are appropriate for all; we do not have to be Rangers to live by that code. I repeat it here.

      Recognizing that I volunteered as a Ranger fully
    knowing the hazards of my chosen profession, I will

always endeavor to uphold the prestige, honor, and high esprit de corps of the Rangers.

Acknowledging the fact that a Ranger is a more elite Soldier who arrives at the cutting edge of battle by land, sea, or air, I accept the fact that as a Ranger, my country expects me to move further, faster, and fight harder than any other Soldier.

Never shall I fail my comrades. I will always keep myself mentally alert, physically strong, and morally straight, and I will shoulder more than my share of the task whatever it may be—100 percent and then some.

Gallantly will I show the world that I am a specially selected and well-trained Soldier. My courtesy to superior officers, my neatness of dress, and care of equipment shall set the example for others to follow.

Energetically will I meet the enemies of my country. I shall defeat them on the field of battle for I am better trained and will fight with all my might. Surrender is not a Ranger word. I will never leave a fallen comrade to fall into the hands of the enemy and under no circumstances will I ever embarrass my country.

Readily will I display the intestinal fortitude required to fight on to the Ranger objective and complete the mission, though I be the lone survivor.

Rangers Lead The Way!

The Rangers who comprised Task Force Ranger lived the Ranger Creed.

WHY MEN FIGHT

… the sense of what it meant to be a man, and that the shame of being thought a coward, or having let down your pals, was more to be dreaded than death itself.[32]

—James Bowman, Writer

Why men fight, why they are willing to face danger or almost certain death, is a question that has been asked thousands of times and will continue to be asked as long as there are wars and men who study wars. Those who ask that question have some ideas or explanation. Yet we know that there is no definitive answer because the reasons vary with each individual Soldier.

> Character—who you are—contributes significantly to how you act. Character helps you know what's right and do what's right, all the time and at whatever the cost. Character is made up of two interacting parts: values and attributes. Stephen Ambrose, speaking about the Civil War, said "at the pivotal point in the war it was always the character of individuals that made the difference." Army leaders must be critical individuals of character themselves and in turn develop character in those they lead.[33]

The Infantry Officer Basic Course has a class entitled "Why Infantry Fight." The instructor elicits responses from the students, some of which are "for each other," "for survival," "for the unit," "for patriotism," and "for their leaders." These comments, of course, are appropriate for the more inclusive question: "Why do men fight?" The Infantryman is not the only Soldier who faces serious injury or death.

Joshua Lawrence Chamberlain, one of our greatest Soldiers, said, "But as a rule, men stand up from one motive or another—simple manhood, force of discipline, pride, love, or bond of comradeship"[34]

Speaking of the men he commanded, Chamberlain wrote that they charged "down from the Round Tops of Gettysburg into the maelstrom of death swirling around the 'Devil's Den,' from which but half their numbers emerged, and those so wrought upon that they were soon released from service in the field to recover strength....The same tendency of thought and feeling was, no doubt, in the hearts of our adversaries....The prime motive for these men was no doubt, like ours, grounded in the instincts of manhood."

The answer to "Why do men fight?" varies. There is no simple answer. Commanders can use all those reasons listed by Chamberlain and the explanation given by Bowman as bases for inculcating the desire—or at least, willingness—to close with and destroy the enemy.

Section V

TRAINING

PART I:
INDIVIDUAL TRAINING

AARs Are a Valuable Teaching Tool

Any fault recognized is half corrected.[1]

—Anonymous

The after action review (AAR) can be a very valuable training tool. According to Training Circular 25-20, *A Leader's Guide to After Action Reviews*, "The real benefits come from taking the results and applying them to future training.... After action reviews are the dynamic link between task performance and execution to standard."[2]

FM 22-100, *Army Leadership*, states, "Individuals benefit when the group learns together. The AAR is one tool good leaders use to help their organizations learn as a group. Properly conducted, an AAR is a professional discussion of an event, focused on performance standards, that enables Soldiers to discover for themselves what happened, why it happened, and how to sustain strengths and improve on weaknesses."[3] Training Circular TC 25-20 contains an AAR format that will be useful in planning and conducting an AAR.[4]

Debriefs and AARs that are positive—not a harangue filled with criticism—can be a learning experience. The proper AAR environment—one in which participants feel free to be self-critical, to comment freely on mistakes they have made—was demonstrated clearly to me when I observed my first live-fire exercise as the Honorary Colonel, 75th Ranger Regiment.

The time was 0200, the weather cold. The location—K22—at Fort Benning, GA. Company B, 3-75th had just completed the night live-fire iteration of an attack on a fortified guerrilla complex. The company commander was Captain Jim Johnson, a very conscientious and dedicated officer who is destined to go far. Looking on was the battalion commander, Lieutenant Colonel Frank Kearney.

We were in a tent located in the training area. Major Steve Townsend, S3, 3-75 conducted the AAR. Participating with Johnson were members of the supporting aviation units, leaders of other supporting elements, Ranger platoon leaders and sergeants, and squad leaders. The atmosphere was completely relaxed. Johnson and members of his company spoke freely about their thought processes and actions sometimes saying, "I should have ..." or "If I had to do it again, I would...." Amazing! Here were subordinates unafraid to admit in front of their commander that they had not always made the best decision!

Major Townsend drew from the participants every teaching point that he wanted to make. He was thoroughly aware of all the tactical principles and battle drills that were involved. He was a master at eliciting frank comments from the participants while keeping the discussion on track. His total demeanor was one of a friendly mentor with one goal only—to help his Rangers learn!

When Townsend completed his summation, Lieutenant Colonel Kearney spoke briefly. "You did a great job. I was pleased with the way you performed. You learned a lot and improved your skills. You know what you did right—those things that you need to sustain. You know what needs improving. Let's get on with it and do better next time." Lieutenant Colonel Kearney demonstrated what Warren Bennis wrote in his *Training and Development Journal*: "Leaders value learning and mastery, and so do people who work for leaders. Leaders make it clear that there is no failure, only mistakes that give us feedback and tell us what to do next."[5]

I remember Colonel Ken Keen, commander of the 75th Ranger Regiment, and one of the best critiquers I ever saw. I listened to him on numerous occasions during field exercises with some of our Rangers. He was a master at drawing frank appraisals from the participants. He used leading questions such as: "what happened when you reached that trail junction? What did you do? Was that what you had planned to do? What had you rehearsed? What caused you to deviate from your plan? If you had to do it over would you take the same action?" None of these questions were put forth in a "You should have …" vein. They were noncritical. When the responses did not cover the points that Keen wanted, he asked additional questions. When appropriate, he summarized the responses. It was only rarely necessary for him to state the teaching points that he wanted to emphasize because the Rangers had stated them for him. Colonel Keen was a firm believer in what General MacArthur had said, "A good Soldier, whether he leads a platoon or an Army, is expected to look backward as well as forward, but he must think only forward."[6]

Having attended several AARs in the 25th Infantry Division and the 75th Ranger Regiment in the last few years, I am favorably impressed with what I witnessed. Because of the way the AARs were conducted they were the positive training devices they were meant to be. They were a far cry from the critical, almost totally one-sided harangues that I had observed in the Army in the 1950s and 1960s.

After each tactical exercise during the training of the Eighth Army Ranger Company, we conducted a thorough critique. We encouraged each Ranger to comment on the orders he had received, the actions he had taken, and any difficulties he may have encountered. More important, we encouraged him to make suggestions about how we might do better the next time. If it were a company exercise, I encouraged them to comment on my performance. We both knew that I had a lot to learn about being a company commander. The primary focus was the answer to the question, "How can we do better next time? Then we "did it again," incorporating appropriate suggestions from our Rangers.

Lieutenant Colonel Sean Jenkins, commander of the 3-75th, employed a good technique to focus on the question of "how can we do better next time?" In his wrap-up of an AAR of a platoon night blank fire exercise he asked the platoon leader and squad leaders in turn, "What one thing are you going to improve in the live-fire exercise?" This question caused these leaders to select the one most important shortcoming that needed improvement. Concentrating on the most important training objective would not preclude improvement in other areas. It did help ensure that these leaders would remember and do at least one thing better than before.

The point of doing it again after the critique (even if done on a parade ground or chalkboard) is critical and usually omitted in most of the training that I have seen. "We learn by doing. If we only talk about doing it correctly after doing it in a less satisfactory way, learning is much shallower, and actual experience (the less desirable performance) may take over under stress. It is also entirely possible that you may discover that your 'improved' solution is not as good as you thought it was."[7]

"The AAR is one of the most effective techniques to use in a combat environment."[8] Properly conducted it can improve performance thereby reducing casualties. "An effective AAR takes little time … and can be conducted almost anywhere consistent with unit security requirements. Conducting AARs helps overcome the steep learning curve that exists in a unit exposed to combat and helps the unit ensure that it does not repeat mistakes. It also helps them (sic) sustain strengths."[9]

In the Eighth Army Ranger Company, we held short critiques after each contact with the enemy if time permitted. Although we could not repeat the combat action, we assembled our Rangers and critiqued what we had done. We wanted to do better the next time. Frederick the Great summed it up when he asked, "What is the good of experience if you do not reflect?"[10]

The value gained from an AAR depends on the ability of the person conducting the review, the participation in the discussion by the individuals being trained, and the environment in which the AAR is conducted—and what steps are taken to incorporate lessons learned into future actions.

INSTILLING ARMY VALUES CAN HELP PREVENT ATROCITIES

Of all the thousands of things that come under the heading of "leadership," what is it that's "most important?" Simple ... Soldier's values.[11]

—Colonel Dandridge M. "Mike" Malone

FM 22-100 tells leaders that "one of your key responsibilities as a leader is to teach Army values to your subordinates. The old saying that actions speak louder than words has never been truer than here. Leaders who talk about honor, loyalty, and selfless service but do not live those values—both on and off duty—send the wrong message that this 'values stuff' is all just talk."[12]

FM 100-1 adds, "Leadership in war must be framed by the values of the profession—tenets such as duty, honor, country—that are consistent with the larger moral, spiritual, and social values upon which our nation was founded. These (values) define the fundamental character of our nation ... an Army which springs from such a nation must reflect and be governed by these values."

The commander is responsible for everything that his unit does or fails to do. We have heard that almost from the first day we entered the service.

General Charles Krulak, former commandant, USMC, said, "The conduct of a nation's military during both war and peace defines and sustains its very character."[13] Instilling that character is our responsibility. That responsibility extends to our Soldiers regardless of where they are and whether we are present. It is a major responsibility and must not be slighted. It is one of the many characteristics that distinguish the military profession from the civilian world.

What do we mean when we use the term "ethics"? Philosophers use "ethics" to describe the study of the meaning of life. Our ethics are our character. Character significantly affects how we react to extreme pressure. General Ronald Fogelman, former chief of staff, USAF, and a former fighter jock with 315 combat missions in Vietnam, defined character as "doing the right thing when nobody's looking."[14]

Stressing the importance of character, former Army chief of staff, General John A. Wickham, Jr., said, "Character is what enables us to withstand the rigors of combat or the daily challenges that might tempt us to compromise our principles. Strengthening values will allow us to strengthen our inner self, our bonding to others, and our commitment to a purpose beyond that of ourselves."[15]

Socrates devoted his life to the examination of the meaning of life. Ethics is the systematic inquiry into moral behavior with the purpose of discovering the rules that ought to govern human action.[16] "Do the right thing" expresses that goal in one rule.

How do we know what is the right thing? If we are imbued with high moral standards—if we have lived a moral life—knowing right from wrong is generally easy. There may be times, however, when our Soldiers and we will be pressured to resort to illegal or unethical behavior.

Clausewitz wrote that when Soldiers are subjected to the heartrending spectacle of dead or wounded comrades, it is then that the strength of character inherent in a moral person becomes critical. If our Soldiers lack character, "the mass will drag [us] down to the brutish world where danger is shirked and shame is unknown."[17]

Moral standards in our society have deteriorated. Situational ethics reign. Values change with the situation. "Go with the flow." "If it feels good, do it."

The Wall Street Journal described this decline. It quoted Brigadier General R. Stephen Ritchie, USAF Retired, the only Air Force ace from the Vietnam War, who said that many young people have "little respect for anything … they don't respect themselves, their colleagues, their schools, their teachers, or their country."[18]

The military, on the other hand, several times in the last few years has been voted in polls as the most respected institution in our country. Members of our profession are expected to lay down their lives in the defense of our country when necessary. I have long believed that we have a different set of values from much of the civilian world. I believe that we do and must hold ourselves to higher standards.

As one officer expressed it,

> War places men under unparalleled pressure, no matter where in the forces they serve. At all levels tough decisions must be made—decisions that can cost lives. There is no room for anything but an eye toward the common good here. Mutual trust is indispensable if the forces are to operate the way they must. The whole structure of discipline and esprit de corps will disintegrate if officers cannot see past their own wants and aspirations.[19]

The rules of land warfare define correct, moral, legal behavior in war. However, combat stress, the hatred or anger that builds within us as we see our Soldiers killed, the adrenaline rush that accompanies the fear aroused by an enemy who is trying to kill us, may influence us to react in unacceptable ways. Many combat veterans have experienced these pressures. Moral character developed through the years will determine how our Soldiers respond.

Our Soldiers come from all walks of life. Some may have little if any moral virtue. They may show little restraint under pressure. They may be induced to beat, to manhandle, and to kill prisoners. After all, some Soldiers believe that the enemy are just "gooks;" they are less than human.

In the movie *Platoon*, an American patrol comes under fire

as it approaches a village. One Soldier is killed. When the patrol reaches the hamlet, all the villagers are either very old or very young. They repeat again and again "No VC! No VC!" (Vietcong) to convince the Americans that there is no enemy present and that the villagers are friendly. When the Soldiers find huge stores of rice they know that the village is a Vietcong logistics base. The animosity and stress that had been aroused by combat, the loss of a member of the patrol, and the obvious lying by the villagers is almost too much for the Soldiers. One begins to beat a villager. The atmosphere becomes more and more charged. It seems that soon the Soldier and his buddies will explode and "waste" all the villagers. Fortunately, the patrol leader is able to calm his men who are about to go ballistic. He prevents a major atrocity.

Violations of the Geneva Conventions are illegal. What do we commanders do to prevent this unacceptable violence by our Soldiers when we are not present? How do we develop within our Soldiers the standards of behavior, the strength of character that will stand them in good stead when the chips are down? That will cause them to act in an ethical manner?

As commanders, we are responsible for instilling a strong moral compass within our troops. We begin the day we take command. We cannot stop until we are no longer in command. We develop this moral compass in training before our Soldiers are subjected to the pressures of combat.

Russell Baker, writing in the *New York Times,* said that it is impossible to train Soldiers to kill the enemy and expect them to be ethical at the same time. He is wrong.

George Will, a pundit of national renown, placed the responsibility for correcting this deficiency on us (the Army) when he wrote, "Basic training must correct consequences of contemporary society's defects."[20] He also said "never before in this nation's experience have the values and expectations in society been more at variance with the values and expectations that are indispensable to a military establishment."[21]

To combat the decline of moral standards in our society, our Army has initiated training in "Army values." There are seven of them. They are loyalty, duty, respect, selfless service, honor, integrity, and personal courage.[22] None is more important than any other. We begin instilling the core Army values within our Soldiers the day they enter the service.

The Army leadership manual explains that Army values are more than a system of rules. They tell us what to do every day in every situation. They are our internal compass for navigating "through defining moments" and become the foundation of who [we] are as a person and as a leader."[23] They form the basis for ethical behavior. In other words, these Army values tell us how to live. Living them, we will "do the right thing." Our conduct will be ethical.

Our Army is a values-based organization. Army values are the solid rock on which everything else stands. They are nonnegotiable. They remind us and all who see us who we are and for what we stand.[24] Inculcating these values in our Soldiers is of paramount importance.

Being a person of honor, a person of high moral character, can be risky. William J. Bennett wrote, "Honor never grows old, and honor gives the greatest joy, because honor is, finally, about defending noble and worthy things that deserve to be defended, even at a high cost. In our time, the cost may be social disapproval, public scorn, hardship, persecution, or even death."[25] Soldiers defend noble and worthy things. Clausewitz said, "The Soldier's trade ... has to be anchored to an unshakable code of honor."[26]

Former Army Chief of Staff General John Wickham stressed that the ethical climate in our units has more impact on our Soldiers than any other influence.[27] If we inculcate high ethical standards in each of our Soldiers—character grounded on the Army values—it will do more to improve the combat efficiency of our Army than an increase in people, weapons, or budget.

Army values are the foundation on which we build our strength. By living these values we develop within ourselves the character that is the solid bedrock of our being.

How do we instill these values in our Soldiers? We begin by setting the example. It is the *sine qua non* of leadership. Setting the example is the most important principle of leadership. We cannot be a "do as I say, not as I do" commander. Our example, the way we conduct ourselves every day, will have greater effect on our men than anything we can say. General Douglas MacArthur said, "No nation can safely trust its martial honor to leaders who do not maintain the universal code which distinguishes between those things that are right and those things that are wrong.[28] *The Battalion Commander's Handbook* states, "A Soldier may not always believe what you say, but he will never doubt what you do."[29]

"You help build subordinates' character by acting the way you want them to act. You teach by example, and coach along the way.... When you hold yourself and your subordinates to the highest standards, you reinforce the values those standards embody."[30]

The commander involves himself in that training to which he attaches great importance. If he believes that physical fitness is of great consequence, he participates with his troops. If marksmanship is important to him, he is at the range. So it is with ethical training. He demonstrates the importance he places on this training by setting the example and being an active participant in that training. Because of that, the commander may be the one who both introduces and ends the training module. Leaving the instruction to the chaplain indicates to the commander's Soldiers that he places less importance on ethics than, say, land navigation.

Instilling ethical standards requires more than classroom instruction. The commander strives to get it across to everyone in his command—particularly officers and senior noncommissioned officers—that he expects from them unflinching adherence to the highest standards of conduct and that they be an example to their Soldiers.

Whether it is a report of survey for lost or damaged equipment, an accident investigation, or a training or readiness report, there can be no equivocation. If we bend the rules, if we deviate from the strictest standard or accept such a performance from one of our subordinates, returning to an acceptable standard will be extremely difficult.

Soldiers see what other Soldiers have done and the consequences, rewards, or admonishments of those actions. Soldiers need clear guidelines as to what is acceptable. They can discern if informal norms are consistent with traditional Army values. They will be confused by ambiguous or conflicting standards. We can develop Soldiers of moral character only by demonstrating by our own conduct what a good Soldier is.

Combat places a significantly greater pressure on Soldiers. There is pressure to submit high although inaccurate body and weapons counts. There is pressure to appear to have been more effective than was the case. As commanders, we must ensure that our subordinates know that falsifying or "fudging," as some might say, is unacceptable. We take strong, corrective action when and if there is deviation from the standard we have set.

Because of the sometimes-rapid turnover of personnel and the absence of adequate opportunity in combat, ensuring that our standards are understood and met is more difficult. That does not excuse us from this responsibility, however.

In the My Lai investigation, Major General Sam Koster, commanding general, Americal Division, relied upon his staff. He told me that his staff had assured him that there was nothing to the rumor of an atrocity. Because I know and have served with General Koster, I believe him. The division chaplain, Lieutenant Colonel Francis Lewis, also agreed. Hindsight tells us that General Koster should have personally checked when he was informed that an atrocity might have been committed. However, if a commander cannot trust his staff whom can he trust?

We are responsible for enforcing the rules of land warfare and for limiting civilian casualties. Permitting violations of these rules starts Soldiers and their commanders on the slippery slope of a war with no limits. Violations degrade and weaken cohesion and discipline, and may provoke reprisals. Violations hurt combat effectiveness.

We can expect that there may be violations of the Geneva Conventions. When there is a report or even a rumor of an atrocity or violation of the rules of land warfare, we are responsible for conducting a thorough investigation. Because of its importance and the possible pressure for a cover-up by those involved, we need to assure ourselves that the investigation is proper. We must see for ourselves. If a violation has occurred, strong corrective action is necessary. Otherwise, abuses become contagious and widespread.

As commanders, we are responsible for ensuring that our Soldiers obey the rules of land warfare. We develop the moral basis for ethical conduct through training in garrison and by continuing explanation and emphasis in combat. Setting the example in everything that we do and say is our most effective tool in achieving ethical conduct in the Soldiers we lead.

ARMY VALUES AND A WARRIOR WHO LIVED THEM

Duty, Honor, Country. Those three hallowed words reverently dictate what you ought to be, what you can be, what you will be. They are your rallying points: to build courage when courage seems to fail; to regain faith when there seems to be little cause for faith; to create hope when hope becomes forlorn.[31]

—General Douglas MacArthur

We hear and read about values every day. Often it's in reference to the declining values in our society. Recruits come to us from a society that no longer has the absolutes of past generations. For that reason, teaching values is more important than ever.[32]

There are seven Army values. The values are loyalty, duty, respect, selfless service, honor, integrity, and personal courage.[33]

Good leaders set the example. You can't fool the troops. You can't just talk the talk. You must walk the walk. Your every action must be an example of the Army values.

If we have the right values—if these values are part of us—we will be better able to face the challenge of combat when it comes.

Joshua Lawrence Chamberlain lived those values every day in every way. He is one of the greatest Soldiers that this country has ever produced. Many of us were first "introduced" to Chamberlain when we read *Killer Angels* or watched the movie *Gettysburg.* I am convinced that if any Soldier deserves the sobriquet "warrior," it is he.

Chamberlain was a man of total integrity, the unflinching adherence to the highest ideals of duty, honor, and country. He had personal courage. His actions at Little Round Top on July 2, 1863, were certainly those of a brave man. He was awarded the Medal of Honor many years later for his actions that day. His exploits were almost unbelievable. During the Civil War he was wounded five or six times (sources vary), twice so badly that newspapers reported that he had been killed. He had four to six horses shot from under him (again, sources vary). If there was ever a man who "led from the front," it was Chamberlain.

During the attack at Petersburg, Chamberlain was seriously wounded. "The ball passed through his body, exited his hip, and left a trail of red on the ground. Within minutes he was faint from the loss of blood … his brigade was shattered. It was, as many of them later remembered, a 'massacre.' Chamberlain was dragged out of range of the point-blank rebel fire but then was left on the field between the lines. He was spotted, finally, by artilleryman John Bigelow, who ordered four men to retrieve him.

"Chamberlain was almost unconscious but protested to his rescuers to take others first. 'You are not in command, Sir,' one said. 'Captain Bigelow's order to us was to bring you back, and that is what we must do.' Two hours later, Joshua Chamberlain was behind the Union lines at a field hospital, attended by brigade and division surgeons, including one from the 20th Maine, who worked furiously to save his life."[34] These surgeons were exploring new medical territory. They were certain, as were the senior commanders, that Chamberlain would die. Grant promoted Chamberlain "on the spot—to brigadier general—the only time he did so, for any officer or Soldier, during the war."[35] Chamberlain's obituary was published in the New York papers. Remarkably, though, he recovered, [36] although he would suffer from the wound the rest of his life. His devotion to duty caused him to return to combat as soon as he was able.

This personal courage was manifested not only in combat. In the election of 1879, the outcome of the campaign for governor of Maine was contested. Emotions were strong. Men formed armed groups and threatened the peace. Chamberlain, who had been appointed major general in the state militia, was given the mission of quelling the dissension. He moved rapidly to resolve the deteriorating situation. [37]

By the end of the second week of the crisis, he was receiving death threats. As he was leaving his office one night, Chamberlain was told that there was a gang of men waiting to kill him. Hearing this news, Chamberlain went into the dark, cold night to meet his adversaries. He said:

> Men, you wish to kill me, I hear. Killing is no new thing to me. I have offered myself to be killed many times, when I no more deserved it than I do now. Some of you, I think, have been with me in those days. You understand what you want, do you? I am here to preserve the peace and honor of this State, until the rightful government is seated—whichever it may be, it is not for me to say. But it is for me to see that the laws of this State are put into effect, without fraud, without force, but with calm thought and purpose. I am here for that, and I shall do it. If anybody wants to kill me for it, here I am. Let him kill![38]

"Chamberlain then threw open his coat as an old veteran who knew him stepped from the crowd: 'By God, General, the first man that dares lay a hand on you, I'll kill him on the spot.'"[39] The crowd dispersed! His commitment to selfless service caused him to risk his life to maintain law and order.

Because of the many major battles in which he had been involved, the many wounds and the many hardships he had endured, Chamberlain knew or could envision the impact of each of his orders on his Soldiers. While this empathy would not cause him to avoid a tough battle that might result in many casualties, he never forgot or failed to consider what his Soldiers (and he himself) would face.

He was an aggressive fighter. He wanted to carry the fight to the enemy. His courage enabled him to "lead from the front." Yet he was not foolhardy and was concerned for the safety of his Soldiers.

At Petersburg, for the only time in his career, Chamberlain questioned an order to make a frontal attack on an entrenched enemy. Scrawling an appeal to General George Meade, Chamberlain explained that he believed that Meade could not be aware of the situation that faced Chamberlain. However, a messenger soon returned with verbal confirmation that Chamberlain was to attack. He complied with the best of his ability. [40]

Chamberlain was physically tough. He trained at a breakneck speed, thriving on the pace.[41] In combat, Chamberlain seemed to be unaffected by or ignored the harshest winter weather. [42] He often spent twelve to fifteen hours each day in the saddle. [43]

He was very calm under the direst circumstances. His command presence exuded confidence and was infectious in his Soldiers. No matter what was happening, Chamberlain was never rattled.

On the contrary, he was a quick thinker. On March 29, 1865, at Dinwiddie Court House, Chamberlain received one of the several wounds of his Civil War service. He was hit by a minie ball that struck his horse, Charlemagne, and then pierced Chamberlain's arm before slamming him in the chest. He slumped, unconscious, over his horse's neck as the federal lines were disintegrating under the heavy rebel fire. General Charles Griffin, the division commander, thought Chamberlain was dead. However, Chamberlain revived himself, dismounted, and ran into the farmyard where he was confronted by a squad of rebels who demanded that Chamberlain surrender. Coolly, Chamberlain shook his head and yelled at them, "'Surrender, what's the matter with you? What do you take me for?' His faded uniform, nearly gray from the dust and heat, served him well. He convinced the rebels that he was a Confederate officer, then took them in hand and led them into the Union lines as prisoners." [44]

He was compassionate; he demonstrated his respect for others by treating them the way he wanted to be treated. Recall the novel, *Killer Angels*, and the movie, *Gettysburg*, based on it, Chamberlain's hypothetical talk with the deserters who had just been given to him before the battle of Gettysburg was certainly compassionate. However, we don't really know what he said. No matter; there are many, many other examples of his compassion and respect for others.

After each battle (if the Federals were still in command of the terrain), Chamberlain walked the battlefield looking and caring for the casualties. He assisted the medics in finding and retrieving the wounded. *The Soul of the Lion* has a great anecdote about his finding General Sickles after the latter had been wounded.

> Then he rose, spoke to several of the wounded, and suddenly discovered "brave old Sickles lying calm and cheerful, ... refusing to have more attention than came in his turn." Chamberlain sat down beside him to cheer him as best he could. But Sickles, who could still smile despite his pain, thought Chamberlain needed comforting rather than himself. "General," he whispered, "you have the soul of the lion and the heart of the woman."
>
> "Take the benediction to yourself," Chamberlain replied gently; "you could not have thought that, if you had not been it."[45]

Chamberlain put the welfare of others first; he took care of his men.

He demonstrated his compassion—his respect for others in battle after battle. This compassion did not come to the fore only when Chamberlain was fighting. His actions at Appomattox are one of the most poignant scenes I've ever heard described. Chamberlain, because of his great, heroic service, was selected by General Grant to receive the surrender of the rebels. General John B. Gordon, a great and courageous rebel leader, was in command of the Southern troops. As the latter dragged themselves dejectedly toward Chamberlain, he gave the marching salute command "carry arms" to his troops. Wanting to recognize the courage of the Southerners, Chamberlain had planned this movement and informed his regimental commanders before the surrender. Gordon and his Soldiers were startled ...

> Wheeling his horse toward Chamberlain, he [Gordon] touched the animal slightly with the spur so that it reared, and as the horse's head came down in a graceful bow, Gordon brought his sword-point down to his boot-toe. Then wheeling back toward his own column, he gave the command to carry arms. The two armies thus accorded each other the final recognition of gallant opponents. But, said Chamberlain, 'On our part not a sound of the trumpet more, nor roll of drum; not a cheer, nor word nor whisper of vain-glorying, nor motion of man standing again at the order, but an awed stillness rather, and breath-holding, as if it were the passing of the dead.'[46]

As Chamberlain wrote, "For us they were fellow-soldiers as well, suffering the fate of arms. We could not look into those brave, bronzed faces, and those battered flags we had met on so many fields where glorious manhood lent a glory to the earth that bore it, and think of personal hate and mean revenge."[47] The mutual respect that the erstwhile enemies were now showing each other was "honor answering honor."[48]

Chamberlain's comments make a point much ignored today by historians. "Chamberlain recognized ... that henceforth both sides shared in the gallantry, honor and dedication of the opponent. Northerners share in the legendary fighting spirit and élan of Lee's Army and Southerners share in the raw courage and dedication to a just conclusion to a no-holds-barred battle. We are immensely richer for it."[49]

Chamberlain was modest. He was a professor at Bowdoin College when the Civil War commenced. He was given a sabbatical for additional study but decided to enlist instead—another example of his selfless service. Although offered a colonel's rank and regimental command, he recognized that he had no experience; he asked to be a lieutenant colonel and the executive so he could learn. Chamberlain had no inflated opinion of himself.

Chamberlain became knowledgeable, however. He studied and learned the business of fighting. Although he had absolutely no experience or training in the military when he volunteered, he immediately became a student of military tactics. He observed what others did. He learned from their successes and mistakes. He never stopped studying; he continued to learn. He quickly concluded that the frontal attack that seemed almost to be the only way in which both armies fought, left much to be desired. Chamberlain tried to attack weaknesses. He wanted to accomplish the mission with less loss of life. That is one of the reasons why he objected to Meade's order at Petersburg.

Chamberlain was loyal to his country and had a strong belief in the cause. He saw the war at the outset as one to preserve the Union and abolish slavery. He thought it a sin that one man should own another.

Chamberlain was faithful—he was loyal—to his wife. He adored her beginning with his courtship to the end of his life. She was spoiled and caused him a lot of grief. However, he never turned away; he honored his vows always.

While in college he decided not to drink because he wanted to devote his energies to his studies. He also believed that he could not drink with one friend and not another.[50] Chamberlain almost never drank and when he did it was lightly.[51] Chamberlain did not believe as some people do that a man has to drink to show how tough he is or to prove that he is a man. When it comes to courage or manhood, Chamberlain is second to none.

He was ethical and religious. He taught Sunday school. He

believed that "God is over all things and that he will put me where he wants me and where I ought to be."[52] His faith was a major part of his character.

He was a very intelligent scholar. While a student at Bowdoin, he was elected to Phi Beta Kappa. He became an accomplished organist, performed in stage productions, won prizes in oratory and composition, taught himself Italian, and became a member of several student societies.[53]

Chamberlain's appearance added to his ability to lead. While we cannot make ourselves handsome or beautiful, we can ensure that our appearance and bearing are appropriate.

Chamberlain defines "warrior." He strove for excellence in all that he did. His attention to duty and his courage was unexcelled. He respected others. He demonstrated his loyalty and selfless service to his country by volunteering to serve. He lived by a code that brought honor to his regiment, his Army, and our country. He was a man of integrity and epitomized unyielding adherence to the highest ideals of duty, honor, and country.

Few Soldiers can match Chamberlain in all of these qualities. No one can surpass his living our Army values. To become a warrior, we can choose no better role model than Joshua Lawrence Chamberlain.

BASIC TRAINING

Individual training is the foundation on which unit training is built. It is the source of a Soldier's confidence and trust in the Army.[54]

—Lieutenant General Arthur S. Collins, Jr.

The modern battlefield is lethal and unforgiving. The goal of Basic Combat Training (BCT), the initial training that every Soldier receives when he enters the service, is to teach basic skills and habits necessary to survive on that battlefield. The physical and emotional toughening begins in Basic. All recruits, regardless of branch, complete a nine-week BCT program. Following Basic, the Soldier attends advanced individual training (AIT) where he qualifies in some specialty such as rifleman, clerk, or mechanic. For Infantrymen, these two phases are rolled into one, OSUT (One Station Unit Training).

After Basic, the recruit with a non-combat arms MOS (military occupational specialty) is transferred to some post for his advanced individual training. He receives only a modicum of training, if any, in the skills of the basic Soldier—those skills designed to keep him alive on the battlefield and help him defend his unit if required. When he reports to his first unit after AIT, his basic Soldier skills atrophy. He seldom goes to the field to practice those war-fighting skills that he may be required to demonstrate on some battlefield in the future. As a result, the noncombat MOS Soldier who has a much shorter initial entry training cycle will always be less qualified as a combat ready Soldier than his combat arms counterpart.

This shortfall must never be such that this Soldier cannot perform those basic war-fighting skills he may need in combat.

General Peter Schoomaker, the U.S. Army chief of staff, directed a major analysis of the initial entry training. The study accomplished by "Task Force Soldier," among other things, defined the "Warrior Ethos," a statement of what the individual Soldier should be, regardless of branch. This "Ethos" identifies an attitude that has defined the American Soldier since the Revolutionary War. It states that the American Soldier is a Soldier first and foremost regardless of branch. It is the total commitment to victory. In addition, every Soldier is trained to be able to accomplish 40 Warrior Corps Tasks and nine Warrior Drills.[55] The chief of staff summed it up when he said, "You're a rifleman first."[56]

Today's pundits and "old Soldiers" unjustly criticize the new Soldier and his contemporaries. If there are shortcomings, the criticisms should be targeted at leaders and policy-makers. Provide the right environment for the drill sergeants, and they will bring new Soldiers to whatever standard is set by the officer leadership.

On June 27, 1997, Secretary of Defense William Cohen announced the formation of the Federal Advisory Committee on Gender-Integrated Training and Readiness Issues, composed of eleven private citizens and chaired by former Senator Nancy Kassebaum Baker. The Kassebaum Committee in its December 16, 1997, report recognized that the principal mission of military training "is to produce an effective, efficient, and ready force."[57] It acknowledged the importance of training cadre leadership.[58] The report strongly supported a gender-integrated force.[59] A question not asked is: "If coed training is a good way to achieve high standards, why don't male and female Olympic athletes train together?" Because current law prohibits females from being assigned to Infantry, armor, Special Forces, and certain artillery units, basic training for these branches is male only. Basic for other branches may be coed.

The committee reported that some basic trainees contend that basic is too easy and that it failed to prepare them to defend themselves and their unit if the need arises! The committee recommended toughening requirements.[60]

Some trainees today repeat the criticism.[61] That contention should be alarming to the chief of staff of the Army. If the criticism is accurate, basic has failed to develop the self-confidence and competence each Soldier should have. The result will be higher casualties. (Infantry basic has added a rite of passage called "The Bayonet." This demanding addition is a twenty-five-mile course that challenges trainees with situations they are likely to face in combat.)[62]

The committee unanimously recommended changes to improve basic and AIT training. Among these were separate barracks for male and female recruits,[63] single-gender basic, tougher basic training requirements including physical fitness, the enforcement of consistent standards for males and females, and a determination of whether more leeway to discharge recruits should be allowed.[64]

The committee found that monetary enlistment incentives make the maintenance of discipline more difficult because many recruits enlist to get out and return to school.[65] Consequently, the committee recommended a shift in recruiting policy from monetary rewards to more motivational themes of challenge and patriotism.[66] (In 2005, when the Army was experiencing great difficulty in meeting its recruiting goals, the focus was shifted from "benefits" to "patriotism" and "service to country.")

Finding that only 30 percent of the Army's trainers were volunteers for the assignment[67] and recognizing the vital nature of high quality trainers, the committee recommended that a training assignment be made "career enhancing."[68] (In the summer of 2004, numerous drill sergeants at Fort Benning were involuntarily extended. Regardless of their status they continued their great work.)

A major task of Basic is developing a level of physical fitness that for most inductees is far above their physical condition when they enlist. Trainees are tested within seventy-two hours of arriving at their basic training company. The test consists of three events: pushups, sit-ups, and a two-mile run. The average scores in two recent basic combat training companies (noncombat arms) that I observed were 100 and 116 out of a possible 300. "Passing"—the score necessary for graduation from basic—is 150 points.

Some critics believe that the 150 standard is too low—that the trainee should meet the Army standard of 180. However, the lowering of the qualification is acceptance of reality; the Army has concluded that 150 points is what can be reasonably expected from recruits after nine weeks of training.[69] The Kassebaum Committee found that PT was often "crowded from" the training schedule because of other requirements thereby lessening the training received.[70] Recruits, drill sergeants, and commanders in conversations with me confirm this criticism.

Some critics of coed basic focus on the difference in physical capabilities between males and females. To equalize the disparities in capabilities the Army instituted gender-normed physical training tests with lower requirements for females. For example, a female twenty-one- to twenty-six-year-old must do forty-six push-ups in two minutes for one hundred points. A male must do seventy-five.[71]

Gender-norming is an admission that most females are less physically capable than most males. Gender-norming is based on "equal points for equal effort."[72] Requiring the same standards for both sexes would do much to diminish the criticisms by males that females receive preferential treatment.

The Army tried coed basic several decades ago. It was unsatisfactory and discontinued.[73] However, it has been reinstituted. Critics believe that basic should be single sex because the pressures arising from sexual attraction should not be added to the other stresses extant in the unfamiliar environment of basic. Although senior policy makers seem to believe otherwise, sexual attraction cannot be easily controlled and sometimes results in sexual problems. Although the Kassebaum Committee recommended that the military have single-sex basic,[74] the Army continues coed basic for the noncombat arms.

The Army's rationale is that Soldiers need to train together if they are going to work together. The tighter control in basic is more conducive to inculcating proper conduct than waiting until AIT or assignment to a unit. There are, of course, widespread criticisms of this approach. Fourteen pro-defense organizations including the American Legion, Veterans of Foreign Wars, and the Center for Security Policy, announced opposition to coed basic.[75]

Developing the mental, emotional, and physical toughness required to succeed and survive on the battlefield begins in basic training. It should be the toughest thing a recruit has ever experienced. Tough—not "chicken" or "Mickey Mouse" or "hazing"— but tough because of a battle-focused regimen with high, realistic standards that the trainee must meet. It means higher standards of physical fitness, care of equipment, military courtesy, marksmanship, and field craft—a myriad of skills that every Soldier must master before he is combat ready.

Inscribed on a small monument at the Infantry Training Brigade (ITB) Headquarters (all Infantry enlistees are trained by ITB) are these words: "Let no man's soul cry out ... Had I been properly trained."[76] It is a constant reminder of the importance of training.

The Army should institute a uniform basic training program of approximately eighteen to twenty weeks to develop the basic Soldier skills supported by the mental and physical toughness needed to survive on today's lethal and unforgiving battlefield. This training should be separated by gender. Our Soldiers deserve the best preparation that we can give them. It is unconscionable to do less.

TO DEVELOP COMBAT-READY SOLDIERS YOU MUST HAVE BATTLE-FOCUSED TRAINING

In no other profession are the penalties for employing untrained personnel so appalling or so irrevocable as in the military.[77]

—General of the Army Douglas MacArthur

When bullets are flying overhead clipping branches and leaves off the trees, and mortar rounds are exploding among your troops causing casualties and screams of pain, frustration, anger, fear will fill the air. The commander by his commands and example must be able to bring order from this chaos. However, his ability to exert influence immediately is probably limited to those few Soldiers nearby. Squad and team leaders are the ones who will control their small part of the battlefield. Their state of training determines in large measure what these leaders and their men are capable of doing. Training may have more to do with success on the battlefield than a leader's actions.

Colonel Joe Votel was commander of the 75th Ranger Regiment when terrorists destroyed the Twin Towers on September 11, 2001. One month later, the Rangers made a successful parachute assault to seize an airfield in Afghanistan. Although the regiment was always in a high state of readiness, it was quickly sharpened even further under Colonel Votel's outstanding leadership. Part of the regiment has been in contact with the enemy in either Afghanistan or Iraq or both since that date. (Brigadier General Votel was later selected to form and head a special agency to develop ways to combat improvised explosive devices [IED] more effectively. Subsequently, he became the assistant division commander of the 82nd Airborne Division.)

Battle-focused training is the heart and soul of combat preparation, contributes positively to combat readiness, and leads to success on the battlefield. Unless his Soldiers are properly trained, physically fit, and emotionally conditioned, the best, most competent leader will fail.

Any team sport coach worth his paycheck toughens his players mentally and physically and drills them on the fundamentals until the team masters them. The coach knows that in the "heat" of the contest, his players must react spontaneously, instinctively, and immediately if they are to dominate the other team. So it is with combat. Your Soldiers either dominate the enemy or the enemy dominates them.

Commanders focus on what is important. Ask your subordinates what the troops need. Your NCOs are particularly adept at sensing the shortcomings of their Soldiers. If the activity does not contribute to effectiveness on the battlefield, the item should be eliminated from the training schedule. General Mikhail I. Dragomirov reminds us that "the troops should learn in peacetime only what must be done in wartime."[78]

Accomplishing this task in a climate dominated by requirements from higher headquarters is difficult. Sometimes the elimination of what you deem superfluous or a waste of time may be impossible. Eliminate what you can; diminish the impact of those inappropriate requirements that must be met.

T. R. Fehrenbach, in *This Kind of War*, wrote, "A nation that does not prepare for all forms of war should then renounce the use of war in national policy. A people that does not prepare to fight should then be morally prepared for surrender. To fail to prepare Soldiers and citizens for limited, bloody ground action, and then to engage in it is folly verging on the criminal."[79]

"A 'modern' Infantry may ride sky vehicles into combat, fire and sense its weapons through instrumentation, employ devices of frightening lethality in the future—but it must also be old-fashioned enough to be iron-hard, poised for instant obedience, and prepared to die in the mud."[80]

Fehrenbach compares the need for tough military training to football practice. Americans fully understand the need for preparation for competition. If a coach is too permissive, his team will lose. Unfortunately, any American officer who works his troops as hard as the football coach trains his team could be severely criticized. "But the shocks of the battlefield are a hundred times those of the playing field, and the outcome infinitely more important to the nation. The problem is to see not what is desirable, or nice, or politically feasible, but what is necessary."[81]

While I agree that some may criticize the officer who "trains hard," I believe that he has little to fear. Put the training on the training schedule, follow the field manual, obey the regulations, enforce the safety policy, and, by all means, participate in the training with the troops—set the example. You won't go wrong.

Boots on the Ground: Man Is the Ultimate Weapon

Men may argue forever on what wins wars,
And welter in cons and pros,
And seek for their answer at history's doors,
But the man with the rifle knows.
He must stand on the ground on his own two feet,
And he's never in doubt when it's won,
If it's won, he's there; if he's not, it's defeat.
That's the test, when the fighting is done.[82]

—Author Unknown

When I graduated from West Point and was commissioned a second lieutenant of Infantry in 1949, I was told that I was obsolete—that the next war would be fought with missiles. This fallacious prediction came from much of the media and, unfortunately, from many military "thinkers." My classmates who had selected the air force to become pilots were told the same thing—the days of the manned aircraft were numbered! I wish that those naysayers had told the North Koreans and the Chinese that, because one year after graduation many of us were slugging it out in tough, deadly ground combat in Korea. My air force friends and their counterparts in the navy and Marine corps were doing all they could to gain air superiority and were trying to help us on the ground with dangerous, close ground support missions.

Less than two decades later, some of us were doing the same

thing in Southeast Asia. We were face-to-face, toe-to-toe with a tough, determined foe in a hot, wet, filthy jungle. My friends in the sky were braving extremely heavy antiaircraft missiles and artillery trying to destroy the will and capability of another resolute foe. I guess somebody forgot to tell the North Vietnamese what we had been told so many years earlier—you're obsolete!

As he began his description of the defeat in Korea of the U.S. Eighth Army in November 1950, historian Brigadier General S. L. A. Marshall used these words: "In the hour of its defeat the Eighth Army was a wholly modern force technologically, sprung from a nation that prides itself as being as well informed as any of earth's people. The Chinese Communist Army was a wholly peasant body composed in the main of illiterates."[83]

In Vietnam, a third world country, U.S. forces significantly outclassed the enemy in technology. Yet the North Vietnamese Army (NVA) was a formidable foe. The NVA believed that men, not weapons, were the decisive element on the battlefield. Bernard Fall described the NVA as "one of the best Infantry combat forces in the world, capable of incredible feats of endurance and raw courage even against vastly superior firepower and under the worst physical conditions."[84]

Although the two Vietnamese regiments that fought at Ia Drang outnumbered the Americans, the Vietnamese were at a major disadvantage when it came to resources. Where the U.S. had 110-mph troop and supply movement, the NVA moved on foot. The U.S. had major USAF aircraft and Army helicopter gunship support; the NVA had none. The U.S. had 105mm and 155mm howitzers; the fire support for the NVA was very limited. The U.S. had radio communication within the battalion (although at times the din of battle was so great only arm signals would suffice); the NVA had field telephones, whistles, and arm and hand signals. The enemy put up a very commendable fight. If the Vietnamese had had the tremendous fire support that the Americans had, the outcome of the battle may have been decidedly different. Lieutenant Colonel Hal Moore, the commander of the 1-7 Cavalry, said that the fire support he had was his advantage over the NVA. The technological superiority of the Americans was a major advantage. Saying that does not detract from the fighting spirit and heroism of Moore and his Soldiers.

In Mogadishu, October 3–4, 1993, a ferocious Somali militia again demonstrated what a dedicated third world force, though technologically inferior, could do against a force with modern equipment. This battle in which Task Force Ranger was embroiled is another example illustrating that close, dirty, deadly ground combat has not disappeared from the battlefield. A handful of Rangers fought for their lives against a swirling mob of Somali militia, women, and children who outnumbered the Rangers more than ten to one. The Rangers' leadership at all levels and their courage and training status enabled them to extricate themselves from a situation that bordered on a disaster.

Later, in Afghanistan and Iraq, "obsolete," close ground fighting reared its ugly head again as air force heavy bombers high in the sky and fighter-bombers flying lower over the battlefield added their firepower to the embattled Soldiers on the ground. Close ground fighting may be obsolete, but our Army and Marines continue to be engaged in this kind of warfare.

Throughout history, there have been innumerable occasions when the numerically or technologically inferior force has won because of the leadership of the commander and the intrepidity and proficiency of the Soldiers. To name just a few: the Spartans at Thermopylae; Mosby's March 6, 1863, raid that resulted in the capture of a brigadier general, two captains, thirty enlisted men, and fifty horses without a shot being fired; Colonel Joshua Lawrence Chamberlain's leadership and the actions of the 20th Maine on July 2, 1863; Indian Chief Nana's rampage through the Southwest in 1881;[85] and the 101st Airborne Division at Bastogne.

Our experience in Korea, Vietnam, Somalia, Afghanistan, and Iraq, should put an end forever to the belief that the technologically superior force will always win. Despite their tremendous technological disadvantage, third world countries are able to mount and fight momentous battles, inflict significant casualties, and cause major damage.

Soldiers from the third world are usually extremely tough physically and emotionally, highly disciplined, dedicated to winning, very courageous, and seemingly inured to hardship. Being third world does not make them inferior fighters. They are true warriors. Although we may consider them "backward," they may still pose a threat to our country.

Much of the literature in the media and in our military journals describe the Army of the future—the Army after next or the Army of 2010—as being one where everything is high-tech—where the battle is fought from bunkers miles from the enemy and almost devoid of danger. In a recent *Army* article our forces engaged and destroyed the enemy using *Star Wars* weaponry. Our forces sustained no losses. I do not believe that we will reach that level of technology in the next twenty years, if ever. Senator John McCain gave some cogent advice when he said that counting on technology to solve all our problems is wishful thinking. Those marvelous innovations are never ready on time and seldom work as well as advertised.

Our Army is the most technologically advanced force in the world. We see technology as a way to improve combat effectiveness while reducing casualties. Consequently, the emphasis on technology is well placed.

However, we need to remember some of the battles of the past. It is the Infantryman who carries the battle to the enemy. Sooner or later he has to get out of that vehicle and fight on the ground. It's the grunt with boots on the ground that slogs through that cold rain and mud or endures the jungle heat, leeches, and insects. It is he who wins with rifle, bayonet, grenade, and hand-to-hand combat. He gets on the objective and plants his feet there.

There will always be a demand for the physically, mentally, emotionally tough and highly skilled combat-ready Soldier led by confident, competent junior leaders. "The most precious commodity with which the Army deals is the individual Soldier who is the heart and soul of our combat forces."[86] Our focus ought to be on developing that Soldier. He's the man who makes the difference.

He is the ultimate weapon.

DISCIPLINE TAKES OVER WHEN YOUR BODY AND MIND TELL YOU TO QUIT

You teach discipline by doing it over and over, by repetition and rote, especially in a game like football when you have very little time to decide what you are going to do. So what you do is react almost instinctively, naturally. You have done it so many times, over and over and over again.[87]

—Vince Lombardi

Tough training exercises and combat can be so physically, mentally, and emotionally stressful on Soldiers and their commanders that they become "survivors." Their minds become numb. On those occasions, because of the great physical duress under which the unit finds itself, commanders, like the Soldiers they lead, become so tired that their only thought is putting one foot in front of the other. Both leaders and men being led just "keep on keeping on." They are just "survivors." It happens to all of us.

When this condition occurs, commanders may neglect basic security measures such as selecting and preparing proper primary, alternate, and supplementary fighting positions; rehearsing counterattack plans or, at least, having leaders walk the routes during the day; ensuring Soldiers are spread rather than bunched; checking that sufficient numbers are alert (observing and listening for the enemy); resting; coordinating with adjacent units to include physical contact between the leaders; coordinating sectors of fire; and other tasks that increase the odds that we will be victorious. We sometimes slough off these vital actions because of fatigue. When we do, we endanger the mission, the unit, and ourselves. We're "too tired" to do what we know needs to be done. However, it's better to be "dead tired" than "dead."

Those actions and others must become second nature. Soldiers need to do them and leaders from team leaders up need to ensure accomplishment of them. These actions then become automatic; we do them without thinking. Just as the habit of putting on a seat belt every time we enter a car, these little things that are so important need to become automatic. When they are, your Soldiers and the unit are disciplined. Soldiers are doing what should be done in the absence of specific orders. While no commander is relieved of his responsibility for checking and supervising, disciplined Soldiers continue to perform properly when commanders become "survivors."

How do we add discipline to our Mission Essential Task List (METL) without deleting something else? Training requirements already include more than we can accomplish to the standards we want.

Discipline is not added to the METL; developing and enhancing discipline is part of every task. No additional training hours are required. As we do our tasks to standard, we become well-trained and disciplined. Our combat readiness improves as our discipline improves.

In a well-trained, combat-ready unit, discipline takes over when Soldiers become survivors.

EDUCATE THE MILITARY

A teacher affects eternity; he can never tell where his influence stops.[88]

—Henry Adams, Historian

When I moved to Columbus, Georgia, only ten miles from Fort Benning, I became involved with the military right away. My first contacts were with the Ranger Training Brigade (Ranger School) and the 75th Ranger Regiment. One contact led to another, and soon I was speaking to each Infantry Officer Advanced Course and Infantry Officer Basic Course. Graduations and dinings-in followed. The more I spoke, the more I was requested.

I found these contacts to be very enjoyable because they afforded me an opportunity to meet and get to know some of the military. I also had the opportunity to speak with and learn from the experiences of the many fine Soldiers in our Army.

My subjects were, appropriately, military in nature. They included history, biographical sketches, and combat actions. I concentrated on fundamentals because I believe that if you accomplish those indispensable actions better than the enemy, you will win. I also always complimented and thanked the Soldiers for their service to our country.

I worked hard to make my talks interesting and relevant. When appropriate (for example, presenting a class to students) I always limited my prepared remarks to no more than half of the allotted time. The remainder of the period I reserved for questions and comments. To ensure that this portion of the period would not lag, I always prepared questions that I could ask the audience.

I never considered myself a polished speaker. Consequently, I worked diligently in preparing my notes and rehearsed several times. But as much as I rehearsed, I was never satisfied. I believed that I could always do better. I knew it would be difficult to say something both interesting and worth remembering to these Soldiers. My diligence, however, paid off. I am always pleased to have Soldiers remark to me years later that they remember me speaking to them when they were in Officer Candidate School (OCS) or at Ranger School graduation or some other function. Some can quote phrases that I used!

Talking with Soldiers can pay dividends. Do it.

CALLING FOR AND ADJUSTING SUPPORTING FIRES

_____

Colonel Wainwright of the First Corps entered in his diary that the rebel barrage "was by no means as effective as it should have been, nine-tenths of their shot passing over our men." While this was surely an exaggeration, it did suggest that on this afternoon even the best-plotted shot was not likely to hit what is was aimed at.[89]

—Stephen W. Sears, Author

One of the most valuable skills that an Infantryman can have is the ability to call for and adjust supporting fires. This capability should not be limited to his own supporting weapons but must extend to artillery and Tac Air (Tactical Air Support). Relying totally on an FO (forward observer) is shortsighted; he may become a casualty. Major General John Maher, when commanding the 25th Infantry Division (Light), wrote that his lieutenants demonstrated a consistent weakness in calling for and adjusting fires. He said that they should "take charge" and not always rely on their Fire Support NCO because he might not be available.

All Soldiers need to know how to call for and adjust supporting fire. The best example I know of showing the benefits of this skill is described in the book, *We Were Soldiers Once … and Young.*

Sergeant Ernie Savage, a young rifle squad leader, was the fourth man to take command of Lieutenant Henry Herrick's 2nd

Platoon, B/1-7 Cavalry, during the Ia Drang Valley battle in Vietnam on November 11, 1965. Immediately after landing, Lieutenant Herrick spotted a couple of Vietnamese men running away from his platoon. Herrick led his men in an all-out run trying to capture the enemy. Suddenly, Herrick and his men came under fire and soon found themselves isolated and surrounded. The platoon suffered numerous casualties, Lieutenant Herrick being one of the first. The command of the remnants of the platoon devolved to Sergeant Ernie Savage. It was a desperate situation.[90] Savage called for artillery fires and pulled them as close to his very small perimeter as possible. Whenever he heard voices or saw any movement, he called for artillery. He said, "It seemed like they didn't care how many of them were killed. Some of them were stumbling, walking right into us."[91]

Lieutenant Colonel (now Lieutenant General) Hal Moore, the battalion commander, described the thoughts that were spinning in his head.

> I checked on Sergeant Ernie Savage and his band of survivors in Herrick's cut-off platoon. The report came back by radio that they had taken no additional casualties and were hanging tough. I mulled over possible options for their rescue: a night attack; night infiltration to reinforce the platoon; or a fresh attempt to fight through to them early in the morning. They would be on all our minds this night, that brave handful of men surrounded and alone in a sea of enemies.[92]

When dawn arrived, dozens of khaki-clad Vietnamese Soldiers were strewn around the lost platoon. Sergeant Savage and his men had survived the longest, most fearful night that any of them would ever experience.[93] There can be no doubt that the supporting fires and Sergeant Savage's calm leadership saved the platoon from annihilation.

The importance of artillery support was brought home forcefully to me early in my career. On November 25–26, 1950, the Eighth United States Army in Korea was in North Korea about 40–50 miles from the Yalu River. I was the company commander of the Eighth Army Ranger Company. My company was attached to Task Force Dolvin, the assault element of the 25th Infantry Division. My company secured its objective, Hill 205, late in the afternoon of November 25. Shortly after dark, the Chinese, who launched their first major offensive that night, made five attacks on my company with what was later officially estimated to be a force of five hundred Chinese. My Rangers, exhibiting great courage and skill, repulsed five assaults. A major factor in their success was the artillery support that I called for and adjusted as each enemy assault began. As the Chinese launched their sixth attack at approximately 0230 hours on November 26, I called for artillery as I had done before. Unfortunately, the one available battery was firing another mission, and we were unable to get that support that had proved so valuable in turning back the previous assaults. The enemy overran our position. While I cannot say for certain, I believe that if the support had been available, we would have been able to hold our position during that sixth assault.

All leaders should be capable of calling for and adjusting supporting fires. This support can make the difference between success and failure—between living and dying. Without that capability, the battle may be lost; men may die unnecessarily. The time to develop the skill is in training before it is needed.

OVERCOMING THE
RELUCTANCE TO KILL

A revealing light is thrown on this subject through the studies by Medical Corps psychiatrists of the combat fatigue cases in the European Theater. They found that fear of killing, rather than fear of being killed, was the most common cause of battle failure, and that fear of failure ran second.[94]

—Brigadier General S. L. A. Marshall

First Lieutenant Tom Courtney, the executive officer (XO) of B/2-502nd, and I had been at one of the Navy Officer Clubs in Vietnam for about an hour and a half before returning to our billets. It was about nine o'clock in the evening. After dropping Tom off in his company area I returned to my tent. Bud Connett, one of the brigade chaplains, stopped in to shoot the breeze. After about thirty minutes, I had a call from Tom. He said that Second Lieutenant Jim Smith (not his actual name) had a problem that Tom wanted me to discuss with Jim. I told Tom to come on up and bring Smith with him.

Smith was in the rear area because he had had a significant reaction from a bee sting. When Jim and Tom arrived, Bud left. Smith spoke first. Although he had been very proud when he earned the right to wear the crossed muskets of the Infantryman, he said that he could not bring himself to kill. He cited a couple of times when he had had an enemy in his sights but pulled off on purpose. Expressing his feelings at some length, he said the effect on him was such that he had considered suicide. Jim was not close to his father, a Methodist minister, and had not discussed his feelings with him before leaving the States for Vietnam. However, before arriving in Vietnam, Jim had convinced himself that he could overcome his conscience. He said that he wanted to stay with the brigade even though he knew that he might be subjected to some verbal abuse.

I empathized with his feelings and believed that it took courage to say what he had just told me. I wanted him to discuss his problem with Lieutenant Colonel Dan Danford, his new battalion commander and see if he could use him elsewhere in the battalion. There was a position as assistant adjutant, the position he had filled before I had sent him to the field to take Lieutenant Fred Myers's place after Fred was wounded. Jim said he knew that he had to discuss his problem with Lieutenant Colonel Dan Danford but wanted to talk to me first—said I was still "the Ranger" to the battalion. (Dan and I had just changed positions.)

We talked for more than an hour during which time Tom and I convinced Jim that he should talk with Father Murphy or Chaplain Connett. Murph might be the better choice since he was older and had been in Vietnam longer. I called Murph and then accompanied Jim to Murph's tent. I arranged a ride to take Tom to his company area and then I went to see Major Dick Kupau, the Brigade S1.

Dick knew of four jobs in the brigade where Jim could be used. Dick and I agreed that Jim could earn his pay although we had some concern that "reluctance to kill" might become "catching."

The next morning while Colonel Rip Collins, the brigade deputy commander, was shaving, I discussed the problem with him. He believed that the danger was too great to keep Smith in the brigade, so I asked Dick to contact Lieutenant Colonel Bill Walby, G1, Americal Division. Bill could use Smith. I was glad that we were able to come to some solution.

Jim's problem may have been fear of being wounded or killed rather than reluctance to kill, but I believed in giving him the benefit of the doubt. He did not "misbehave" before the enemy. Regardless, he needed to be taken off the line. As I went over the problem in my mind, I wished that I knew more about human nature.

Many company commanders today recognize and take steps to prevent or sublimate the problem. *Army* magazine, in its "Company Command" column published numerous letters from company commanders who had faced the problem and taken preventive and/or corrective actions. They stressed acknowledging the problem, talking to their Soldiers, and using all resources to help with what can be a serious predicament.

As I was facing this problem, as chance would have it, my wife, Jeannie, sent me a clipping about one of Billy Graham's columns. The Reverend Graham discussed the conflict that others like Smith have. I forwarded it to Smith. While I knew that the clipping would not resolve all the questions that he had, it might be helpful. My sending it would also let him know that he was not forgotten.

Shortly thereafter, Lieutenant Smith contacted me to express his appreciation and told me that he was making a contribution in his new job. I'm glad we did what we did. Smith was "gainfully employed." We had removed him from a situation where he could have had a detrimental effect on his company. There had been no negative impact on our brigade because of his transfer.

What can we learn from this incident? The first thing that came to my mind at the time was that the problem, "reluctance to kill," is real. According to Brigadier General S. L. A. Marshall, (see quote above) it is widespread. It is a potential problem of which commanders should be aware. Discussing it with the Soldiers before and during combat can be worthwhile, as it may be something that is affecting several members of the command. Discussing it may allay somewhat the concerns that the Soldiers have when they realize that others may have the same apprehension. The chaplain can also be helpful. Addressing the problem head-on can be beneficial.

PART II:
UNIT TRAINING

CASUALTY PLAY IN FTXs

It is right to be very concerned about the wounded. If we neglect them, we will find the rest of the troops will deliberately not fight well, and our remissness will cause us to lose some who could have been saved.[95]

—The Emperor Maurice, East Roman Emperor and General

Proper medical evacuation in combat saves lives and has tremendous impact on morale. Realistic casualty play in FTXs (field training exercises) has immediate and future benefits. Casualty play deserves the commander's attention. Soldiers will note this concern (or lack of it), and their confidence and morale will be affected. As Major General Baron von Steuben wrote:

> There is nothing which gains an officer the love of his Soldiers more than his care of them under the distress of sickness; it is then he has the power of exerting his humanity in providing them every comfortable (sic) necessary, and making their situation as agreeable as possible.[96]

Slicks (troop carrier or logistics choppers) are often used to evacuate casualties. While frowned upon by some, commanders in command-and-control (C2) choppers may be the best way to evacuate casualties.

In the 1-7th Cavalry's battle in the Ia Drang Valley in Vietnam on November 1965, Lieutenant Colonel Hal Moore, the battalion commander, went to great (and appropriate) lengths to ensure that all his casualties were recovered, properly treated, and evacuated. Those efforts during and after the battle had a significant, positive impact on his Soldiers. This influence carried over into future battles.

I have observed the 75th Ranger Regiment at the Joint Readiness Training Center (JRTC) on three occasions and in numerous other exercises. On my first visit, Colonel Bill Leszczynski, the Regimental Commander, placed considerable emphasis on casualty play during the exercise. His concern did not go unnoticed by the individual Rangers and had a beneficial impact on them. The emphasis resulted in worthwhile training that stood the Rangers in good stead later. All subsequent commanders have made casualty play a high priority.

When your men see the emphasis you place on care and evacuation, their confidence in you will increase and their morale will rise. Do not "go administrative" during your training evacuations.

A good idea is also to practice CASEVAC (casualty evacuation) with numerous casualties—so many that the combat unit and the MEDEVAC (medical evacuation) unit are stretched to the limit of their capability and beyond.

Minimize the time that MEDEVAC choppers are on the ground. Maximize speed. Provide them security. Pilots will be more reluctant to come to your aid if they have had bad experiences with your unit.

Play fratricide to the hilt in training. Inform the troops of the results of the investigations, how many reports were submitted, and what actions were taken. Can the troops react while they are in the current exercise? To obtain the most training value, the information must be timely. Commanders must see that it is disseminated.

The first responder (the individual providing first aid—the medics and anyone who provides that initial, immediate care to the wounded and injured) has a difficult task. He must determine what is wrong with the casualty and, using whatever knowledge he has, treat that problem. He may have to move the casualty from a position exposed to enemy fire before he can accomplish his initial assessment and begin appropriate first aid.

Medics, both in training and in combat, often give little or no thought to their own safety. While we admire that courage on the battlefield, if the Medic becomes a casualty himself, what was a bad situation becomes worse. The medic must take all reasonable precautions to avoid becoming a casualty. The enemy threat must be neutralized or minimized first. Move the casualty to a covered position before treating him.

Another concern is "manhandling" the casualty when there is no great danger from the enemy. I know from firsthand experience the difference between a situation in which the casualty and rescuer are in imminent danger and one in which they are in a relatively protected position. Sometimes the rescuer treats the casualty very roughly even when danger is not imminent. Rough treatment can exacerbate the injury. Rough treatment can contribute to shock, sometimes called "the killer on the battlefield." "[Shock] can threaten life even though the injuries or conditions that caused the depression may not otherwise be fatal.... The degree of shock is increased by abnormal changes in body temperature, by poor resistance of the victim to stress, by pain, by rough handling, and by delay in treatment."[97] Follow-up care (after immediate treatment) includes reassuring the victim; being gentle, being kind and understanding also play an important role in treating a victim in shock.

Treat the dead with dignity. During combat, as the situation permits, place the remains in a safe area. Cover them with a poncho and put them in the shade. (Lieutenant Colonel Moore's example at Ia Drang is worth emulating.)

Commanders should closely observe casualty play in the FTXs and discuss their concerns with the battalion surgeons and the medics. When appropriate, commanders should quickly initiate corrective training in first aid and evacuation. Proper casualty play in FTXs increases a Soldier's confidence and aggressiveness because he knows that he will be properly cared for if he becomes a casualty.

CHAIN OF COMMAND

Mission accomplishment depends on information passing accurately to and from subordinates and leaders, up and down the chain of command and NCO support channel, and laterally among adjacent organizations or activities.[98]

—FM 22-100

Every unit (and section) has a commander (or chief) and subordinates. The subordinates are there to help the commander. He cannot do the job of his unit without this help. If he could, these subordinates would not have been included in the composition of the unit. The successful commander develops and uses these subordinates effectively. One way is working through the chain of command—the issuing of orders to the immediate subordinates, supporting their efforts, and holding them accountable.

As a rule, give instructions, orders, or corrections using the chain of command. By so doing, you emphasize leader responsibility. You also enhance the prestige of the leader; he will be the one who knows what is going on.

Following this principle sometimes becomes very difficult if not inappropriate under pressure of combat. Circumstances may force the leader to issue orders directly to the Soldier who is to carry out those instructions. Only then is the chain jumped. As soon as possible, the leaders are informed. The situation may arise in training "when a subordinate is about to make a mistake that could result in serious injury or death."[99] As in combat, your immediate intercession is vital.

For the chain of command to function properly, Soldiers must receive a proper order. One way to determine if your chain of command is functioning properly and emphasize its importance is to locate the Soldier who you consider is least likely to have "gotten the word." Ask him about his specific task, that of his squad, his platoon, and the other platoon. If you discover that he has not received an order or is not knowledgeable, locate the recalcitrant leader and impress upon him his responsibility for ensuring that his subordinates are well-informed.

This technique is also effective in making certain that your Soldiers are informed of administrative and logistical policies and procedures.

The Eighth Army Ranger Company was composed of a disparate group of low-ranking volunteers primarily from service units in Japan. I set the development of a strong, functioning chain of command as a priority task in reaching the training goals that I established for the company. By following the principles enumerated above, our chain of command was strong and effective. At the completion of our training, Colonel John H. McGee, the commander of the Eighth Army Ranger Training Center, wrote G3, Eighth Army, "Unity to include a chain of command and the development of a sense of duty responsibility in the noncommissioned officers has been achieved."[100] Achieving this goal was one of the bases for the company's effectiveness.

CHEMICAL WARFARE IS A THREAT[101]

... the second battle of Ypres developed from their (Germans) efforts to break the Allied cordon. During the next three weeks their gas, artillery and Infantry assaults inflicted 70,000 casualties at a cost of half as many.[102]

—Lynn Montross, author

Protective masks and chemical protective equipment are a burden. They are uncomfortable to wear, and they multiply the difficulty of any task—physical or mental—many times. Train with them anyway!

Every time I have asked the chemical officer of any unit if he thought enough attention was given to preparing for the enemy's use of chemical warfare, (or for our use for that matter) the answer was always an emphatic "No!" That's not surprising. Most special staff, like almost every commander, would probably respond the same if asked a similar question about their special area of interest.

Are we neglecting this important aspect of our preparation for combat because training time is always tight or because the training is very difficult to conduct? Could our Soldiers continue to do their jobs whether it is a combat assault or defense? Or would they react as described by Lynn Montross? "The wretched survivors, gasping and choking, threw away their arms and stumbled to the rear ..."[103]

Montross's comment reminds me of the time I was observing

a night live-fire exercise with the 2-75th Ranger Battalion. During the assault of the objective, a heavy concentration of tear gas was released. My escort, Chaplain Paul Lasley, and I were caught without masks. We ran from the site gasping and choking. We also shed a lot of tears.

Could our headquarters personnel operate while wearing a mask? We need to know. We were concerned about Saddam Hussein's possible use of chemical weapons during Desert Storm and Operation Iraqi Freedom. We must be prepared for the eventuality.

Annual training is the minimum; these skills should be covered during common task training (CTT), and also during expert Infantryman badge (EIB) and expert field medic badge (EFMB) training. We need to focus at least one significant training event on chemical warfare during each training cycle. Our chemical officer must be given an adequate amount of time for preparation of that event. Some troops may never have received adequate training. Perhaps all will need a refresher. Focus on skill level one tasks; proper performance will keep people alive. Refresher training is vital for everyone since this skill is perishable.

It is imperative that the Company Nuclear Biological Chemical (NBC) NCO (noncommissioned officer) is given every opportunity to obtain additional schooling in his specialty. There are several schools such as Technical Support and Patient Decontamination that would be appropriate. At a minimum, he should attend the NBC course that every installation has. When the time comes for the NBC NCO to conduct training, he should be the subject matter expert in his field.

An appropriate training event for a light Infantry unit will require at least eight hours. This time includes the warning, the donning of protective clothing, the continuation of operations for at least four hours, and the decontamination after the "all clear" is sounded. The after-action review requires an hour.

Do not cut short this process. Commanders who give the "all clear" because their forces have ground to a halt in their operation are defeating the purpose of the training. Continuing to function while under chemical attack conditions is when the real money is made in your training. The unit must be able to disengage from the enemy if need be, assemble at a decontamination site either run by a supporting unit or internally, and then complete the all-important reconstitution.

This important facet of your preparation for combat deserves your attention.

DADE'S MONUMENT

*Have your musket clean as a whistle, hatchet scoured,
sixty rounds powder and ball, and be ready to march at
a minute's warning.*[104]

—Robert Rogers

Plebes at West Point, in my day (1945), were required to memorize all sorts of "plebe poop" (the slang used by upperclassmen) or "fourth class knowledge" (the authorized terminology for plebes). These subjects included some useful military items such as the "five paragraph field order" and the "estimate of the situation." Other items were of no direct benefit such as the answer to the question, "How many gallons of water are there in the Lusk Reservoir?" Requirements in the latter category were justified as helping to develop memory. At any moment, an upperclassman could demand that a plebe "spout off" any bit of plebe knowledge. There were still other questions the answer to which did not have to be a direct quote from our *Bugle Notes*, the small book that contained all the plebe knowledge we were required to learn. An example was the response to "What is Dade's monument?"

For some reason I remember so well the day when we were marched by Dade's monument that was then located on The Plain, the large parade ground that is the center of much of the activity at West Point. The upperclassman who was in command stopped and explained what had happened to Dade.

Francis L. Dade was a major during the Seminole War. After chasing some Indians out of the Okefenokee Swamp area in

Georgia, he followed them to Florida. On December 28, 1835, he was marching with his command through a heavily vegetated area when the Seminoles attacked. All men were killed except three who lived to tell what had happened. [105]

Dade's men had been outfitted with new equipment and clothing. Because no enemy contact was expected, the Soldiers were allowed to wear their overcoats as they marched. They put the coats on over their cartridge belts and powder horns to protect them from the wet weather. The Soldiers were authorized to hold their weapons under their "great coats." Since speed was of the essence, Dade posted no flankers. However, Dade, on horseback, could see further than flankers had they been used.[106] Dade and his Soldiers "went administrative," always a mistake.

Dade and his command were not forgotten. Five of the officers killed were West Pointers. In 1845, cadets and graduates collected money to erect a monument in the memory of Dade and his command near Cullum Hall. After WWII, the monument was moved to the cemetery.[107] Incidentally, "among those killed in this massacre was David Moniac, class of 1822, a full-blood Creek, probably the first Indian graduate from the Military Academy."[108]

I remember the story so well. I vowed at the time that I would never repeat such an error. It was engraved indelibly in my memory. My first opportunity to use that bit of knowledge came in Korea. I was a green, second lieutenant, who, because of the Eighth Army's unpreparedness and shortage of personnel, had been selected to form, train, and command the Eighth Army Ranger Company. At the first formation on the first rainy day, my Rangers formed wearing their ponchos over their cartridge belt. As a result, my Rangers, just like Dade's Soldiers, would have had to fumble under their ponchos to access their ammunition, bayonet, canteen, and any other item contained on the belt.

I remembered what had happened to Dade. As we stood in the downpour, I retold the story to my Rangers and directed that they remove their ponchos and web gear. They replaced the poncho with the web gear over it. I do not believe that all of my Rangers agreed at the time with the lesson I was trying to impart. However, as we trained and fought the benefit of not making the same mistake as Dade became apparent.

Unfortunately, this lesson was not learned by many of our Soldiers. The inefficiency—the delay in accessing equipment—could result in death but was not recognized by many of them until it was too late. Their commanders, as always, were responsible.

I remember many years later viewing the Korean War Memorial. It is a beautiful, moving sight. I "recognized" every one of the Soldiers depicted there—my classmate, Barney Cummings; Clanton, the machine gunner; the BAR man, the radioman, everyone there. I was chagrined, however, that those sculptured Soldiers were making the same mistake as Dade and his men. Those statues had their ponchos over their web gear and would have had great difficulty in reacting if they came under fire. It appears that the sculptor has memorialized what is a bad habit.

Leaders ensure by constant training, supervision, and correction that their Soldiers are ready to fight. We must be prepared at all times.

PREPARE FOR A DISASTER

...coolness in disaster is the supreme proof of a commander's courage...[109]

—Field Marshall Earl Wavell, British Army

Prepare yourself and your men mentally, physically, and tactically for a disaster. "Disaster" as used here, does not mean a Hurricane Opal mission. It applies to a catastrophe on the battlefield.

In the past, in most of our training, our unit was always triumphant. Sometimes we went on the defensive; we may even have conducted a retrograde movement, but we never "retreated." We were never defeated. We never trained with a scenario where we were clobbered. Scenarios at the National Training Centers are correcting this shortcoming. However, unit training usually does not give enough attention to this possible outcome in combat.

For many real-life examples of disasters, I recommend *The River and the Gauntlet* by Brigadier General S. L. A. Marshall. He described the debacle after the Chinese intervened in Korea in 1950. In this book, he describes "the defeat of the Eighth Army by the Chinese Communist forces."[110] The book is replete with disasters.

What will you do if your company is cut off and being decimated? Suppose you are isolated and surrounded by an overwhelming force? What will happen when many of your leaders become casualties? Suppose you are one of them? How do you prevent panic? What do you do when it begins? What will the company do? It can happen. That is not defeatism. I'm an optimistic, confident person, but I'm being realistic. It has happened before. It's a tough situation. Be ready.

I was involved in a debacle that did not turn out well. The Eighth Army Ranger Company, which I commanded, commenced our attack on Hill 205, one of the Task Force objectives. It was a cold day, November 25, 1950. When we reached our objective, we had forty-seven Rangers and nine KATUSAs (Korean Augmentation to the U.S. Army). During the night my Rangers repelled five counterattacks by what was later officially estimated to be a force of five hundred Chinese.[111] On each attack, the enemy advanced within hand grenade range. On the sixth, they overran the company. That was a disaster. It can happen to you!

When the Chinese overcame the stubborn resistance and swarmed over the top of Hill 205, individual Rangers "grabbed" their wounded comrades and pulled or dragged them off the hill. The company had never received any specific training in reacting to such a catastrophe. I was remiss in never having scheduled the appropriate "disaster" training. If the Rangers had been trained for this circumstance, our performance would have been better. The morning after the battle, there were one officer and twenty-one Rangers present for duty. Lieutenant Barney Cummings, my 1st Platoon Leader, and I were among the casualties. It was a "disaster" that could have been worse but for the high state of training of the Rangers.

Regardless of how well the unit has been trained or plans have been made, the confusion of intense combat results in fragmented groups fighting in what may be uncoordinated actions. Infantry combat often degenerates into small, isolated groups of men who may not have retained tactical integrity. This situation is particularly likely when the unit has taken heavy casualties. The Normandy invasion was replete with examples of junior noncommissioned and commissioned officers collecting and taking command of nearby Soldiers. Clay Blair's *Ridgway's Paratroopers* describes many such actions. Korean and Vietnam War histories also provide additional examples.

Whether these groups win or lose is dependent, though not entirely, on the courage of the individuals, their training, and the emergence of leadership on the spot. The outcome of the overall battle will be affected by how soon these isolated and uncoordinated actions can be brought to a coherent whole by the (acting) commander. Noncommissioned officers and junior officers need experience in organizing disparate individuals and leading them in a firefight. Therefore, appropriate training will provide opportunities for small, disorganized groups to perform on their own.

When casualties occur, subordinates must take command and be effective. The leader rotations the Eighth Army Ranger Company employed in its training paid dividends later. For the first four weeks, leadership positions were changed weekly. During each week, the emphasis was on developing within leaders the knowledge and skill needed to command effectively. After four weeks, every Ranger had been in a position of leadership at least once, and most had been leaders on two or three occasions. The permanent chain of command was selected based on observed performance. This "fall out one" approach paid off in combat. When casualties occurred, there was always a Ranger with some training and experience ready to fill the vacancy.

The desire to give each leader all the training and experience possible in the training time allotted militates against the "fall out one" approach. If our planning and training focuses only on those who currently occupy our leadership positions, we can expect that the loss of key people will have a decidedly deleterious—even disastrous—effect on our performance. How much of the "never enough" training time to be devoted to subordinates who may be unexpectedly required to take charge in combat is one of those command decisions that has no "approved solution." However, some time must be devoted to this very important training objective.

Train each man in the weapons and tasks of other members of his squad. Each Soldier in a squad needs to be proficient in the use of all the weapons and equipment in his squad. Ammunition bearers and assistant gunners may become gunners. Prepare them for that vital life- and mission-saving eventuality. Twelve members of Merrill's Marauders, that legendary force that operated behind the Chinese Army in Burma, when questioned as to what were the three most important training missions, unanimously included this objective.

Train subordinates in calling for and adjusting fire support. All enlisted men and officers need to be proficient in this task, especially in preparation for a disaster. Include not only Army fire support but support from other services. Sergeant Ernie Savage's actions at Ia Drang were classic. (He was the fourth man to take command of Lieutenant Henry Herrick's 2nd Platoon, the Lost Platoon.[112] (The unit had become separated and surrounded very shortly after it had landed.) The effective resistance provided by a handful of survivors plus the artillery barrages and tactical air support that Sergeant Savage called for and adjusted held off the enemy. What would that platoon have done without him?[113]

When everything goes right, success comes easily. A better test of leadership and the status of training of the individual Soldier, the leader, and the combat readiness of a unit are manifested when things go wrong. When casualties are high, when expected relief, supply, or support does not materialize, training moves to a higher level.

General Matthew B. Ridgway said "The whole training of an officer seeks to accomplish one purpose: to instill in him the ability to take over in battle in a time of crisis."[114] What he said also applies to noncommissioned officers.

FM 22-100 emphasizes the importance of preparing junior leaders to take command when the need arises. "At each level, the leaders must let the subordinate leaders do their jobs. Practicing this kind of decentralized execution based on mission orders in peacetime trains subordinates who will, in battle, exercise disciplined initiative in the absence of orders. They'll continue to fight when the radios are jammed, when the plan falls apart, when the enemy does something unexpected."[115]

Army Leadership continues: "The highest form of discipline is the willing obedience of subordinates who trust their leaders, understand and believe in the mission's purpose, value the team and their place in it, and have the will to see the mission through. This form of discipline produces individuals and teams who—in the really tough moments—come up with solutions themselves."[116]

Can junior leaders move up and get the job done? Incorporating unexpected crises into our training can help achieve that goal. Is unit cohesion such that the unit will not disintegrate under extreme duress? Can leaders adapt? If they cannot, your unit is not combat ready!

EXPECT THE UNEXPECTED

Sixty percent of the art of command is the ability to anticipate; forty percent of the art of command is the ability to improvise.[117]

—Brigadier General S. L. A. Marshall

Much of our training becomes mundane. For example, we attack and seize an objective. Our assault, because of the range fan and other restrictions, may be similar if not identical to what the unit did the last time it went through this exercise. The "enemy" counterattacks. A few casualties may be designated. We may take a few prisoners that we have to process, guard, interrogate, and exfiltrate. After a defense phase, we withdraw. However, there are usually no major surprises that make this iteration different from what we have done previously.

Afterwards, there is a thorough critique in which the subordinate commanders and observer controllers discuss various nuances of the exercise. Usually the unit did well although there always are actions that might be improved just as there are others to be sustained. Because of the lack of real challenge to the commanders, the unit probably does not rise much above the level of training that it had achieved prior to the exercise. To improve, we need to progress to a higher level of training.

The unexpected can force a unit and its leaders to progress to greater competence. When Colonel Stan McChrystal was the commander of the 75th Ranger Regiment, he invariably injected into each tactical exercise some surprise element that taxed the

Rangers both physically and professionally. Few things can cause more significant impact than the loss of leaders. "Fall out one" in training unexpectedly shifts the burden of leadership to subordinates. As they are thrust into a position of responsibility one, two, three levels above what they normally occupy, they are forced to rely upon all that they know and have experienced.

The impact of the loss of key personnel will be increased as the number of casualties climbs. The chain of command must be reestablished. The new leaders reorganize fragmented units, perhaps combine remnants of one or two units to make an effective team, and alter areas of responsibility to fit the new reality of a significantly lessened capability. The pressure of this scenario can be magnified tremendously if the unit is now faced with being overrun. If a reaction force or supporting fires are unavailable, the leader may be faced with an unsolvable dilemma. He cannot leave his wounded and dead. If he remains, his entire command may be destroyed. What does the commander do? Obviously, there is no easy "solution." But the scenario does demand innovative leadership and will provide opportunities for subordinate leaders at all levels to gain experience that may help avoid a disaster in the future.

Errors in execution of a plan are certainly unexpected, but they offer a marvelous opportunity to evaluate a leader and his unit's reactions. Here are a couple of examples of mistakes that produced synergistic benefits. When the 10th Special Forces Group was expanded from one operational company to three, there was a large influx of additional Soldiers. Practically none had special forces (SF) experience. Many were not airborne qualified. I was given the task of developing and conducting training programs in each of the primary special forces skills. Each of these three-weeklong courses was followed by a seven-day tactical exercise that began with a parachute assault onto a drop zone (DZ) somewhere in Bavaria. I remember one occasion in which the "A" Team exited the aircraft at some distance from the proper DZ. This premature jump was not the egregious error that it might appear to be at first glance. Bavaria was heavily populated and covered by numerous small villages and farms that were brightly lit at night.

When my operations sergeant, Master Sergeant "Bud" Malone, saw the Soldiers exiting the aircraft at some distance away, he asked, "Shall I go find them, sir?" I said, "No. Let's see what they do." In about an hour the team appeared at the correct DZ. The team leader was embarrassed by his error and apologized. I said, "No apology needed. You discovered your mistake. You have recovered and can continue on your mission—just as you would do in a real situation. This is good training!" I was highly pleased with my team leader and the synergistic benefit of a mistake.

Another special forces team made a similar mistake when I participated as an official observer of a field training exercise (FTX) many years later. I was in ODSCOPS (Office of the Deputy Chief of Staff for Military Operations), Special Warfare Directorate. The FTX called for an SF team to infiltrate onto a "hostile" shore from a submarine. I accompanied the team as we exited the sub and paddled to the beach. Almost immediately, the team leader came to me and, very apologetically, said "Sir, I made a mistake. We're at the wrong landing site!" I said, "Don't worry about it. Do what you would do in the 'real world.'" He smiled, and after a short reconnaissance, he returned and said that he had located the correct spot. I congratulated him on his performance. Once more, an error had added to the learning value of a training exercise.

Here is a "real world" combat example. On September 1, 1967, the 2-502nd was assigned the mission of attacking and rescuing American POWs in two camps hidden in the jungle. A Vietnamese escapee who would accompany my lead company in the assault had reported the locations. We (the three company commanders, my staff, and I) made detailed plans that were thoroughly coordinated with supporting units. Immediately after Company "A" landed, its commander, Captain Steven L. Arnold (he retired later as a lieutenant general) radioed that the indigenous guide proclaimed that the company was in the wrong place! Steve and I did some quick coordination. As Company "B" was landing at another site, we extracted Company "A" and inserted it at the correct location. The mission continued without further difficulty. Landing initially at the improper location was certainly unexpected. However, Captain Arnold was an exceptionally competent and calm combat leader who could adjust his original plan to fit a changing situation. His subordinates were combat experienced and highly qualified. His detailed planning and coordination with higher headquarters permitted him to respond appropriately to the unexpected.

If the "enemy" uses an unexpected weapon or tactic during an exercise, the training value may be increased. For example, the enemy's use of chemicals may be an unexpected turn of events. Our Soldiers will be forced to don chemical protective gear. Fighting for an extended period of time under protective gear can be extremely difficult. Everything takes longer and requires more physical exertion. All members of the command are taxed to their limit.

Unexpected enemy strength raises the level of training to new heights. A mission that appeared initially to be well within the capability of the unit may now be extremely difficult if not impossible.

A surprising success by the enemy is an excellent way to force leaders to take immediate, unplanned action. Suppose one undetected enemy puts one RPG (rocket-propelled grenade) into the turbine of the last friendly chopper as it leaves the pickup zone with the last of the friendly force. We now have a significant number of casualties on the ground and no forces immediately available (unless the commander planned a reaction force if something went wrong). Regardless of whether planned or not, the training moves to a higher level.

There are some precautions of which commanders need to be aware when they consistently inject the unexpected. As I saw in one highly trained and combat-ready unit, some subordinate commanders begin to "second-guess" their commander. Instead of focusing on the assigned mission, they began to plan for the "unexpected" that the commander might inject into the exercise.

Commanders can assure themselves as far as possible that the "unexpected," while it may tax the ingenuity and skill of the subordinate, does not unnecessarily embarrass that subordinate. Be sure that he has the experience to handle the extra stress. Do not humiliate subordinate leaders and their Soldiers by a challenge that sometimes is overwhelming. A little "humble pie" can be beneficial. Too much can be devastating.

Unexpected events occur in the real world. Preparing for them in training not only increases the interest and value of the training but also improves the leadership and combat effectiveness of the unit for the day when it will face these scenarios on the field of battle.

LEAVE NO MAN BEHIND

When a Soldier was injured and could not get back to safety, his buddy went out to get him, against his officer's orders. He returned mortally wounded and his friend, whom he had carried back, was dead. The officer was angry. "I told you not to go," he said. "Now I've lost both of you. It was not worth it." The dying man replied, "But it was, sir, because when I got to him he said, 'Jim, I knew you'd come.'"[118]

—Leslie D. Weatherhead, Professor

I can speak on this from personal experience. It was early morning, about 0230 hours, on November 26, 1950. I was commanding the Eighth Army Ranger Company. We were part of Task Force Dolvin, the lead element of the 25th Infantry Division. My company consisted of forty-seven Rangers plus nine KATUSAS (Korean Augmentation to the U.S. Army). We had taken our objective, Hill 205, in the late afternoon and dug in our usual 360-degree defense. We were alone with the closest U.S. Army ground unit about a mile away.

By 0230 hours we had withstood five assaults from what was later officially estimated to be a force of five hundred Chinese.[119] I had been wounded by a hand grenade during the first of those attacks. Each attack force had advanced to the perimeter before being repulsed. The sixth attack came like the previous five. We heard the bugles that the Chinese used to control their troops. As in the previous five, a barrage of mortars followed by automatic weapons fire and hand grenades came next. The Chinese swarmed over the top of our defenses; they were everywhere.

When I radioed for the artillery support that had been so helpful during the previous assaults, the artillery liaison officer, Captain Gordon Sumner, told me that the battery was firing another mission; I would have to wait until it finished. I stressed the urgency of our need and was again told that I would have to wait. At that moment, two mortar rounds landed in my foxhole, severely wounding me in both of my feet and in my legs, buttocks, and arm. I hopped from the foxhole, leaving what in retrospect was probably my safest position, and fell to my hands and knees unable to move further. As I lay there, I could see three Chinese about 15 yards away bayoneting some of my wounded Rangers, as they lay unable to protect themselves. One Ranger, Private First Class Bill Judy, ran by where I lay. He asked how I was. I told him I could not move and ordered him to leave me behind. He ran to some other Rangers to get help and told them about me. Two of them, Privates First Class David L. Pollock and Billy G. Walls, charged up the hill and shot the three Chinese who were then only 10 yards away from where I lay.

Walls came over to where I was lying and asked, "Sir, are you hurt?" I thought that was the dumbest question I had ever heard, but I did not say that to Walls. I said, "I'm hurt bad. I can't move. Leave me behind." With that, Walls handed his rifle to Pollock, picked me up in his arms, and began staggering down a steep, rugged mountain face. He went about 40 yards before putting me down, saying, "Sir, you're too heavy! I can't carry you any further!" With that, both Pollock and Walls grabbed one of my arms and began dragging me unceremoniously on my backside down the mountain 200 yards to safety. They lived the Ranger Creed— "I will never leave a fallen comrade to fall into the hands of the enemy"—although it had not yet been written.

I, of course, have always been very appreciative of what they did. I'm thankful for their "insubordination" in refusing to comply with my order to leave me behind. Walls and Pollock were awarded the Silver Star for rescuing me under fire. Needless to say, I have always been sensitive to the issue of "leaving no man behind."

The extraordinary heroism of Master Sergeant Gary Gordon and Sergeant First Class Randy Shughart was recognized by the posthumous award of the Medal of Honor for their attempt to save downed air crewmen and "leave no man behind" in the Mogadishu battle on October 3, 1993. Their unselfish and self-sacrificing actions are an inspiration to all who hear of them.

Lieutenant Colonel Hal Moore, Commander of the 1-7th Cavalry at the Ia Drang Valley battle, went to great efforts to ensure that all casualties were treated with respect and that no man was left behind. After that battle, Moore and his troops swept the battleground several times and made headcounts in the rear to ensure that all had been accounted for.[120]

Developing the "leave no man behind" mentality does not have to be limited to tactical exercises. It can be emphasized even in physical training (PT). Incorporating "buddy runs" where one Soldier picks up and carries a buddy for a significant distance is excellent PT. It also serves as one more way of emphasizing "leave no man behind." Command Sergeant Major Greg Birch, the regimental sergeant major, 75th Ranger Regiment, developed a battle-focused physical training test to be used in addition to the Army's standard test. The sergeant major's test includes one Ranger carrying another Ranger and a team carrying a Ranger on a litter.

How do we instill this "leave no man behind" mind-set into our troops? As always, the answer is "Training." The mind-set is developed during the casualty play in field training exercises (FTXs). That mind-set is nurtured and strengthened by the commander's attention to that vital aspect of his training and his personal example. Give it the attention it deserves. The payback will come in combat.

LONG RANGE SURVEILLANCE UNITS

The U.S. Army combat reconnaissance and ranger campaign of the Vietnam War represented an important military adjunct to regular operations throughout the prolonged conflict. Patrol units were formed as field expedient organizations out of battlefield necessity, and their employment varied according to higher command objectives and terrain dictates.[121]

—Shelby L. Stanton, Author

Long Range Reconnaissance Patrols (LRRPs) were a special breed of men. I admired their courage and their professionalism. (The LRRP designation has been changed several times since the Vietnam War. However, for consistency I will use LRRP.)

Lieutenant General John Hay wrote that the LRRPs in Vietnam were one of the most successful—one of the most efficient—efforts in the war. The information that they gathered led to many major battles. LRRPs were "one of the most significant innovations in the war."[122] Major General William Peers, who commanded the 4th Infantry Division, said that in 1967 before he had the "people sniffer" (an aircraft that could sense significant levels of urine from the air indicating a possible location of enemy) and the air cavalry scout unit, every major battle in the 4th Division was initiated by action of a LRRP. That included the battle of Dak To, one of biggest battles of the war.[123]

Although usually assigned a reconnaissance mission, LRRPs often engaged in close combat. The effectiveness with which the teams accomplished recon missions coupled with their combat operations resulted in incredible body counts and the capture of many weapons and supplies. The LRRPs were one of the most effective uses of manpower during the Vietnam War.

LRRPs were very proficient in operating quietly and unseen. They were utterly fantastic in their ability to out-guerrilla the guerrillas. The enemy held them in high regard. Some enemy units established bounties on LRRP members as high as $1,000. They set the same amount for a colonel.[124] I'm flattered that they thought that I might have been as important as a LRRP!

Our Army recognized the contribution of the Long Range Reconnaissance Patrols. In 1986, the Infantry School, while working on LRRP doctrine said that no other project could make such a giant step in combat effectiveness.[125]

The battlefield commander relies heavily on accurate, timely intelligence to give him the time needed to plan and prepare. The better the intelligence, the better his chance of being successful. He expects the best from the LRRP. He is depending on it. LRRPs are duty-bound to get the job done once assigned a mission.

The Long Range Reconnaissance Patrol leader is sometimes required to make decisions usually reserved for more senior non-commissioned and commissioned officers. He will have to decide because there is no time to ask higher headquarters. Although we have sophisticated communications, LRRPs may be forced to operate without it because it may not be working when they need it most.

A LRRP is a very small, very vulnerable team. It will be alone and far away from any expected resupply, relief, or reinforcement. This isolation can have an adverse psychological impact on the team members. To overcome this feeling of isolation, teams require a strong bond; each member must completely trust every other member; each must believe in every other member. Discipline must be 100 percent.

Each member must be highly trained and totally reliable if the team is going to succeed. He must be physically, mentally, and emotionally tough. He must have achieved an extraordinarily high level of proficiency in individual skills. Similarly, the team must have mastered all its small unit tactics and techniques if it expects to succeed and survive on the battlefield. Weakness in any of these can and probably will lead to failure. All members of the team must be aware of this reality and have accepted it without reservation. Success or failure—life or death—will depend on how well each member and the team performs.

A LRRP Soldier can be as great as he wants to be. The Long Range Reconnaissance Unit is an elite team trained to do a special, tough job. As an elite unit, it is "different;" it is "separate;" it is "unique." Because it is all of these, LRRPs and everything they do will be under constant scrutiny. People will look for something they can criticize.

A LRRP patroller is a "quiet professional." There is no place for the route step, slovenly, big mouth boasting of his prowess. He demonstrates how good he is by performance; a solid performance speaks louder, more convincingly than bragging. He shows that he is the best by his discipline, neatness of dress, and courtesy to superior officers and sets the standard for others to meet.

Because of this professionalism, commanders permit more freedom for the team to do special training. LRRPS, by their professional performance, earn this confidence. As a result, their Army experience will be more exciting and rewarding!

Good Marksmanship and Fire Superiority

Men, you are all marksmen—don't one of you fire un-til you see the whites of their eyes.[126]

—Israel Putnam, Battle of Bunker Hill, June 17, 1775

At Throg's Neck thirty riflemen stopped the British Army in their tracks, then held them while another 1,500 American Infantry hurried to their support. The British Army was stymied.[127]

—David Hackett Fischer, Author

Good marksmanship can make the difference between success and failure. Some Soldiers, particularly those who are inexperienced or frightened, often equate a high volume of fire with effective fire. This mistaken judgment is supported and enhanced by much of our training in which leaders and observer controllers comment favorably on gunners who fired almost continuously on the same target throughout a training exercise although the first burst would have "killed" the enemy. I have often seen this faulty performance on live-fire exercises. By the time the objective has been taken and the supporting weapons moved to a defensive position, these weapons are almost if not completely out of ammunition.

Putting an automatic rifle into the hands of every rifleman contributes to confusing high volume with effectiveness. In Vietnam, Soldiers sometimes held the rifle over their heads and fired a full magazine without ever having seen a target or without having much of an idea where the enemy was located. While in the initial moments of contact in an ambush or similar situation a high volume of fire in the general direction from which the enemy's fire is coming may be appropriate, continuing to fire indiscriminately is a waste of ammunition and will soon leave the unit helpless. On one occasion in Vietnam, one of my rifle companies was out of ammunition within twenty minutes of making contact. For that situation to arise, the Soldiers were probably firing "full automatic" from the beginning.

A couple of combat examples emphasize the importance of good marksmanship.

An example from Vietnam demonstrates how effective a lone rifleman can be. One of my rifle companies was withdrawing from an objective after finding and destroying a rice storage site. We were leaving one platoon as a "stay behind," something we had done successfully before. A lone Vietcong, as he returned to the area thinking that the entire company had departed, saw the platoon leader sitting on the side of his foxhole talking to his Soldiers, a direct contravention of specific instructions I had given during my briefing of the lieutenant. The VC took the platoon under fire, killing several and wounding others before he left the area. His effective rifle fire had pinned down and inflicted numerous casualties on an American Army rifle platoon with all its firepower!

The next example is from Korea. On November 25, 1950, I commanded the Eighth Army Ranger Company as it assaulted across 800 yards of open, frozen, rice paddy to seize the company objective, Hill 205. As we scurried across that open space we received small arms fire—rifle and automatic weapons—and mortar fire.

We were unable to pinpoint the location of the enemy machine gun that kept firing at us. I ran back and forth across an open area drawing fire so my men could locate the enemy machine gun. On the third trip, my BAR (Browning automatic rifle) man, Corporal Barney Cronin, saw a puff of smoke, took the enemy under fire, and put the enemy machine gun out of commission. My Ranger's accurate fire had accomplished what the enemy's poor marksmanship had been unable to do for him.

The enemy, if it had had good marksmen, could have devastated my company as we ran across the open rice paddies. We lost four Rangers from mortar fire in those 800 yards; we lost none from small arms fire although it took us an hour to cover that distance.

A similar situation occurred during the defense of the objective after we had captured and secured it. My Rangers sustained and repelled five counterattacks. Between assaults, the Chinese crept within 20 yards of our perimeter. If we had "owned the night" as our present Rangers do, we would have been able to spot the enemy and kill him. Unfortunately we were as blind as they were.

On one of my rounds of my perimeter, I was at Ranger Bill Judy's foxhole. He pointed to a tree about 20 yards in front of him stating that an enemy was hiding behind it. Intermittently, the enemy would stick his head around the tree and fire a shot. Fortunately, he was a poor marksman. Bill had been unable to catch him in the act. Remembering the success I had had that afternoon, I decided to give it a try. On my third dash across an open area, Bill caught the Chinese Soldier and killed him with one shot. Again, the enemy's poor marksmanship had proved inadequate, while Judy's good marksmanship had succeeded.

One of the most memorable scenes in the old movie *Sergeant York* starring Gary Cooper was the action in which Sergeant Alvin York earned the Medal of Honor. His superior marksmanship was instrumental in his victory over the Germans. Nothing could bring home the value of good marksmanship better than Sergeant York's superb performance.

There is no question that we want to gain fire superiority over our enemy. We want our fire to be so devastatingly effective that our adversaries are unable to return fire. Effective fire control is vital, particularly with crew served weapons in a support by fire role. The best performance I ever observed was on a live-fire exercise by the 2-75th Rangers. First Lieutenant Taylor, who commanded the weapons platoon, "played" his weapons like a concert orchestra director! Constantly moving about his fire support position, he controlled the rate of fire and shifted it from one threat to another, a task that also requires skill and experience on the part of the gunner. Competence in this activity as in every other comes through good training.

As I have watched so many live-fire exercises, I wondered just how effective the fire was. Is it on target? Are team leaders making corrections when bullets are going astray? Are they shifting to new targets when they appear? Would they have killed the enemy if the situation were real? Are they wasting ammo that may be needed for another target of opportunity in the attack or later in the defense of the captured objective?

Emphasize marksmanship in your training. Well-aimed shots are much more effective than many rounds that miss the target. Assess accuracy of first-round shots. You may cause an enemy to duck behind cover, but you won't kill him or root him out unless your firepower is on target. While we can't expect every rifleman to match the "one shot, one kill" of the sniper, we can do better than we do. Night firing can always be improved. Today, our Night Observation Devices (NOD) give us a marked advantage over our enemies. We may not always have that benefit. Good leaders exercise good fire control. After each live-fire exercise, count your hits; how effective was your fire? In training, if under stress, fire from all positions. Practice rapid magazine change under stress. Train while wearing body armor; it affects the way you hold your weapon. As Colonel Martin Stanton expressed so aptly and succinctly, "Troops must be trained to shoot while wearing a flak vest and helmet. Train your Soldiers to run a hundred-yard dash in full LBE (load-bearing equipment), helmet, and flak jacket, then stop, aim, and hit a target in three seconds. This is normally all the time they will have."[128]

Lieutenant Colonel Don Bowman, U.S. Army Retired described how he trained his Soldiers in maintaining fire superiority during magazine and belt changes. While lying on blankets in the squad bay, he had each rifleman say "bang" each time he pulled the trigger. When he called "reload," his buddy increased his rate of fire to cover the reload. Automatic riflemen did the same, except they called "magazine." His assistant gunner picked up his rate of fire as did the leader for the other automatic rifle thereby maintaining fire superiority. Over time they learned to work as a team, maintaining an appropriate volume of accurate fire even with all the noise and distraction of live fire. Later, he assessed casualties to teach succession to both the leader and gunner positions. He required riflemen in both the assault and final protective fires to fire one aimed shot every four to five seconds counting aloud to emphasize discipline. Bowman said that, with practice, they heard the changes in rates of fire and instinctively covered magazine and belt changes when called.[129]

Good marksmanship will help destroy your enemy and keep your Soldiers alive.

MASTER THE FUNDAMENTALS AND WIN

Fundamentals win it. Football is two things: it's block-
ing and tackling. I don't care anything about forma-
tions or new offenses or tricks on defense. If you block
and tackle better than the team you're playing, you'll
win.[130]

—Vince Lombardi, Green Bay Packers' coach

Accomplish the fundamentals better than the enemy you are fighting, and you will win. Win and you enhance the probability of your unit's survival.

Fundamentals are individual and small unit tasks that include fire and maneuver, patrolling, first aid, map reading, use of supporting fires, marksmanship, and many others.

Few things can produce more dramatic results than improving the performance of these crucial tasks. Until they are mastered, the unit will experience unnecessary casualties and may fail to accomplish assigned missions. Unfortunately, a high level of competence is often achieved only after the unit has experienced these casualties. Training is the place to develop the required competence. Lessons learned in training are cheap. Lessons learned in combat are expensive.

As a combat commander, I saw that units that were well grounded in fundamentals did well. Poor performance or violations of basic skills generally resulted in unnecessary casualties. In training and, later, as the Honorary Colonel of the 75th Ranger Regiment, I focused on these essential individual and small unit tasks knowing that they would be the skills most often improperly performed and where most emphasis would be needed. In almost every training exercise, I saw some of the same shortcomings. These included failure to use available cover and concealment, failure to support the movement of team members or another element by fire or from an over-watch position, or failure to remain dispersed (bunching up). I am convinced that if commanders concentrate on fundamentals their Soldiers will be much more effective in combat and suffer fewer casualties.

Violations persist not because the Soldiers are not trying. They persist because proper performance has not become habitual. It is not part of the discipline of the individual Soldier. The violators, for the most part, are our most junior and inexperienced Soldiers. They err because they have not been properly trained. Proper execution of what is sometimes erroneously referred to as "the little things" has not become ingrained in the Soldier.

What to do? Correct every violation every time it occurs. By so doing proper performance becomes a habit—something executed without conscious thought. Like a well-trained football team, the fire team, squad—what have you—practices the drills until proper performance becomes habitual. Repeat the action even though you reach the standard. Repetition develops the discipline to do it correctly without having to think about it. June Jones, the former Atlanta Falcons coach, stressed this principle saying:

> Champions execute the fundamentals with unconscious competence. That means they've practiced the moves so many times in the past that they can do them almost perfectly without thinking about it. When you can perform brilliantly without thinking, you can perform at a very high level.[131]

This level of performance is the result of repetitious training under the watchful eyes of the junior leaders. They must make constant corrections; they cannot let any error go uncorrected. Repetition develops "muscle memory."

Most people never got very good at hitting a baseball. But even the most limited competence at the task required repeated trials, efforts in which the most recent attempt was compared to its predecessor. This was what physical learning was all about—the refinement of technique by feedback. And what made it possible was the fact that each attempt to hit the ball *changed* the neurological framework of the memory itself. When the novice finally made contact, the relevant neurons encoded the information as a successful attempt. Whereupon, the encrypted data became a kind of template for all future at-bats.[132]

Mastering the fundamentals pays great dividends. It brings success on the battlefield and saves lives! Accomplish the fundamentals better than the enemy you're fighting and you will win.

TOUGH TRAINING SAVES LIVES

We must remember that one man is much the same as another, and he is best who is trained in the severest school.[133]

—Thucydides Athenian Admiral and Historian

The man who spends more sleepless nights with his Army and who works harder in drilling his troops runs the fewest risks in fighting the foe.[134]

—The Emperor Maurice, East Roman Emperor and General

The first day in camp I was afraid I was going to die. The next two weeks my sole fear was that I wasn't going to die. And after that I knew I'd never die because I had become so hard nothing could kill me.[135]

—Anonymous American Soldier

America's Army was not ready when it went to war in Korea. Lieutenant General Bernard E. Trainor, USMC, Retired, characterized that Army as "a sorry, under-strength, under-trained, under-equipped, and poorly led ghost of the Army that had brought victory against Germany and Japan in 1945.... It was basically a teenage occupation Army that had gone to rot."[136] Army Colonel John Michaelis, (later general) one of the most successful commanders in Korea, described the performance of the U.S. Army in

Korea as "lousy."[137] However, that lousy Army became tough and battle-hardened.

I was extremely fortunate in my Korean War duty. Although a new second lieutenant recently graduated from the Infantry Officer Basic Course (IOBC) and Jump School, I was selected to form, train, and command the Eighth Army Ranger Company, the first Ranger unit established after WWII. The majority of the volunteers were service troops on occupation duty in Japan. They needed to master the basic skills required of any combat Infantryman and to be physically and emotionally tough. The training regimen was hard on all of us, but it paid off in combat. Some of my Rangers have said, "Ralph, I thought you were going to kill us with that tough training, but it saved our lives in combat!" We're disregarding that most valuable insight today.

For the last seven years (1999 to 2007), I have been involved in "Operation Appreciation," a program in which St. Luke United Methodist Church, Columbus, Georgia, hosts monthly approximately 80–200 Soldiers from the Basic Combat and the Infantry Training Brigades at Fort Benning, Georgia. I estimate that I have asked the question, "Is basic tough enough?" at least 30 times. In every instance, every Soldier except two has answered in the negative! Basic training should be tough and battle-focused—the most difficult thing the trainee has experienced.

There is some truth in T. R. Fehrenbach's statement that any officer who trains his Soldiers as hard as a football coach trains his team will be called on the carpet.[138] In 1954 when I was assigned to the 65th Regimental Combat Team (RCT) in Puerto Rico I was directed to establish and conduct the 65th RCT Orientation School and the 65th RCT Noncommissioned Officer Academy. The former training program was for all privates and privates first class who were filling the RCT as the Puerto Rican Soldiers who composed almost the entire regiment were being transferred. The Orientation School training goal was to teach the basic skills that our incoming Soldiers had not learned and to toughen them physically.

Although the term "politically correct" was not in use at the time, politicians had much to say about what the Army did. It was not unusual for some company commander to have to respond to a "Congressional," as we called a letter of inquiry. The subject was usually some alleged mistreatment that some Soldier had received. As the Commander of the Orientation School I received my share.

On one occasion, I reported to the regimental commander who handed me a Congressman's letter describing alleged inappropriate treatment in the form of severe physical exercise to which one of his constituents had been subjected. I explained to the regimental commander that the training was in accordance with the field manuals and was on the training schedule that I had submitted to his S3. I concluded by saying that I led the PT and did all the exercises and runs with the trainees. My regimental commander was not mollified and warned me that I must be careful. He concluded by saying, "If you get into trouble I won't try to protect you." (My commander was not always this timid. He had previously demonstrated great moral courage in defending a battalion commander whose tactical deployment of his battalion on an FTX was being severely criticized by the division commander.)

"Tough training saves lives," and "more sweat less blood" are true aphorisms. Soldiers will grumble. Some parents may write their elected officials in Washington complaining about the "inappropriate" physical demands placed on their child. Most Soldiers—unless they are hardened combat veterans—and their parents have no comprehension of the great, almost unceasing physical demands placed on the Infantryman in particular. Commanders who, because of these pressures or because they want to be "liked" by their Soldiers, do not train as realistically and as "hard" are doing their troops a disservice. In fact, these commanders are guilty of dereliction of duty. This negligence on some future battleground will result in unnecessary casualties.

President Clinton's desire to have a military that looks like America, Secretary of Defense Cohen's placing the goal of having a defense establishment in which anyone who wants to serve can serve *ahead* of the goal of having a military force capable of defending this nation, and DACOWITS' (Defense Advisory Committee on Women in the Services) trying to eliminate all vestiges of *machismo* in the services hurt the military. Political correctness reigned; social engineering was the goal. The result could be the same as from negligence in training—unnecessary casualties.

Army Leadership states: "Organizational leaders are personally dedicated to providing tough, battle-focused training so that the scrimmage is always harder than the game. They must ensure that in training, to the extent that resources and risks allow, nothing is simulated. Constant assessments refine training challenges, forge confidence, and foster the quiet, calculating and deadly warrior ethos that wins battles and campaigns."[139]

As commanders, we have the responsibility to prepare our Soldiers for combat. The program we implement must stress the mastering of fundamentals in a realistic, progressive, physically and emotionally demanding, battle-focused regimen. This "tough love" can prepare our Soldiers for combat. To do anything less is a serious dereliction of our duty and our responsibility to the Soldiers, whose lives are ultimately in our hands.

Veterans Can Be Great Trainers

It takes very little yeast to leaven a lump of dough.... It takes a very few Veterans to leaven a division of dough-boys.[140]

—General George S. Patton, Jr.

Veterans can be both an inspirational and instructional resource for training. As they recount their "war stories," their practical experiences can inspire both commissioned and enlisted Soldiers to greater effort to "be like them." This desire to emulate the veterans can be a prime motivation in encouraging trainees to greater effort to master the fundamentals and meet training standards.

Likewise, as veterans recount "the way we did it," they pass on to those with little or no experience the so-called "tricks of the trade" that are true combat multipliers that contribute to success in battle.

Lieutenant Colonel Keith Antonia, while commanding the 5th Ranger Training Battalion, Camp Frank D. Merrill (the Ranger Mountain Camp), formalized his use of veterans as a training resource. Antonia said that he used the veterans similar to the way the 75th Ranger Regiment Commander used the Honorary Colonel. They participated in, observed, and commented on what they had seen. Some veterans accompanied Ranger student patrols and joined in the critiques. Many offered suggestions on improving the training program.

Working directly with individual veterans and also through

the Mountain Ranger Association, Antonia encouraged participation by Vietnam veterans who were also former Mountain Ranger Instructors. He wrote:

> Since the United States has not been in a war where Ranger-type patrolling techniques were used for twenty-five years, I wanted to validate the TTPs (tactics, techniques, and procedures), relearn forgotten TTPs, get a combat vet's perspective on how we were training, and provide mentors for our Ranger instructors. I wanted the vets to pass their war stories on to instructors as well as students. I felt that a student would remember a technique much more vividly if it were related in a real-world story. You can tell a Ranger student all day that it's important to stay awake. But when a war vet describes a situation where some of his comrades were killed because of lax security, it makes a Ranger pay attention …
>
> Another example is how to use artillery and mortars in the mountains. We were always wrestling over this, but when we had a Vietnam vet platoon leader from the 173rd explain to us how he employed it in Vietnam, the problem was virtually solved for us. Essentially, how close you bring the indirect in is based on the commander's analysis of risk. Army doctrine with regard to min safe distances does not work in the mountains."[141]

When describing his use of the veterans, Lieutenant Colonel Antonia spoke highly of their contributions. He added an appropriate caveat: "We listened to and considered all that our veterans offered. We accepted and implemented what we deemed appropriate."

Lieutenant Colonel Antonia knew that some "lessons learned" were not always something that should be taught to trainees. He knew that because some technique worked on some occasion it might not be a fundamental that is generally applicable. There might be better ways to accomplish tasks than how the veterans suggested.

Veterans can be a valuable, inspirational teaching resource. Liberal use of them while remembering Antonia's caveat can enhance training.

Section VI

TAKING CARE OF SOLDIERS

HURRY UP AND WAIT

One thing you can't recycle is wasted time.[1]
—Anonymous

Time is the most valuable thing a man can spend.[2]
—Theophrastus, Philosopher

Anyone who has been in the Army for any length of time has heard the complaint characterized by the phrase, "Hurry up and wait." Individually or as a group, we have hurried to meet an appointed time and then had to wait what sometimes seemed an interminable length of time for the person in charge to arrive or for all elements of an activity to be readied. Often it seemed that the people responsible had no concern for or interest in the individuals whose time was being wasted. Perhaps the most prevalent example of "Hurry up and wait" occurs at a formation or ceremony.

The troops are assembled, inspected, and readied for the activity with time to spare, the reason being that it is much better to be early than late. The padding of time at each echelon increases the total amount of time wasted until it sometimes reaches an almost unbelievable total.

When I was a company commander in the 65th Regimental Combat Team (RCT) in Puerto Rico, we had a regimental parade once each month. A detailed letter of instructions had been issued to each unit defining the uniform and equipment to be worn and the schedule of the events to include assembly in the company area. I remember my first one of these ceremonies.

We formed at the appointed time, inspected the troops, and sized them—put the tallest in the right front and tapered the remainder to the shortest in the left rear. This arrangement helped insure that each Soldier would be better able to guide to the right front (align himself with the remainder of the company properly.) After we had completed these activities, we stood at "rest" for more than ten minutes, waiting for the bugle to sound the next movement. As I waited in the heat, I thought to myself, "I have about 150 Soldiers wasting ten minutes each in the hot sun. That's twenty-five man-hours! I'm going to change that."

At the next parade, I decided to assemble my company ten minutes after the appointed time. We would be in the company area out of sight of anyone on the parade ground. I was a little nervous about what I was doing and wanted to ensure that nothing went awry. Consequently, I was in the area well before the time for the ceremony. Surprisingly, my battalion commander came walking through the area! I reported as smartly as I could.

He asked, "Where are your Soldiers?"

I replied, "They're in the barracks, sir."

He asked, "Aren't you going to the parade?"

I responded, "Yes, sir! We will be forming in a few minutes and will have time to accomplish the inspection and sizing."

I then explained to him why I had chosen to do as I had done. I don't think he was satisfied, but he said nothing more as he walked away. My Soldiers formed, and we completed our duties in sufficient time to meet the schedule.

Padding a schedule with time to spare is common with many commanders and staff. The reason is understandable. Being on time is not just a virtue in the military; sometimes it is a life and death matter. However, we should be aware of what we are doing when we insert that padding. It behooves us to limit it to the safe minimum. The troops—and you—will reap the benefits when you do.

Lightening a Soldier's Load Is a High and Continuing Priority

---

Fatigue makes cowards of us all.
— Lieutenant General George S. Patton, Jr.[3]

Our combat Soldiers are overloaded. This weight produces great fatigue, lessens mobility, and results in unnecessary casualties.

Every officer should read Brigadier General S. L. A. Marshall's *A Soldier's Load and the Mobility of a Nation*. It is a classic and should be in the professional library of every officer.

According to the Infantry School at Fort Benning, Georgia, "The average Infantryman carries eighty-five pounds of gear into battle.... This includes weapons, ammunition, water, protective gear, and so on." The recent additions of enhanced plates, side-panel plates, and shoulder and side protection to body armor add eleven pounds, increasing the total to 96 pounds.[4] Studies conducted in the past indicate that about 40 pounds is the optimum weight for a combat load.[5]

Some Soldiers pride themselves on the heavy rucksack they carry. No matter how much of a stud he may be, that load will affect him negatively. Because he tires more quickly, his mental capacities will decline, his courage will sag, and he will be more prone to injury. These degradations of performance will impact negatively on the combat effectiveness of the unit.

Scrutinize that mission essential equipment list. Is all of it really essential? Nobody wants to be caught short. However, do we really need all those items? How well does resupply work? Some of the blame for carrying too much gear results from the Soldier's fear of being caught short. "No logistical system is sound unless its first principle is enlightened conservation of the power of the individual Soldier."[6] Despite the fact that technology has improved tremendously "... *it is conspicuous that what the machine has failed to do right up to the present moment is decrease by a single pound the weight the individual has to carry in war* (emphasis in the original). He is still as heavily burdened as the Soldier of 1000 years BC."[7]

Carrying what may be an excessive amount of ammo "just in case" is a continuing problem. Do we really need all of it? Better fire discipline permits us to lighten our loads significantly. In Vietnam, many Soldiers fired blindly "full automatic" without having any idea from where the enemy fire might be coming.

While the noise of that heavy volume of fire may have been soothing to the Soldier, his ineffective fire often had little impact on the enemy.

We haven't made much progress; the Soldier is still overloaded. Much of that is the commander's fault. Lightening a Soldier's load should be a continuing priority. Reviewing our SOP equipment lists should be accomplished periodically. Lists prescribing what each Soldier will carry are of no benefit if not enforced. Almost everyone agrees that the load must be lightened but determining what will be left behind is difficult. As always, the noncommissioned officers can shed valuable insight concerning changes being considered. Take care that the "We've always done it that way" syndrome does not taint the review.

Lightening a Soldier's load is a high payoff goal resulting in increased combat effectiveness.

REALLY LISTEN TO YOUR SOLDIERS

There is among the mass of individuals who carry rifles in war a great amount of ingenuity and efficiency. If men can talk naturally to their officers, the product of their resourcefulness becomes available to all.[8]

—General Dwight D. Eisenhower

Make listening one of your highest management priorities. [Emphasis in the original.] Speak less and say more. You don't learn anything new when you are the one doing the talking. Listen carefully so you can be open to unencumbered awareness. Part of this awareness is listening to circumstance; becoming cognizant of what is really going on; hearing the nuances, the subtleties of experience. Winston Churchill captured it when he observed: "Men stumble over the truth from time to time, but most pick themselves up and hurry off as if nothing happened." Unvarnished listening is perhaps the single best empowerment tool available to leaders today.[9]

—Bil Holton, PhD

Commanders use various structured means to communicate with the troops. They most often rely on the chain of command to move information up and down within the unit. They may conduct formal briefings after which they encourage questions and comments from their Soldiers. Some commanders find helpful unstructured "bull sessions" during which Soldiers are urged to say what is on their minds—to ask questions about matters that concern them. All of these have their place and can be of benefit. However, the commander who really listens to his troops will have the best feel for what they are thinking.

Command Sergeant Major David E. Wright offered this advice: "You must talk to your Soldiers.... I don't just mean in formation or in groups, but one-on-one. Take time (at least fifteen to thirty minutes a day) to really talk to a Soldier, one Soldier a day."[10]

Some commanders have an "open door" policy in which all in the command are told, "You can come see me any time." While many commanders establish this policy, benefits vary from none to few. It also can lead to contravention of the chain of command. Talking to Soldiers one-on-one and in small, informal groups as you move about your command is more beneficial. When Soldiers see that their commander "really listens" and is interested in what they have to say, they begin to open up and provide insights that may not be available otherwise.

A concern no matter what you do to stay informed is that you do not undercut your noncommissioned officers.

Whenever you learn about something that needs action, take that action, and inform the Soldier who brought the matter to your attention. If his suggestion made a significant improvement in the unit, give him credit publicly. By so doing, you will be repaid a hundredfold.[11]

One of my earliest experiences of talking informally to small groups occurred when I was the Headquarters Company commander in the formative days of the Ranger Department. At first, I could see that the cadre were hesitant to make comments and suggestions. When I asked them why, one Ranger commented frankly, "It won't do any good!" I challenged him, "Try me and see!" With that, there were several suggestions to improve the mess hall. One example: "Why can't we have pitchers of coffee for each table so that we won't have to return to the line for a refill?" Satisfying this request was easy. I secured small pitchers for each of the tables thereby instituting what I thought was a feasible and beneficial suggestion. It was only one of several and served notice that I "really listened" and would consider all that my Soldiers suggested. I tried to be this accessible during the rest of my career. Being so always paid dividends in opening up the communication between my Soldiers and me.

As Bil Holton wrote, the commander needs to "speak less." He needs to listen more. He has to be cognizant of "the nuances." He has to learn how to "read between the lines." What the Soldier is saying may not be what he is thinking. Developing the talent— the ability—to have your Soldiers relax enough to say what they really mean is very difficult. Unless it comes naturally, developing that skill can prove to be one of the most difficult tasks that you ever confront. You have to "really listen." When you can do that, your Soldiers will know that you are truly interested in what they have to say.

When your Soldiers will talk to you freely, you will have tapped a resource that can prove to be most beneficial. In particular, many of your noncommissioned officers have an uncanny ability to feel the pulse of your command. They are able to advise you on problems. They can help you avert difficulty by alerting you to potential problems. This valuable resource is available to officers who "really listen" to their Soldiers.

MAKE CARE OF THE
FEET HIGH PRIORITY

Our feet were our most precious assets because they were our transportation, so without healthy feet we could not continue in the course.[12]

—Brace E. Barber, Author

Keep your mouth wet, feet dry.[13]

—Benjamin Franklin

An Infantryman whose feet are not toughened to long distance marching while bearing a heavy load is not physically fit for combat. Whenever I talk to Soldiers who will soon be going to Ranger School, I discuss with them this vital aspect of preparation for the training. If they have to worry about their feet, they will have difficulty meeting both physical and leadership standards required to complete the program of instruction successfully.

I have never felt that this vital objective—care of the feet—received the emphasis in training and in combat operations that it deserved. There were thousands of casualties in Korea resulting from frozen or frostbitten feet. Foot problems were widespread in Vietnam. Many of these may have been prevented by proper attention from leaders.

I have often recommended that part of a Ranger trainee's leadership evaluation include this important responsibility of command. While medics on the Ranger Training Brigade staff check the students' feet daily, I believe that this responsibility should be borne by the student leader with the medic in an "overwatch" role, ensuring that the task is performed properly. There is probably no better way to convince the budding leader that foot care is his responsibility than to make it part of his evaluation. When it affects his "go, no go" grade, he will recognize the importance of this often overlooked task.

Just as we see to the care and cleaning of our Soldiers' weapons, so must we also ensure proper care of the feet. A daily check is not too often. If it goes unperformed, Soldiers may let foot care ride. They may be too tired to take the time for proper foot maintenance. When that happens, be assured that you will soon have Soldiers who are incapable of performing their duty because foot problems have incapacitated them.

Accomplishing this vital task is a requirement of competent command.

MENTORING

Leadership is a quality that one nurtures with experience and the proper guidance. Senior officers must act as mentors to their youthful counterparts, trusting them with real responsibilities, and allowing them to make their own decisions.[14]

—David M. Abshire, Educator and Presidential Advisor

According to FM 22-100, "Mentoring (in the Army) is the proactive development of each subordinate through observing, assessing, coaching, teaching, developmental counseling, and evaluating that results in people being treated with fairness and equal opportunity. Mentoring is an inclusive process (not an exclusive one) for everyone under a leader's charge."[15]

Mentoring can help set up your subordinates for success. That result is not a completely altruistic goal. When they look good you look good.

We hear that word, mentoring, a lot today. I never heard it when I was coming along. Although some of my commanders mentored me, it had not attained the importance we place on it today.

How did that word originate? When Odysseus was departing for Troy, he entrusted his household and the education of his son, Telemachus, to a friend. That friend's name was Mentor. Hence, a mentor is a trusted friend or counselor.[16] Your subordinates need a trusted friend and counselor to talk to them, to advise them, to listen to them in a nonthreatening environment.

As a commander (my focus is company and battalion commanders, although these comments apply generally at any level), you can help ensure mission accomplishment by establishing a supportive environment in which your subordinates operate. They need to know that they can focus on their mission of preparing for and leading their troops in whatever task is assigned. Whether in combat or garrison, they need to be confident that you will be there to see that they can do their job without having to worry about support—combat power, administrative, or logistical.

Mentoring can help develop this supportive relationship. The Army definition implies a structured approach—and it is. Nothing as important as mentoring should be left to chance. However, it is more than that. It includes everything you do and say. You may be mentoring without knowing it.

Your mentoring may occur extemporaneously and occupy only a brief moment. At the end of the climactic battle in *Saving Private Ryan*, Captain Miller, played by Tom Hanks, says, almost inaudibly, to Private Ryan, "Earn this! Earn this!" The captain was enjoining Ryan to live his life so that he would deserve the sacrifice that had been made directly and indirectly for him. In one of the final scenes, the aged Ryan returns to the Normandy American Cemetery at Omaha Beach and, while kneeling at the gravesite of Captain Miller, asks his wife, "Have I lived a good life? Tell me I am a good man." Captain Miller's command had had a deep and everlasting effect on Ryan.

FM 22-100 tells us that how you, the commander, live the Army values determines whether the mentoring is positive or negative.[17] Everything you do consciously and unconsciously affects the leadership environment that you develop. It affects the way your subordinates feel about you—whether they are comfortable in your presence or whether they believe that they must always be "on guard' to avoid a slip of the tongue or inadvertent action that will affect your appraisal of them in a negative way. They want mentoring—a personal relationship with their seniors—and not a strictly hierarchical one.

While a "warm and fuzzy" feeling may not be your goal, your

subordinates need to be able to relax and be themselves. Ultimately you would like them to feel free to come to you to discuss anything that affects them. Your most junior officers will probably see you as someone who has "been there, done that" and consequently have "the answer" or, at least, a helpful suggestion for whatever they face. Mentoring is a way we can share the knowledge gained over time. We influence not only our immediate subordinates but also the people with whom they come in contact. Great leaders are characterized by having a beneficial effect to the second, third, or more generations as compared to immediate impact. That is their legacy.

How do you establish this supportive environment? You establish it by being supportive rather than critical, by listening more and talking less, by suggesting more and directing less. You create this environment by doing what you can to set your subordinates up for success. When you help them succeed, you will be helping yourself succeed. Establishing that relationship takes effort, but the improved performance of your junior leaders will more than repay you.

How do you judge your progress? There are obvious signs. One of the most observable and strongest indicators of success is for a junior during an AAR to speak openly about his decisions that were not as effective as he would have liked. He needs to be able to say without fear of retribution, "I made the wrong decision here. If I had to do it over again, I would do thus-and-so." In such a leadership environment, it is easier for you to be more supportive, more complimentary, and less critical. He has seen his mistakes; he knows what he needs to do to improve.

Mentoring is a combat-force multiplier. It can support you in the achievement of your goals. It can prepare your junior leaders for greater challenges. While the beneficial effects may not be immediately apparent, it may pay higher dividends for the time and effort expended than anything you do.

MISFITS MAY HAVE A PLACE

Talented people are difficult, from start to finish. They require special care and feeding—not consistently, but often unexpectedly.[18]

—Ralph Peters, Author

Many individuals have, like uncut diamonds, shining qualities beneath a rough exterior.[19]

—Juvenal, Roman Poet

Misfits may have a special skill or capability that can be used by an astute commander willing to take the appropriate steps to tap that competence. These individuals are often seen as "quirky," or "route step," or "indifferent." While there may be some accuracy in each of those adjectives, these Soldiers may have talent that can assist in mission accomplishment.

Because the Soldiers are seen as different from the generally accepted norm, some commanders conclude that the appropriate action is to discharge them or, at least, transfer them to some other unit. (Let that commander face the problem.) If the Soldier is not an irreconcilable disciplinary problem or security risk, discarding him may not be in the best interests of our Army or the Soldier.

In its discussion on punishment, FM 22-100, *Army Leadership* states: "If you were surprised to find a discussion of punishment under the section on motivation, consider this: good leaders are always on the lookout for opportunities to develop subordinates, even the ones who are being punished. Your people—even the ones who cause you problems—are still the most important re-source you have. When a vehicle is broken, you don't throw it out; you fix it. If one of your people is performing poorly, don't just get rid of the person; try to fix the problem."[20]

When I was the S2 (Intelligence Officer), 10th Special Forces Group in Germany, the Headquarters and Headquarters Company (HHC) commander brought one of these "problem" Soldiers to my attention. He was Sergeant First Class Jones (not his actual name). The commander said that Jones was a security risk and recommended that I withdraw Jones' clearance, thereby paving the way for him to be transferred from the group.

I knew Jones. He was an African-American disliked by many in our group. I believed that part of this low regard came from Jones dating a very attractive white girl. His speech, which was grammatically correct and spoken without "black" accent, was an-other cause of resentment. He was better educated than many. These characteristics made him a little "uppity" (a racist term used to describe him) to some. I concluded that his race was more the "problem" than his performance that, from all I could determine, was exemplary.

After several discussions with Jones and others in the group, I decided that he was no security risk. He and I had some very frank discussions about how he was perceived and why. I suggested ways in which he might improve his image; he agreed. I believe that we developed respect for each other.

At this time, the group was expanding from one operational company to three. The influx of commissioned and noncommissioned officers contained many who had no special forces experience. To remedy this shortcoming, the group commander, Colonel Salve Matheson, decided to form a provisional company to train these Soldiers in four special forces skills areas: weapons, operations and intelligence, demolitions, and medical skills. He selected me to be the commander of this training company.

In addition to the obvious preparation and implementation, we had a lot of administration (typing and filing) to accomplish. A good administrator, who could type well, even in civilian life, is hard to find. However, there was one man who I believed was capable and responsible: Sergeant First Class Jones.

He would be perfect to assemble the vault files of all our training classes (one of training company's missions) and maintain training records. The appropriate place for him would be working directly for my operations sergeant, Master Sergeant Bud Malone, a mature and very capable noncommissioned officer. Before going further, I discussed the idea with Malone. He saw no problem. We both agreed that Jones would work directly under, report to, and answer to no one but Malone. After talking to the Headquarters Company commander, Jones was transferred to Training Company. The solution worked like a charm.

Jones had an essential job for which he was well qualified. He knew he was important; he saw what he had to do. I often expressed my appreciation to him for his good work; we would be hard-pressed to operate without him. And, vital to success, there was a clear and inviolable "chain of command" to his supervisor, Master Sergeant Malone.

Our "solution" to a sticky problem—the HHC commander who wanted to rid himself of what he saw as a "problem Soldier" and our requirement for a good administrator—was not unique or original with me. Other commanders had described how they had solved similar problems.

Those "misfits" who cause us many moments of anguished contemplation may be turned around and become very productive members of our team if we can only find the right job and environment for them. All that it may require is a specific task that uses that Soldier's capability, a clear line of authority, and the realization that he is important to his commander and the unit's mission. It's always worth a try.

SEND YOUR SOLDIERS TO SCHOOL

Always be ready to send folks to school, no one is irreplaceable, as we are all just one bullet away from getting replaced anyway.[21]

—Command Sergeant Major Greg Birch

Make peace a time for training for war, and battle an exhibition of bravery.[22]

—The Emperor Maurice, East Roman Emperor and General

Officers are well aware of how attendance at military schools is a benefit to their careers. Schools that are in the professional development military education program are of great importance. Consequently, officers are eager to attend as soon as possible.

Schools for enlisted Soldiers have the same effect on their careers. These Soldiers must attend certain schools in order to qualify for promotion. Unfortunately, some commanders hesitate to do what they can to have a Soldier assigned to a school at the earliest opportunity. They are reluctant to approve the Soldier's release because he is "irreplaceable," "vital to the operation of the unit," or "cannot be spared" at the time because of a planned deployment, some important field training exercise (FTX), or other activity.

FM 22-100 advises: "The Army school system provides formal education and training for job-related and leadership skills. The Army school system is progressive.... Institutional training is critical in developing leaders and preparing them for increased positions of responsibility throughout the Army."[23]

When I was a company commander in the 65th Regimental Combat Team, the regiment received a quota for one officer to attend Ranger School. Since I was the only Ranger-qualified officer in the regiment, I was asked if I wanted to fill the quota. Although I had only one other officer, Lieutenant John B. Tower, I jumped at the chance. I submitted Tower's name. Almost immediately, my battalion commander reminded me that this particular course was scheduled during a big maneuver. He felt that I should not be sending my only officer. I differed with my commander saying that completion of the Ranger course would be beneficial to Tower and would be a reward to an outstanding officer. In addition, the experience of commanding the company with no officer would be good training for me! However, the quota was refused.

Send your men to school. Refusing to release them is unfair to them. They deserve the opportunity to improve their professional knowledge and to get ahead. They and their predecessors are responsible for your being where you are. Turnabout is fair play.

THANK THE COOKS AND KPs

No amount of rhetoric can replace an act of simple decency bestowed by a leader on a subordinate.[24]

—Bil Holton, PhD

And don't forget a good word for the cooks.[25]

—Lieutenant General Sir Leslie Morshead, Australian Army

Many of the Soldiers who make it possible for us to succeed never share in the limelight; they perform behind the scenes, accomplishing vital supportive tasks. Some of these support Soldiers do tasks that seem mundane and, to them, unimportant. The thoughtful commander will see to it that they are not forgotten, that they receive deserved recognition, and that they share in the acknowledgment of a job well done.

Our big consolidated messes (dining facilities) are impersonal compared to the company messes that used to be where we fed the troops. Because of the large size of the facility and the large number of people fed at each meal, there may be little personal contact between those doing the cooking and cleanup, and the Soldiers eating there. Regardless, commanders need to try to establish rapport with the cooks and kitchen police (KP), even though they may be civilian contract personnel.

Commanders, who make it a habit of getting to know the people preparing the food and acknowledging their contribution, will affect these vital people most positively. Get to know them the same way we knew our mess personnel in those bygone days of the company mess. After a meal, make it a habit to walk through the kitchen and cleanup area to say "thanks" to the people who made it possible for you to eat. It will only take a few minutes. They will be surprised—at least the first few times you do it—and they will be very pleased. They will respond with a huge grin that says, "You're welcome" in the most positive way. Your "thank you" will be most appreciated.

You Never Know the Impact You Are Having

He made us all better than we thought we could be.[26]
  —Jerry Kramer, Green Bay Packers football player

It is said of Caesar that he never lacked a pleasant word for his Soldiers. He remembered the face of anyone who had done a gallant deed and, when not in the presence of the enemy, joined his men in Soldier games. Such little human acts as these inspired his legionnaires with the devotion that went so far to account for his success as a great captain.[27]

  —General Maxwell D. Taylor

We never know what unrealized influence—for good or bad—that we have on others.

Whenever I reflect on my life—not only my youth but also my adult years—I am amazed at the things that I remember. Things that happened and what people said may have seemed inconsequential at the time. However, those scenes reappear with a clarity that surprises me. It takes only a moment of thought to understand why they return again and again. It is because those seemingly unimportant events had a marked effect on me.

My father had by far the most influence on me. He never "preached." He never spent much time on what today we would call counseling or mentoring. However, some simple statements imbedded themselves in my subconsciousness and often reappear. I remember interactions with teachers and coaches, friends, fellow Soldiers, and others. I doubt that any of them would recall what I remember, even if I described the scene to them. Yet I will never forget.

Conversely, I am amazed at what some individuals remember about something I said in a speech or class, or in a conversation we were having, or some task in which both of us were engaged. Soldiers, both officer and enlisted, often say, "I remember when you..." To them, what I said was so profound that they never forgot it and have used it as one of those guiding principles for their actions in similar circumstances.

Command Sergeant Major John D. Woodyard asked,

> How can you know if you've made a difference? Sometimes—rarely—the results are instant. Usually it takes much longer. You may see a Soldier again as a seasoned NCO; you may get a call or a letter or see a name in *Army Times*. In most cases, you will never be sure how well you succeeded, but don't let that stop you.[28]

I've tried to figure out in my own mind why these memories are so strong. I can only conclude that they placed much more importance on what we were doing and saying. Perhaps something that was "old hat" to me because of my age and experience was enlightening to them. Whatever the reason, I have concluded that we who are in a leadership or supervisory position are always "on stage," regardless of how little importance we may place on what is happening. We are having an impact often of much greater significance than we would ever imagine. Saying this does not mean that we can never be "at ease" around those who look to us for guidance and leadership. It does mean that our impact on others may be much greater than we can ever imagine. Consequently, we must always be discrete and circumspect in what we say and do.

Section VII

PERSONAL DEVELOPMENT

BE ALL YOU CAN BE

---

*A man can be as great as he wants to be. If you believe
in yourself and have the courage, the determination, the
dedication, the competitive drive, and if you are willing
to sacrifice the little things in life and pay the price for
the things that are worthwhile, it can be done.*[1]

—Vince Lombardi, Green Bay Packers Coach

*The man [Vince Lombardi] was a perfectionist ... he
was never satisfied simply by victory. He always wanted
us to play as well as we were capable of playing.*[2]

—Bart Starr, Green Bay Packers Football Player

"Be all you can be!" was the recruiting slogan for the Army for
many years. I thought it was the best that we ever had. It
sums up in a few words encouragement for a Soldier to do his best
in all endeavors. It is an admonition for all of us to remember and
live by. We need words to guide and inspire us in our daily lives.
When we succeed in following these words, we are better for it.
We may never be "all we can be"—we may never reach our potential—but striving for the goal will make us better than we are.

Most of us probably have not written a creed that expresses our
expectations for ourselves. On the other hand, we are inspired by
the words of others. We may have collected quotes over the years
and kept them in some file somewhere. We may, on occasion,
return to that file to read what we have saved. It helps us refocus
our thoughts as we find inspiration in what others have said. We

may use the time for reflection, to "clean out the cobwebs," and to strengthen our resolve to do better.

Soldiers often prepare inspirational creeds that express a particular group's standards, responsibilities, and expectations of itself. The Noncommissioned Officer Creed, the Drill Sergeant Creed, and the Athenian Warrior Creed are examples of what some groups have prepared to define what they expect all that members of that group to be.

The Creed of the Noncommissioned Officer, "I realize that I am a member of a time-honored corps, which is known as 'The Backbone of the Army,'" reminds us of the vital mission performed by our incomparable noncommissioned officers. Can there be any more stirring words than those contained in an ancient Athenian oath: "I will not disgrace the Soldier's arms nor abandon the comrade who stands at my side; but whether alone or with many, I will fight to defend things sacred and profane. I will hand down my country not lessened but larger and better than I have received it."[3] From "I Am the Infantry," we read, "My bayonet ... on the wings of power ... keeps the peace worldwide. And despots, falsely garbed in freedom's mantle, falter ... hide.... FOLLOW ME!"

Task Force Soldier, an initiative of the chief of staff of the Army, formulated the Soldier's Creed to assist in developing the warrior ethos in every Soldier and to increase combat effectiveness.

THE SOLDIER'S CREED
I am an American Soldier.
I am a warrior and a member of a team.
I serve the people of the United States and live the Army Values.
I will always place the mission first.
I will never accept defeat.
I will never quit.
I will never leave a fallen comrade.
I am disciplined, physically and mentally tough, trained and proficient in my warrior tasks and drills.
I always maintain my arms, my equipment and myself.

I am an expert and I am a professional.
I stand ready to deploy, engage, and destroy the enemies of the
United States of America in close combat.
I am a guardian of freedom and the American way of life.
I am an American Soldier.

Each of us can put together our own words to live by. We may assemble them into a formal creed, or we may just collect those that move and appeal to us. However we do it, developing a clear picture of what we want to be helps. We must not disappoint ourselves; we are the most important people to meet the standards of our own creed. Undoubtedly there will be times when we fall below our expectations. However, these words serve as a reminder of what we expect of ourselves. They can remind us never to be content with less than our best. Collecting and organizing them is a worthwhile task. Turning to them on occasion will encourage us to exert ourselves even more strongly to live to be all that we can be.

BECOME THE LEADER YOU WANT TO BE

---

*The present is the result of the past. The future is the
result of the present.*

—Alfred North Whitehead, British Mathematician,
Logician and Philosopher

The Cherokees tell us, "We are who we are by what we choose
to cultivate, and all worthy performances are made up of very
little parts."[4] *The Book of Virtues* restates this truism: "We are the
sum of our actions, Aristotle tells us, and therefore our habits make
the difference."[5] We determined what we are today by the way we
lived our past.

We will determine what we are to become by how we live today and tomorrow. If we build the habit of doing the right thing,
of striving for excellence, we will become people of character who
are all that we can be. When we accept less than our best, we are
establishing a standard of mediocrity.

A significant goal in basic training is instilling Army values
in each trainee. Our Army will be better if our Soldiers live these
values. The values are loyalty, duty, respect for others, selfless service, honor, integrity, and personal courage. Rangers, Soldiers,
noncommissioned officers, and others have creeds that tell them
who and what they are. It tells them what is expected of them
as members of those groups. If they live by their creed, they will
bring credit onto themselves and this great Army in which we are
privileged to serve.

What we do each day of our lives—our attention to duty; our

leisure activities; our relations with our peers, superiors, Soldiers, and families; our language—is determining our reputation, what others think of us, and our character, who we are when no one is looking. The words of Albert Camus are appropriate here: "Try not to seem, but to be."

Each decision we make, whether large or small, shapes our character in some finite although infinitesimal way, just as the drops of water in a limestone cave form a stalagmite and stalactite. General Maxwell D. Taylor said, "Professional competence is more than a display of book knowledge or of the results of military schooling. It requires the display of qualities of character which reflect inner strength and justified confidence in one's self."[6]

How can we model our lives so that we will be the persons we want to be? We may begin by considering people whose character we admire. While each of us is an individual, heroes can help us define what we want to be. We tend to emulate them both consciously and unconsciously, so choose them wisely. We are known by our heroes.

To become the leader we want to be, describe that person in specific terms. What would we like for our Soldiers to say about us when we are not present—when there is no possibility for the words they speak to get back to us? Do we want our Soldiers to say that we stick up for them? Then we must go to bat for them where rewards, recognition, and other benefits are concerned. Going to bat for them also includes the times when they are in trouble. What specific actions could we take to elicit those comments? Begin to live that way. If we want to be described as honest and truthful, we must be honest and truthful in everything, large and small, that we do. What would we like for our boss to say? Demonstrate those characteristics. To be known as someone who has the courage of his convictions, we "stand tall" when those convictions are challenged—we can't be one who tells his boss what he wants to hear.

Perhaps most important of all, we want to be respected for the persons we are. Many civilians believe that all an officer has to do to get something done is to give an order. It's not that simple, particularly when carrying out that order may be very difficult or cause great discomfort or even death. It takes respect, and respect has to be earned.

There may be no occurrence throughout our lives that by itself determines what and who we are; but we can be confident that everything we do—in every decision we make—is shaping us into what we will ultimately become. We have it within our power to be all that we want to be.

In short, be what we want to become. Live every moment in recognition that our every deed, every thought, is a stone in the makeup of who and what we are. In that way one can become the leader one wants to be.

How Can We Develop Courage?

There are two kinds of courage, physical and moral, and he who would be a true leader must have both. Both are the products of the character-forming process, of the development of self-control, self-discipline, physical endurance, of knowledge of one's job and, therefore, of confidence. These qualities minimize fear and maximize sound judgment under pressure—with some of that indispensable stuff called luck—often bring success from seemingly hopeless situations.[7]

—General Matthew B. Ridgway

FM 22-100 tells us "Leaders who demonstrate personal courage show physical and moral bravery; take responsibility for decisions and actions; and accept responsibility for mistakes and shortcomings."[8]

Courage comes in many forms. I believe that moral and physical courage are different. I define moral courage as the ability to withstand the scorn, ridicule, derision, or condemnation from peers, subordinates, or superiors for "doing the right thing," for choosing "the harder right instead of the easier wrong." I believe that moral courage is rarer than physical courage—facing physical danger and bodily harm.

I agree with Mark Twain who said: "It is curious that physical courage should be so common in the world and moral courage so rare."[9] Field Marshal Viscount Slim said, "I have never met a man with moral courage who would not, when it was really necessary, face bodily danger. Moral courage is a higher and a rarer virtue than physical courage."[10]

I don't know why. It seems to me that men are more likely to "knuckle under" when differing with their superiors than when confronted by physical danger. Fear of disapproval from one's boss can be a debilitating emotion. In most cases, the subordinate is alone; he does not have "buddies" on whom he can depend. His future—his career—may be threatened. In such a situation, not standing up for what one believes is sometimes seen as the easier decision. "Discretion is the better part of valor."

When Senator Carl Levin, Senate Armed Services Committee, asked General Eric Shinseki, then Army chief of staff, how many troops would be needed to keep the peace in Iraq, General Shinseki answered, "Something on the order of several hundred thousand Soldiers are probably, you know, a figure that would be required." The number was based on experience gained in Vietnam, Bosnia, and in NATO. That answer was not what his civilian boss, Secretary of Defense Donald Rumsfeld, wanted to hear. In fact, it ran counter to Rumsfeld's opinion that fewer men would be required. The general could have supported the position of his boss. Instead, he did what was right. He gave an honest opinion to an important question. Because of previous run-ins with Rumsfeld over other matters, General Shinseki knew that his response would arouse even greater antipathy in his boss. The general never wavered. Subsequent events have proved him correct.[11] Subsequently, many pundits have reminded the public what General Shinseki had predicted as the occupation of Iraq became more deadly to our troops. I have never read or heard that the General has ever said, "See! I told you so!" That he has not is another indication of his upstanding nature. General Shinseki is an example for all of us.

We sometimes face a situation where our opinions, though not as important as those of the chief of staff, are of consequence. Not being true to our duty and ourselves can cause great harm. We must "choose the harder right instead of the easier wrong." The fate of our Soldiers may depend on it.

In the 1800s, a Frenchman left a sizable sum of money to the *Academie Francaise* to be used each year to recognize "virtue." The *Academie* usually was partial to those individuals who demonstrated simple and chronic virtue rather than acknowledging spasmodic and dramatic actions. Many of those selected were simple housewives who went about their daily lives under tremendous burdens imposed by poverty, illness, dependents, or other unrelenting hardships. William James commented, "Human nature, responding to the call of duty, appears nowhere sublimer than in the person of these humble heroines of family life."[12] I agree. This continuing pressure can cripple a person who is in no physical danger. Instead, there may be the morale crushing strain of a problem for which there is no apparent solution. To carry on under this burden may require greater courage and emotional stability than that demonstrated by the Soldier who takes great physical risk. This "chronic virtue" is an example of "moral" courage.

I describe physical courage as "standing up to" bodily harm and often think of it in the context of combat. Some Soldier with a burst of energy leaps to the front of a group of men who fear for their safety. He may expose himself, may take risks that seem foolhardy to any thinking person. Yet he may not see himself as brave; he may look upon his actions as only doing his job. Adrenaline coursing through his body brings an almost unbelievable boost to his physical capability that may leave him completely exhausted once the danger is past. Although he demonstrated his courage when it was needed, he cannot say that he will have that strength the next time danger surrounds him.

To me, the most courageous person is one who carries on day after day under the strain of some continuing, seemingly neverending physical danger. (Seemingly unrelenting as was the moral stress recognized by the *Academie Francaise*.) This situation can confront every Soldier, particularly a combat Infantryman, who must go about the most dangerous job in the world every day that he is in a combat zone. This constant worry can grind him down as it impacts with never-ending pressure on his confidence and morale.

Nowhere is this continuing, grinding pressure better expressed than in the words of General Omar Bradley.

> The rifleman fights without promise of either reward or relief. Behind every river there's another hill—and behind that hill, another river. After weeks or months in the line only a wound can offer him the comfort of safety, shelter and a bed. Those who are left to fight, fight on, evading death, but knowing each day of evasion they have exhausted one more chance of survival. Sooner or later, unless victory comes, this chase will end on the litter or in the grave.

The rotation policies during the Korean, Vietnam, Afghanistan, and Iraq Wars are an approach to reducing this morale debilitating pressure. Most Soldiers have probably asked themselves, "How do I ensure that I have the courage to face the perils of combat?" All of us have faced fear. Shakespeare expressed so well the egregious effect it can have on us: "Cowards die many times before their deaths; the valiant never taste of death but once."[13] We ask ourselves, "How can I ensure that I will rise to combat's challenge?"

I must respond, "I do not know." I wish that I did. For some, it's a matter of faith, a belief that some Supreme Being, God, is watching over them. While I do not believe that those fortunate individuals never experience fear, some seem to be able to control concern for themselves by turning to God. I do not know how to develop that faith. I do not believe that a minister, rabbi, or priest has the secret, but he may be able to help. I encourage you to talk to your spiritual leader.

There are concrete actions that may help us. I want to discuss some suggestions from others that may be of assistance. I will also describe something that helped me, although I can assure you I have no magic formula. I was very afraid on many occasions. Let me begin with a personal experience.

I was a new second lieutenant in the Infantry Officer Basic Course (IOBC) at Fort Benning, Georgia. The year was 1950, before the Korean War. I was visiting Lieutenant Colonel Louis G. Mendez, a member of the faculty at the Infantry School. It was a social occasion. Colonel Mendez had become a mentor to me. I had contacted him shortly after I arrived at Benning at the suggestion of a West Point roommate, Doug Bush. Doug had been a Pathfinder First Lieutenant in Lieutenant Colonel Mendez's 3rd Battalion, 508th Parachute Infantry Regiment. Lieutenant Colonel Mendez and his wife, Jean, were a warm, friendly couple that opened their home and hearts to young officers. I was fortunate to be included.

When I had the opportunity, I asked my mentor a question that had bothered me for some time. "Sir, I know that I will be afraid in combat. How do I control that fear?" Colonel Mendez answered, "If you are thinking about yourself, you're not doing your job. You have a responsibility for your men. When you begin to become fearful, get up and check on the men. You'll be so busy that you won't have time to worry about yourself." Not a lot of help there, I thought, but I remembered it and told myself that I would give it a try when the occasion arose.

I didn't have to wait long. In a few months that occasion did arise—many times. Shortly after graduation from IOBC and Jump School, I was on my way to Korea. I was selected to form, train, and command the Eighth Army Ranger Company. Whenever the bullets began to fly, the adrenaline rushed through my body and apprehension began to rise. I remembered what Colonel Mendez had said. I was not doing my job because I was thinking about myself. I ran from Ranger to Ranger "checking." While I still felt trepidation, it was not overwhelming; it was not paralyzing. I have silently thanked Colonel Mendez many times for his sage advice.

Colonel Joshua Lawrence Chamberlain, one of America's greatest Soldiers, expressed similar sentiments when he said, "An officer is so absorbed by the sense of responsibility for his men, for his cause, or for the fight that the thought of personal peril has no place whatever in governing his actions. The instinct to seek safety is overcome by the instinct of honor."[14]

Chamberlain also wrote, "Curious people often ask the questions whether in battle we are not affected by fear, so that our actions are influenced by it; and some are prompt to answer, 'Yes, surely we are, and anybody who denies it is a braggart or a liar.' I say to such, 'Speak for yourselves.' A Soldier has something else to think about."[15] There are probably more people who would disagree with Chamberlain than concur with this last statement. However, he is emphasizing Colonel Mendez's advice to me.

I must admit, that when I did not follow Colonel Mendez's counsel, my fears became significant. When I failed to heed General Patton's advice, "Do not take counsel of your fears," only physical action helped me regain emotional control.

Despite all our efforts, seeing men die day after day has an effect on the most stalwart. We will be beset by doubts—by the natural concern for our own safety. Charlton Ogburn, in his book, *Merrill's Marauders*, wrote about courage.

> How does one make himself continue when he has to realize that he is not indestructible—that sooner or later like all the other men he has seen die, that he, too, will "get it"? Sam Wilson, an heroic Intelligence and Reconnaissance (I&R) Platoon Leader, responded:
> "I can only speak for myself, but as far as I was concerned, it wasn't possible. At least it wasn't when once you had got over the idea you were different from the rest and nothing could touch you. You couldn't face it. Maybe that kind of courage is made. But I haven't got it. There was one ability I found I did have, though. It was a very modest one, to be sure—but it had to serve. I could command one foot to move out in front of the other one.
> There's no great trick in that, is there? A matter of elementary muscular control! You can tell your

leg what to do, certainly. What's a step? A child can take one! You advance one foot so ... and then the other ... and now the first again. And that is all you have to do, except wipe your hands off from time to time so they won't be too slippery to hold your gun. That's all that is required of you. You just have to take the first step."[16]

Perhaps it is, as James Bowman stated so well, "namely the sense of what it meant to be a man, and that the shame of being thought a coward, or having let down your pals, was more to be dreaded than death itself."[17]

We can enhance our ability to overcome or control our fears by forcing ourselves to face those fears. "Few men are born brave; many become so through force of training and discipline."[18] If we are nervous about speaking in public, we can build confidence by doing more of it. As we become better at it, we are more relaxed. We can diminish our fear of the water by improving our ability to swim. In combat, we will improve our self-control as we force ourselves "to get up and check on the men." "Courage is not the absence of fear, but the capacity to act despite our fears."[19] We are sublimating those emotions that, if left unchecked, may paralyze us.

Ms. Eleanor Roosevelt expressed her thoughts on developing courage this way: "I gain strength, courage, and confidence by every experience in which I must stop and look fear in the face.... I say to myself, I've lived through this and can take the next thing that comes along.... We must do the things we think we cannot do."[20] Sequichie Comingdeer, a Cherokee Indian, agrees. "The death of fear is in doing what you fear to do."[21] "We become brave by doing brave acts."[22] Senator John McCain compared courage to a muscle. "The more we exercise it the stronger it gets."[23]

Lieutenant Colonel Don Bowman, U.S. Army Retired, when reviewing an earlier draft of Words for Warriors, offered this insight:

> While daring new things can help build a sense of assurance, courage as such can be spent and not replenished.... Both moral and physical courage can be exhausted by constant stress and demands. The result may be erosion or collapse, but it can occur.... You cannot expect a valorous action from someone in every situation simply because he has done it once or twice before.
>
> I recall a young Soldier named "Mouse" Cowan in Company A, 2-12th Cavalry. He was an extraordinarily alert and a deadly point man ... in the mountains and jungles.... Then one day, he said, "No; no more." His company commander was wise enough to allow him to rejoin the ranks and let another step forward.[24]

We can learn to control our fear by doing what we fear. We just "keep on keeping on." We develop the ability to control our emotions the same way we learn to control our muscles. We develop that capability through practice. We also can attenuate the self-preservation desire by doing our job, by taking care of the men. It works! Try it.

Learn from Your Mistakes and Those of Others

The only man who makes no mistake is the man who does nothing.[25]

—Theodore Roosevelt

Schools and their training offer better ways to do things, but only through experience are we able to capitalize on this learning. The process of profiting from mistakes becomes a milestone in learning to become a more efficient Soldier.[26]

—Former Sergeant Major of the Army, William G. Bainbridge

President Theodore Roosevelt was correct; the only person who never made a mistake is the person who never did anything. (Some people say that doing nothing is a mistake!) All people— even the best—make mistakes. Some can be devastating with their impact. They may result in a loss of a battle, loss of life, failed inspection, or in rewarding or punishing the wrong Soldier. No matter how hard we try, we will err. The focus in learning from one's mistakes is to avoid repeating those errors while improving our performance

President Warren G. Harding said, "A regret for the mistakes of yesterday must not, however, blind us to the tasks of today."[27] President Franklin D. Roosevelt expressed it so well, saying, "We shall strive for perfection. We shall not achieve it immediately—

but we still shall strive. We may make mistakes—but they must never be mistakes which result from faintness of heart or abandonment of moral principle."[28] Every mistake can be a learning experience. Placing blame on oneself or others is usually counterproductive.

In training, one of the best ways to learn from mistakes is to conduct an after-action review (AAR). If the focus of the review is the answer to the question, "How do we do better next time?" improvement is more likely. Once the actions that need improving and those that will be sustained have been determined, repeat the exercise incorporating those decisions. Repetition helps inculcate proper habits and responses. It supports learning from one's mistakes. Anyone who has ever played a sport has experienced his coach requiring the team to repeat a play again and again. Doing it correctly does not stop the coach from saying, "Do it again." He wants the actions to become automatic.

Thomas A. Edison, the inventor of the electric light and many other useful items, was once asked how he felt about his many failures in trying to discover something that would serve as the filament for his electric lamp. He said that he did not consider the unsuccessful trials as failures; each was a success. He had learned one more material that would not work. "I have not failed. I've just found 10,000 ways that won't work."[29] He learned from his mistakes just as we can if we analyze what we have done and look on the mistakes in a positive manner.[30]

It is better to learn from the mistakes of others; we do not have to limit our learning to our own errors. To derive the most benefit from mistakes (and successes) of others, analyze what that person did on the basis of what he knew at the time. Examine the decision and actions from that perspective. Monday morning quarterbacks have the benefit of hindsight. Any decision that they make avoids the pitfalls of the person whose actions are being examined.

Playing "what if" is another good way to learn. One may examine his own decisions or those of others using this technique. It can be very beneficial because it requires us to decide the course(s) of action we would take in light of changing situations. The number of scenarios is limited only by our imagination.

No one wants to make mistakes. Everyone wants to avoid repeating a mistake. We can improve our probability by learning from our mistakes and those of others

You're a Problem if You're Not Physically Fit

Truly then, it is killing men with kindness not to insist upon physical standards during training which will give them maximum fitness for the extraordinary stresses of campaigning in war.[31]

—Brigadier General S. L. A. Marshall

We do PT (physical training) to prepare us for the physical and emotional demands of combat. Our Army was woefully unprepared for the Korean War.

On 5 July 1950, U.S. troops, who were unprepared for the physical demands of war, were sent to battle. The early days of the Korean War were nothing short of disastrous, as U.S. Soldiers were routed by a poorly equipped, but well-trained, North Korean People's Army. As American Soldiers withdrew, they left behind wounded comrades and valuable equipment; their training had not adequately prepared them to carry heavy loads.... If we fail to prepare our Soldiers for their physically demanding wartime tasks, we are guilty of paying lip service to the principle of "train as you fight." Our physical training programs must do more for our Soldiers than just get them ready for the semi-annual Army Physical Fitness Test (APFT).[32]

Later, poor physical fitness made it more difficult and more unlikely that our Soldiers would control the high ground, a fundamental principle of the first order of importance.

When the Chinese slammed the Eighth Army on November 25 and 26, 1950, some of our units attempted to withdraw through narrow defiles without controlling the high ground. The Chinese, located on the high ground, established ambushes and roadblocks and slaughtered the retreating Americans.

An entire Chinese division outflanked the 2nd Division and established itself in a five-mile narrow stretch of the road near Kunu-ri. The southern end was so narrow that it was called "the pass." The Chinese were heavily armed and were, in some instances, only one hundred yards from the road. They destroyed the lead vehicle of the American convoy and plugged the pass and then slaughtered the Americans. Approximately 4,000 of the original 7,000 made it through the pass.[33]

In the east, the Marines faced similar odds. However, they made a correct tactical decision. They decided to control the ridges and fight their way through the gauntlet as they "attacked in a different direction." They came out with their dead and wounded, weapons and equipment, having survived a major ordeal of the war.[34]

"Those who wage war in mountains should never pass through defiles without first making themselves masters of the heights."[35] Unless Soldiers are physically fit they will be unable to control the heights.

FM 21-20, *Physical Training*, states that physical fitness consists of:

> Cardiovascular (CR) endurance: the efficiency with which the body delivers oxygen and nutrients needed for muscular activity and transports waste products from the cells.

Muscular strength: the greatest amount of force a muscle or muscle group can exert in a single effort.

Muscular endurance: the ability of a muscle or muscle group to perform repeated movements with a submaximal force for extended periods of time.

Flexibility: the ability to move the joints (for example, elbow, knee) or any group of joints through an entire, normal range of motion.

Body composition: the amount of body fat a Soldier has in comparison to his total body mass.[36]

The Physical Training Standing Operating Procedure (SOP) for the 3rd Battalion, 75th Ranger Regiment expresses the characteristics prescribed by FM 21-20 in real-life terms.

A Ranger needs to have the strength to withstand an air drop in full combat load, have the aerobic capacity to move great distances with heavy loads, have the anaerobic capacity to repeatedly sprint and move in a tactical sense, have the agility to maneuver around obstacles, have the core strength to not sustain injuries, and have the power to deliver a lethal blow to overcome the enemy.[37]

Command Sergeant Major Greg Birch, when he was the command sergeant major of the 3rd Ranger Battalion, developed and implemented a physical fitness test containing events that replicated physically demanding requirements of combat. His Ranger Physical Assessment Test (RPAT) included six events. They were a three-mile run wearing individual body armor and helmet, a twenty-foot caving ladder climb, a fifty-meter Skedco (a plastic collapsible stretcher used to drag wounded Soldiers from the battlefield) pull, a twenty-foot fast rope climb, a hundred-meter sprint, and an eight-foot wall climb. There was no "passing" grade; each Ranger was expected to do better each time he took the test.

Lieutenant Colonel Paul LaCamera, commander of the 3-75th (later commander of the 75th Ranger Regiment) was leading the way as a member of one of the teams.

I believe that the best PT program is one that duplicates or replicates the demands of combat. We "train for the test." When I was the commander of a "B" team in the 10th Special Forces Group, I tested my team and the subordinate "A" teams each quarter. To provide a base line, we took the then current five-event Army PT test. In subsequent quarters, based on suggestions from my noncommissioned officers, I prescribed a special test composed of challenges similar to those we faced in our field training.

No matter how we get into battle, once we are committed on the ground, our mobility depends on our strength and physical stamina. Outstanding physical fitness saves lives. Without it, an Infantryman is nothing.

For the combat Soldier—in particular, for the Infantryman—stamina is the most important facet of physical fitness. He must be able to continue with a maximum performance day after day for weeks at a time. PT and tactical training need to focus on developing stamina more than strength. However, we may be unable to match the stamina of third world Soldiers no matter how much PT we have.

Commanders of the 75th Ranger Regiment emphasize physical fitness; it is one of the "big four." Colonel Stan McChrystal, a former commander of the Regiment, always injected some requirement into the Emergency Deployment Readiness Exercises (EDRE) that placed great demands on stamina. Colonel McChrystal would ensure that his Rangers would meet the goal stated in FM21-20: "He must have the ability to meet any combat or duty situation, accomplish his mission, and still have a reserve of strength."[38]

Trainees in Ranger School learn that stamina is determined in large measure by a person's will. That is one of the reasons why the Ranger course is so beneficial to all Soldiers regardless of branch. In reality, we know that there are limits. Commanders must not push men beyond those limits.

Since Vietnam, some of our conflicts have lasted only a few days. (Afghanistan and Iraq are notable exceptions.) This fact should not lull us into believing that maximum physical fitness is not required. The Soldier has to be able to give 100 percent every day. If he is concerned about physical fitness, if he is so physically tired that it affects his thought processes, he will not be up to standard for combat.

The Army continues worthwhile efforts to improve our physical training. While expensive equipment and training areas can help, they are not essential. Bayonet, hand-to-hand training, and obstacle courses are battle-focused and will improve any program.

Outstanding physical fitness permits us to do our jobs and saves lives.

Reducing Stress

You must have a room, or a certain hour or so each day, where you don't know what was in the newspaper that morning ... a place where you can simply experience and bring forth what you are and what you might be.[39]

—Joseph Campbell, Author

Stress is essential to leadership. Living with stress, knowing how to handle pressure, is necessary for survival. It is related to a man's ability to wrest control of his own destiny from the circumstances that surround him.[40]

—Vice Admiral James Bond Stockdale

FM 22-100 counsels us that:

Effective leaders develop techniques to identify and manage stress well before actual combat occurs.[41] ... [I]f you think about combat stress and its effects on you and your Soldiers ahead of time, you'll be less surprised and better prepared to deal with and reduce its effects. It takes mental discipline to imagine the unthinkable—the plan going wrong, your Soldiers wounded or dying, and the enemy coming after YOU. (Emphasis in the original.) But in combat, all of these things can happen, and your Soldiers expect you, their leader, to have thought through each of them.... And the will to win serves you just as well in peacetime, when it's easy to become discouraged, feel let down, and spend your energy complaining instead of using your talents to make things better.[42]

A memo entitled "Planning Document for the Leaders and Operational Stress Panels" stimulated the following comments. Just reading the memo caused a ratcheting up of my stress level! The jargon about a Service's perspective on stress "in a joint context" and thinking "out-of-the-box" made me realize once again that I am two generations behind the current thinking. I never knew that there was a joint context for thinking about stress. I have always envisioned stress as being something fairly individual and personal. I did agree with the guidance that "commanders play the key role." What else is new? Commanders always have been the ones to "play the key role." That is as it should be.

Despite the guidance to "think out-of-the-box," I recalled techniques that I had used. Calm commanders are a great stress inhibitor and have a calming effect on their subordinates. I concentrated on trying to appear calm no matter how dire the situation although at times my emotions were churning inside. If the boss is calm then everything must be OK. My troopers in the 2-502nd in Vietnam expressed it this way: "No need to fear danger! Here comes the Ranger (my code name)!"

One of the greatest stress inhibitors is a commander in whom subordinates have complete trust. The junior knows that his boss is going to see to it that the junior receives all the physical and moral support that he can use. Nothing can be more soothing to a junior facing a tough battle than to hear his commander say:

I have arranged for Puff, the Magic Dragon (AC-130 aircraft fitted with Gatling Guns) to be on standby. We have gunships and all the artillery you can use available and waiting for your call. Dustoff (rescue and evacuation helicopter) has been alerted that we expect a big battle tonight. You fight your war. I'll see that you don't have to look over your shoulder for support.

Outstanding physical fitness is a stress inhibitor. Physical training that develops stamina will help us face stress with more equanimity.

Training, both physical and mental, that develops confidence in oneself, in our buddies, in our leaders, and in our subordinates is a great stress inhibitor and is an appropriate part of our training. We are not alone. We know that there are others on our team who will help us bear the challenges we face.

Confidence in our equipment, like confidence in people, inhibits stress. We fret less when we know that we can count on our equipment. We develop that confidence by training and maintaining.

Some Soldiers, particularly commanders, principal staff officers, and senior noncommissioned officers, pride themselves on their perceived ability to perform with little sleep or rest. These Soldiers sometimes decide to stay on duty—to stay awake—for an entire two- or three-day exercise claiming that they can function without loss of efficiency. They are fooling themselves and endangering the troops. Pragmatic, knowledgeable commanders require staff to rest during off duty.

A rested body and mind inhibit stress. In this regard, "snatches" of rest—a ten-minute sleep break—can do wonders for the tired body and mind.

While a seeming contradiction to resting when you can, a brisk workout or quick walk in the fresh air can help clear the cobwebs from one's mind and relax physical tension. Even a big, lengthy stretch at the desk helps.

All Soldiers like mail. Although e-mail has replaced regular mail in some circumstances, the latter is still highly desirable. Mail connects a Soldier with home, the "real world," the world to which he wants to return. Commanders who see that mail delivery is a priority will benefit from the reduced stress and higher morale in their troops.

Discipline that comes from ingrained habits reduces stress. The "do it again" approach to training helps develop this discipline. Soldiers do not have to stop and think when faced with certain contingencies. They have always reacted in a certain way. They have always "taken a knee" or gotten into a firing position at every halt. They have always cleaned their weapons and equipment when the opportunity arose. Battle drills are instinctive. Troops have always done what was required because the junior leaders have always checked. Consequently, troops do what is required without constant supervision. Training produces a disciplined mind. Imagine the stress if you had to decide each and every action that you took—if you had to think about rising in the morning, about how to lace your shoes, about brushing your teeth, and about washing your face. What a strain to have to make a conscious decision to hook your safety belt in an auto and to look to the rear before backing. That is stress that you do not need and do not have to endure.

Working with the same supporting units develops familiarity that reduces stress. You and they have developed confidence in each other. You know that you can depend on each other. You understand each other's thought processes and know what each wants. Anything that increases this favorable familiarity is a stress inhibitor.

Chaplains and medics have big roles to play. A chaplain's presence can exert a calming influence. They need to be where the troops are most miserable. The religious services that the chaplains conduct—particularly the quick, impromptu ones—can work wonders. Most of us have some belief, weak or strong, in some outside power greater than ourselves. The chaplains help put us in closer touch with that power.

What a blessing to know that we have highly skilled medics who can and will look after us. This confidence is developed in training. When the troops see that the commander stresses medical training and "plays" CASEVAC (casualty evacuation) to the hilt in field exercises, they feel confident that the "old man" is going to do everything in his power to see that they do not get hurt and, if they do, he is going to do his best to look after them.

There is no "joint" or "out-of-the-box" in these ideas, but they work! Commanders can get more ideas by recalling what has reduced their stress levels in the past. Reducing stress is a worthy goal.

Strive for Excellence
(Excellence Is Its Own Reward)

I discovered in the flying fraternity, particularly military flying, a brotherhood based on the idea that all that counted in life was the excellent performance of routine duties, which consisted of defying death daily in the air. Rank meant nothing. Money meant nothing. Yeager, when he ascended to the top of this pyramid, was a captain in the Air Force. Excellent performance of your duty as a military officer was everything; to Chuck Yeager, this was all that mattered. He told me at the time, "Everything I ever did I did for this blue suit," and he grasped the lapel of his blue Air Force officer's uniform.[43]

—Tom Wolfe, Author

In 1973 when General Creighton Abrams, chief of staff of the U.S. Army, directed the activation of the 1st Ranger Battalion, he gave the following guidance:

> The battalion is to be an elite, light, and the most proficient Infantry battalion in the world. A battalion that can do things with its hands and weapons better than anyone. The battalion will contain no "hoodlums or brigands" and if the battalion is formed from such persons it will be dis-

banded. Wherever the battalion goes, it must be apparent that it is the best.[44]

To be the best, to be all we can be, we must "continually pursue excellence."[45]

The Rangers of the 1st Ranger Battalion and later the regiment have lived that charter. The regiment is better today than it was when formed; the Rangers themselves are also better qualified. When a Soldier reports to the regiment, he is immediately immersed in a culture of excellence that is almost palpable. He recognizes that he is expected to do his best always. He knows that if he fails to meet standards, he will be relieved. Those returning to the regiment for additional tours after serving elsewhere in the Army must pass mental, physical, and psychological tests to qualify for acceptance.

> People create organizations, and the creators of organizations also create culture through the articulation of their assumptions. Although the final form of an organization's final culture reflects the complex interaction between the thrust provided by the founder, the reactions of the group's members and their shared historical experiences, there is little doubt that the initial shaping force is the personality and the belief system of the founder.[46]
>
> Once an organization has evolved a mature culture because it has had a long rich history, that culture creates the patterns of perception, thought, and feeling of every new generation in the organization and therefore, also "causes" the organization to be predisposed to certain kinds of leadership. In that sense, the mature group, through its culture, also creates its leaders. As scholars we must understand this paradox: leaders create cultures but cultures in turn create their next generation of leaders.[47]

It is in the striving for excellence that we make the greatest contributions in the performance of our duties. I have heard so many times, "It's good enough for government work," meaning that the performance of the task was acceptable, but not the best that the person could do. He was doing just enough to "get by." If this level of ambition is widespread in the unit then our unit will be mediocre. It may have the most up-to-date weapons and equipment, its Soldiers may have been highly trained, it may out-number its enemy—it may have all the advantages. If, however, officers and noncommissioned officers who do only enough to "get by," lead it, then it can and probably will be defeated by a less advantaged force composed of men dedicated to excellence. Good enough is never good enough until it is the best that you can do. When we settle for less than our best, we are cheating our men, we're cheating our Army, and we're cheating this great country in which we live.

YOUR WORD IS YOUR BOND

In a conference with Indians, Washington could say: "Brothers: I am a Warrior. My words are few and plain; but I will make good what I say." As he would do so often in years to come, whether the issue be pay for his officers or passage of the Constitution, the sole guarantee Washington would give was his word, as though that alone were enough. It is a measure of the man's standing that it almost always was.[48]

—William B. Allen, Editor

The American people look to their military leaders to be people of integrity.[49]

—General J. Lawton Collins

Washington was a man of his word; his word was his bond. He earned that reputation by the way he lived his life. Historian Forrest McDonald described Washington as "the most trusted man of the age."[50] President Theodore Roosevelt said Washington "never spoke a word which he did not make good by an act and always acted with serene, farsighted wisdom and entire fearlessness."[51] President John Adams said, "For [Washington's] fellow citizens, if their prayers could have been answered, he would have been immortal."[52] French Foreign Minister Talleyrand wrote that Washington's death deprived "the world of one of its brightest ornaments, and removes to the realms of history one of the nobler lives that ever honored the human race."[53] Douglas Southall

Freeman, when he finished his seminal work, *George Washington*, wrote "[I]n Washington this nation and the Western Hemisphere have a man 'greater than the world ever knew, living and dying' a man dedicated, just and incorruptible, an example for long centuries of what character and diligence can achieve." [54]

None of us may achieve that international reputation. However, we, like Washington, can live our lives in such a way that our word is our bond. We must live that way if we expect to earn the trust and respect of the Soldiers we lead. They deserve no less than a leader with unshakable honesty

The disappearance of high moral standards can destroy our Army. General Matthew B. Ridgway wrote, "The 'integrity of the military profession' ... means that we must have an officer corps of such character and competence as will promote the highest professional and spiritual leadership to our citizen armies." [55] Major General John LeMoyne, commanding general, Fort Benning, Georgia, had this to say about trust:

> I remember when I was a young Soldier and as a junior NCO that there was no substitute for absolute trust in another person's spoken word. In combat that translates to: When you tell me on the radio at 2:30 in the morning to do the following thing, and I've never met you before, never seen your face, all I know is your radio call sign, and you're telling me to do something and my life's in jeopardy, and I'm trusting you with my life, I have never, in thirty-six years, ever had that trust violated by an American Soldier. Ever. [56]

The future security of our country depends on a military trusted and respected by the citizenry. This faith is earned by years of honorable performance in times of great stress. It must be constantly reaffirmed by everything that we do.

Some public opinion polls indicate that the military has the highest reputation for integrity of any institution in America.

That reputation had to be earned; it was not bestowed upon the military. Each of us is responsible for ensuring that the military's reputation remains unsullied.

Whenever you do something that is not ethical, it becomes easier to repeat that unethical behavior. You begin to establish an internal standard of mediocrity. We are creatures of habit. Build the habit of doing the right thing, of striving for excellence.

What we are today was built day-by-day in the past. What we become in the future is determined by what we do today and tomorrow. To become, like Washington, a man of our word, we must, like Washington, live that way every day of our life.

Section VIII

HOME FRONT

ARMY WIVES

I know how to do anything—I'm a mom![1]

—Roseanne Barr

When I was a lieutenant, it was fashionable to say, "If the Army wanted you to have a wife, the Army would have issued you one." I often repeated that glib remark. But I knew then and I know now that I could never have made it through my Army career without the support of my wife. When I think of her I am often reminded of the words (paraphrased) of a popular song. She is my hero and is the wind beneath my wings.

I have left my wife, Jeannie, more than once. I left her for a year when I went to Colombia, South America. I was there during *La Violencia*, The Violence. In a ten-year period, almost 300,000 Colombians were killed. Later, in special forces, I was away on numerous exercises and missions lasting several months. I left her for a year when I went to Vietnam in 1967. She has experienced the loneliness and concern for my safety just as wives are feeling those emotions today

The day I left for Vietnam was the saddest day of my Army life. I was going to war again. I knew that she was concerned about me. She never forgot that I had been wounded three times in Korea, that I had spent almost eleven months recuperating in the hospital, and that my wounds continue to bother me today. While I tried to allay her fears, telling her that all that battalion commanders did was fly around in helicopters far above the battlefield, she was not convinced. She knew better. (I was wounded twice in Vietnam.)

Shortly before I left, I reminded her that she would be "in charge"—that no matter what problem arose she would have to solve it. It would take days for her to get in touch with me. I knew she knew that, but I felt that I needed to say it. I wanted her to know that I was depending on her as I had done so many times in the past. So were the kids. I had complete confidence in her. I knew she would come through like she always had.

And she came through. My wife is wonderful. She's special! She took care of everything just like military wives today are taking care of everything.

The poet Milton wrote, "They also serve who only stand and wait."[2] Our wives don't stand and wait when their husbands leave. They take on all the tasks that their husbands performed while continuing to do what the wives have always done.

The Family Readiness Group (FRG) is an organization that was not around during my active-duty days. The FRG is similar to a mini-business. Army wives, knowing the stresses and challenges that they face, particularly when their husbands are away, participate in the FRG. It offers support to the wife and her family by providing orientations about the various support agencies that are available on post and nearby. Members also provide moral support. In the 75th Ranger Regiment, with its three battalions widely dispersed on both the east and west coasts, the FRG brings the wives together annually for orientation, training, and bonding.[3]

Wives support the troops by planning and hosting social functions, looking after the children when the mother is ill, and visiting the sick and wounded. In this regard, they are following the example set by Martha Washington who, while spending each winter with the General (including the winter at Valley Forge) visited "sick soldiers in their huts, braving camp fever and the odors of decaying horses and open latrines."[4]

Army wives look after the kids—get them to school, help them with their homework, nurse them when they are sick, comfort them when they are sad, take them to soccer practice, clean the house, do the laundry. Time management experts need to talk to wives to learn about real efficiency.

When I asked Don Bowman, a retired Army Officer and close friend, to review what I had written, his comments were so eloquent that I asked his permission to include them in this essay. Here is what he had to say.

> What makes [Army wives] so special [is their] courage, tenacity of purpose, talent, imagination, management skills, ability to communicate, self-sacrifice, patriotism—yes, patriotism. Think what they are risking for their country!—and most of all, love. The risks they run which are completely out of their control require a special courage. This courage is not the adrenaline rush of battle or the intensity of a powerful team in action. This is the courage of the prisoner who may never be released from [confinement]. It is the acceptance of the risk of destruction of a part of [themselves] that [they] love more than [themselves] and not crumbling under that burden. A medal would not do them justice.
>
> It is a thing of great beauty, this force of character that strengthens them to do what they do. Our nation owes them a debt beyond price. Only with effort can we understand how clearly they understand the price they may have to pay.
>
> I have stood by the gravesites of my friends and stumbled to give some small measure of comfort too many times. But while there might be tears these women stand in composure and strength to buttress our courage and save the pain for the innermost recesses of their hearts.

I don't know how wives do all that they do. They just do it. We can't do without them. They are wonderful. They just keep on keeping on until their men come home. Army wives lead the way!

EDUCATE THE PUBLIC

It is not only the right but the duty of those who have served to make our voices heard, to speak for those still in uniform who cannot speak for themselves.[5]

—Ralph Peters, Author

When I moved to Columbus, Georgia, in 1990, I was chagrined at how little people knew about "the world situation." They were poorly informed about the Army, although Columbus is about ten miles from Fort Benning, the home of the Infantry. It is one of our biggest military installations and has a multimillion dollar impact on Columbus and the surrounding area. Why were they so poorly informed?

There were several reasons. There was little contact between the rank-and-file of the military and the civilians. There was little or nothing in the local newspaper about Fort Benning and the military in general. With the exception of a short commentary about the changes in the highest commands on post, the newspaper ignored the Soldiers. There was little or nothing about military history. Independence Day, Washington's Birthday, and other memorable dates were ignored except for the advertisements that heralded the sales event in the local retail outlets. Civilians seldom came to the post except on holidays such as the Fourth of July, when a significant number might come to the fort for the activities. The fireworks, in particular, were a drawing card.

There was a military-civilian council composed of business leaders and the senior military. The main Rotary Club always had as members the commanding general, the chief of staff, the post chaplain, the protocol officer, the public affairs officer, and the commandant of the Western Hemisphere Institute for Security Cooperation (formerly the School of the Americas). Each week, the Rotary Club also had a military guest—almost always an enlisted Soldier—from one of the units on post. I thought these contacts insufficient. The ordinary civilian and military did not mix. In fact, some civilians who had lived in Columbus forty to fifty years remarked to me that they had never spoken to a Soldier.

I thought the situation unconscionable; it had to be detrimental to the Army whose well-being is affected significantly by the way in which it is perceived by the citizenry. In Columbus, that citizenry knew little and seemed uninterested. It also meant that many civilians were missing the enjoyable experience of meeting and mixing with Soldiers. I wanted to do something and vowed to accept every request to speak to any local group.

I made myself available by showing interest in various organizations around town. My speaking to one group often resulted in an invitation to another. While I am far from an accomplished speaker, I was available and willing to fill the need for some program chair at a local gathering. As my willingness became known, the invitations from different civilian groups grew rapidly to about one a month. (I was speaking at least that often to military groups at Fort Benning.)

Being the Honorary Colonel of the 75th Ranger Regiment gave me additional "exposure." Colonel Ken Keen, who had been the regimental commander (RCO), invited me on two occasions to come to Colombia, South America, where he was the Chief of the U.S. Military Group. Colonel Craig Nixon, while he was the RCO, arranged a visit to Afghanistan for me. Colonel Paul LaCamera, who followed Nixon as the regimental commander, invited me to Iraq. These trips and others caused me to be invited to speak to other groups.

My speeches focused on military, historical, and patriotic themes. They were well received. I enjoyed myself and made many acquaintances that I would not have met but for my willingness to speak.

In addition to speaking, I began to write articles for the newspaper. Not being talented in this regard, writing was hard for me, but it was a labor of love. My articles, like my speeches, focused on military and patriotic themes. I did my best to remind anyone who read the essays that "freedom is not free," and that we owe a great debt to our military. There is no question that these initiatives resulted in a greater interest in and a much better understanding of our military.

Making oneself available—even actively seeking an invitation to speak—benefits our Army because of the better understanding that the speeches generate. Write something for the newspaper. Small town newspapers, in particular, are looking for sources of additional material. Get involved. You'll enjoy it and make a contribution to your Army at the same time.

DEVELOPING BETTER RELATIONS
WITH THE MEDIA

Four hostile newspapers are more to be feared than a thousand bayonets.[6]

—Napoleon

The ancients had a great advantage over us in that their armies were not trailed by a second army of pen-pushers.[7]

—Napoleon

Justice Oliver Wendell Holmes, Jr., said, "When a nation is at war, many things that might be said in time of peace are such a hindrance to its effort that their utterance will not be endured so long as men fight, and that no court could regard them as protected by any constitutional right."[8] Most commanders and members of the press will strongly disagree on where the line can be appropriately drawn.

Combat affects significantly what should be released to the media. Media representatives are aggressive in getting and reporting "the story," oftentimes in opposition to the military's belief that operational security may be affected unacceptably. Commanders who brief Soldiers at all levels prior to, during, and after combat operations will help prevent unauthorized disclosure of sensitive information.

In 1990, chairman of the Joint Chiefs of Staff, General Colin

Powell, sent this message to Desert Storm commanders, "The media aspects of military operations are important, will get national attention, and warrant your personal attention."[9] His advice is appropriate today and in the future.

General Norman Schwarzkopf directed his Desert Storm commanders to "make sure your subordinates are well briefed on the mission and their role in making a successful public affairs program work."[10]

Dr. Douglas Johnson, a professor at the U.S. Army War College, whom I first met when he was a cadet candidate at the U.S. Military Academy Preparatory School where I was the training officer, expressed the importance of good media relations saying:

> We cannot any longer simply view the media as [an often uninformed perhaps unfriendly group.] They are now a frontline weapon in the war of ideas. Any opportunity we have to set the truth before them or a legitimately inquiring public must be seized upon and pursued in a professional manner knowing that in doing so we are wielding a weapon that can cause death and destruction of the will as much as of the body.[11]

To prepare for the media pressure in combat, former Army chief of staff General Carl E. Vuono recommended that combat training centers include media play in exercises.[12] Injecting media play is a good way to prepare participants at all levels for the real-life battlefield. Real reporters or role-playing individuals can add realism by asking questions that would be asked if the situation were real. You can prepare your officers and enlisted men to withstand these pressures by providing them with answers to the most likely questions before the exercise begins. Newsletter No. 92-7, "Media and the Tactical Commander," prepared by the Center for Army Lessons Learned, Fort Leavenworth, Kansas, has some very helpful suggestions.

I observed many tactical exercises conducted by the 75th

Ranger Regiment in which media play was a significant part. On occasion, the media representatives were "real." On others, Rangers or their wives portrayed them. All, regardless of whether real or "make-believe," were usually very aggressive, some to the point of being obnoxious and obstreperous. I marveled as the young Rangers—both commissioned and enlisted—reacted coolly to this extreme harassment. The preparation they had received prior to the exercise stood them in good stead.

Inform and orient your Soldiers on how they should conduct themselves with the press. Prepare them for many of the questions that will be asked. Emphasize those things that they should not discuss for reasons of security. Soldiers need some guidance in how to respond to the media representatives. Be truthful; "volunteer nothing; tell only what you know first hand" are good guidelines for Soldiers. Remind them to keep classified information to themselves.

Since there are sufficient rules as to what information should be classified whether in war or peace, this essay focuses primarily on developing good media relations in an environment in which national security is not a significant consideration.

Good relations can be built only on a foundation of trust and respect. Commanders would do well to foster this environment. Such a relationship can be invaluable if a death, a serious accident, or some other newsworthy event occurs—particularly if it might ultimately reflect unfavorably on the Army and you. If such a circumstance arises, being proactive and going to the media with the "news" can prove to be beneficial. By providing all appropriate information and promising to keep them informed through your public affairs officer (PAO) you may be able to "head off" inaccurate and damaging conjecture.

Both the military and the media realize the difficulty of establishing good relations. Dusty Nix, associate editor of the *Columbus Ledger-Enquirer* wrote, "It's sometimes hard for a free country's military and its journalists to remember that they're on the same side.… A competent free press is an ally, not an enemy."[13] Many commanders will contradict or at least question that last statement. They have either been "burned" by the media or know of someone who has. Regardless of your personal mindset a continuing effort to build good relations with the media can pay big dividends.

Be proactive. Get to know representatives of the local media—the newspapers, radio, and TV. Meet with them periodically. Invite them to activities you would like for them to see and, you hope, events that they may publicize. Taking the initiative—informing your media contacts before they come to you—helps orient their thoughts based on the accurate information that you have provided rather than what they may have read in some news wire report.

> Let the media do your work for you. Conduct a positive, planned, and even aggressive program of letting the media see your accomplishments. Admit your mistakes, and really get to know the reporters with whom you deal with on a regular basis. That's my prescription for a successful public relations program, provided your command is doing a good job in the first place.[14]

The reporter has a job to do just like you. His job is to get the story. In an article for *Proceedings*, Commander Marcus E. Woodring wrote, "If the media can get a document through the freedom of information act system, do not add to your paperwork—simply release the information via your public affairs shop. Honesty and cooperation before the onset of difficult situations will pay big dividends later."[15] If you have established a good relationship with the media, they are more likely to cooperate with you than if you have shunned and hindered them in their information gathering.

Many reporters—probably most of them—have little or no knowledge of the military. They know little or nothing about the subject on which they are writing. They have little or no knowledge about the units—squads, platoons, companies, and brigades—that compose our Army. They are uninformed about the decorations that are awarded. They know nothing about tactics and doctrine. Because many of the media lack knowledge about the military, providing a "press release" or a fact sheet as a follow-up to any announcement can be helpful.

We can accomplish a lot by trying to educate media representatives on some of the more mundane (to us) aspects of our profession. Offer to help them with whatever they are writing. While it is doubtful that they will let you proofread it before publication, the proffered help, if accepted, may result in an accurate report and may show the military—you and your unit—in a better light.

Never lie to or cover up with the press. Steamrollering or devious behavior can lead to a "feeding frenzy" by the press. They will keep investigating until they have what they believe are the facts. If what you have told them is not the truth, you will look bad, and the situation will be worse when they discover the truth—and they will discover the truth. If you have provided incorrect information, the sooner you correct it, the better. "Maximum disclosure with minimum delay"[16] is a good guide.

Appointing your most junior and inexperienced officer to be your PAO is often a mistake. Once you select your PAO, brief him thoroughly on what you expect. If he is experienced, ask him for his suggestions as to how you might support him in his job.

In building good relations, your PAO is a key player. Unfortunately, he is often left out of the loop. As a result, your key representative may find himself on the hot seat if something occurs that can be detrimental to your unit and our Army. Although not cognizant of all the facts and your views, he will have to deal with the bad press that may result.[17]

The media are a fact of life. Prepare; be cooperative. They can be helpful; they can be extremely harmful. The outcome, in large measure, depends on you.

Honoring Veterans

We owe you everything! America gave us our freedom!
We will never forget you![18]

—Mayor, Trois Ponts, Belgium

I have great admiration for our veterans and our active duty Soldiers. I have always tended to merge the two. I never miss an opportunity to praise them and express my thanks for what they are doing for all of us. In fact, I seek the opportunity and volunteer to speak to civic and social groups, military ceremonies, and informal gatherings. When I see a Soldier in a public place, if appropriate, I tell him how much I appreciate his service to our country. The thanks always hit a responsive chord, and the Soldier's face breaks into a wide grin as he stammers his appreciation for my comment. My words are especially meaningful to wives and parents whose contribution and sacrifice often go unrecognized.

I have been asked to speak at farewells prior to deployments, graduations, memorial ceremonies, and special holidays honoring Soldiers. I often begin with my favorite story about our greatest American, George Washington. It helps explain how I feel about Soldiers. (When I say "Soldier," I usually mean all military.)

The Continental Army, the Army that gave us our freedom, was plagued by one-year enlistments. Because the majority had joined December 31, 1775, Washington faced that reality December 30, 1776. There were six inches of snow on the ground. The cold was severe—more severe than the men could remember. The ranks were thinner; so were the men. They were underfed and ill-clothed. Some were barefoot in the snow. They had endured grinding hardship and were ready to go home. Only one more day!

As the men formed on the drumbeat, they saw Washington standing quietly to the side, alone and on his horse. They knew something was up. Washington rode to the center of the line and began to speak slowly. He congratulated them on their recent victory at Trenton. He told them why they, the veterans, were still needed. When he finished, he rode to the side. The regimental officers called on the volunteers to step forward. *Not one man moved!*

Washington wheeled his horse, rode to the center of the line in front of his embarrassed Soldiers, and began to speak again.

> You have done all I asked you to do, and more than could be reasonably expected; but your country is at stake, your wives, your houses, and all that you hold dear. You have worn yourselves out with fatigues and hardships, but we know not how to spare you. If you will consent to stay only one month longer, you will render that service to the cause of liberty, and to your country, which you probably never can do under any other circumstance. [What we are facing today is] the crisis which is to decide our destiny.

Washington rode to the side again. Finally, one lone veteran stepped forward, saying that he would not go home when the Army needed him. After a moment, all who were able to move stepped forward![19]

Who were these men who gave us our freedom?

Without their courage, their dedication, their sacrifice, and their superhuman effort, the American Revolution would have been lost. Thank God for them all!

Washington, also, was indispensable. He was the inspiration and glue that held the Continental Army together. If the fate of our country had to rest on the shoulders of one man, that man had to be George Washington.

I'm reminded of a passage in the Bible—Isaiah 6:8: "And I heard the voice of the Lord saying, 'Whom shall I send, and who will go for us?' Then I said, 'Here I am! Send me.'"

When America asked "Whom shall I send?" George Washington and his Soldiers answered, "Send me. I am here."

All our Soldiers today are volunteers. They have said again and again, "Send me. I am here."

In the play, *Ben Franklin in Paris*, Franklin wonders about America 200 years hence. Will Americans take freedom for granted because it was handed to them when they were born? Will they be willing to step forward, to sacrifice everything to keep that freedom?[20]

Mr. Franklin, you need not have worried. Americans have always stepped forward. They have always said, "Send me. I am here."

On the first anniversary of the World War I (WWI) truce, President Woodrow Wilson issued a proclamation eulogizing fallen allied Soldiers and referred to November 11 as Armistice Day. The name was changed in 1954 to Veterans Day to recognize its broadened significance.[21]

WWI was the "Great War," the "war to end all wars." Americans went to France singing, "And we won't be back 'til it's over over there!" Victory would make the world "safe for democracy."

I remember the first time I heard about that war. I was about five or six. I was walking with my dad to the drugstore after church to get the Sunday papers. We met a man on crutches; he was an amputee—the first I had ever seen. He was holding a red paper flower.

My dad gave the man some money and took one of the flowers. When I asked Daddy what it was, he explained that it symbolized the poppies in Europe where the war had been fought. The man was a veteran, someone who had been in the war. He had been wounded and had lost his leg. That began to bring home to me the reality of war.

Later, in grade school, I remember our principal, Mr. Frank Kelly, coming into our classroom to talk a few moments about Armistice Day. He told us what it meant and recounted the coincidence of the war ending at the eleventh hour of the eleventh day of the eleventh month in 1918. In a few moments, we would observe a minute of silence. Then the siren on the top of the local water tower would sound in recognition of the significance of the day.

Years later in junior high school, we would study John Mc-Crae's sad, moving poem, "In Flanders Fields." This famous poem was about the Allied dead buried in Belgium.

> *To you from failing hands we throw the torch;*
> *Be yours to hold it high.*
> *If ye break faith with us who die*
> *We shall not sleep, though poppies grow*
> *In Flanders fields.*

It had a great impact on me. The teacher said that the headstones in those cemeteries were almost as numerous as the poppies that grew "between the crosses, row on row." Many years later, I toured those battlefields and visited the cemeteries that were the final resting-place for thousands and thousands of young men killed in battle. And, yes, the crosses seemed almost as numerous as the poppies that I saw along the way.

We observe Veterans Day each year to honor those who have answered the call, "Send me! I am here!" We honor our veterans. We remember them for what they did. We observe Memorial Day to honor those who have given their lives in the defense of this great country. We honor those who still serve.

We should honor their wives, also. They look after the kids, they run the household, they organize family support groups, and they do the myriad things that wives and mothers always do, plus all the things the daddies did. They are the wind beneath our wings.

And now, we have women—mothers—who serve.

I like going to Fort Benning, the home of the Infantry. There I am privileged to walk among giants, real heroes, every day. They are not rock stars or movie actors who play at being heroes. Our Soldiers—both men and women—are the real things.

We live free today. We take for granted the freedom we have, seldom stopping to realize what it has cost. We live free because over a million Americans have given their lives on the battlefields. We live free because millions more have suffered wounds to win that freedom. We live free because thousands of young American men and women today are stationed in more than one hundred locations throughout the world. We live free because thousands more of America's finest stand ready to be deployed to any trouble spot in the world. And they will be deployed! They serve proudly and well. How fortunate we are!

Our service men and women, our veterans, and their families are a national treasure. We owe them everything. We need to let them know it.

Section IX

RACE AND GENDER

BLOOD'S COMMON COLOR

'Tout le Sang qui coule est rouge!'—*'All blood runs red.'*[1]

—Eugene Bullard, African American Combat Pilot, WWI

I remember the men in my Eighth Army Ranger Company. Most were volunteers from service units in Japan. They could have enjoyed a safe existence during the war if they had stayed where they were. However, they were among that breed of men of whom America has always had a plentiful supply—men who wanted a challenge, who wanted to be all they could be.

I remember the pride that I felt when I first saw them together. They came from many ethnic groups. There were WASPS (White Anglo-Saxon Protestants), African-Americans, Hispanics, German-Americans, Native Americans, Japanese-Americans, and Italian-Americans. I never thought of them as hyphenated Americans, and they never thought of themselves that way. They were Americans, and all that the word means.

All I cared about was what was behind their belt buckles and between their ears. Did they have the guts and brains to be Infantrymen and Rangers?

Although President Harry S. Truman banned segregation in the military forces in 1948 his directive had not been widely implemented by 1950. However, I didn't give it a thought when Wilbert Clanton and Allen Waters, both African-Americans, reported. Our company was the first integrated Ranger unit and one of the first integrated units in the Army. I knew the stereotype.

The perception in America was that African-Americans would not fight but somebody forgot to tell Clanton and Waters that.

Clanton's perpetual grin seemed to get bigger as the going got tougher. He was killed on Hill 205, November 26, 1950, as he charged a swarm of Chinese overrunning our position.

Waters was always serious. He was the BAR (Browning Automatic Rifle) man on a patrol one day. As we stopped for a brief respite, five North Koreans jumped up and ran away from us. In a blink of an eye, Waters cut four of them down. Clanton and Waters, like the other Rangers, gave me all I asked and then some. Their blood was the same color, their performance what you expect from Americans.

Today, our Armed Forces contain 17 percent blacks (12.2 percent of our total population). Hispanics are 9 percent of the total force (14.2 percent of our population). Other minorities compose 7 percent of the total force (12.2 percent of total population)[2] As a practical matter, if for no other reason, we need to be "color-blind" where our Soldiers are concerned. Otherwise, we may do an injustice to some of them and fail to tap the great talent in these minorities.

In Vietnam, we saw a higher percentage of African-Americans serving in an American war. During 1965–69, "blacks, who formed 11 percent of the American population, made up 12.6 percent of the Soldiers in Vietnam.[3]

There were many African-Americans, Hispanic, and other minorities in my battalion in Vietnam—many in key leadership positions as both noncommissioned and commissioned officers. I was fortunate to have all of them. So was America.

FRATERNIZATION HURTS COMBAT EFFECTIVENESS

---

*Relationships are ... forbidden if they will have an ad-
verse impact on unit morale or the ability of a command
to accomplish its mission.*[4]

—SFC Connie E. Dickey

In 1998, Secretary of Defense William Cohen issued a policy "prohibiting fraternization between officers and enlisted personnel, active or reserve, which applies to all military branches."[5]

As could be expected, some Soldiers objected. "I think what you do on your off-duty time, as long as it's not affecting the Army, is your own business." "I don't feel like it's any of their business. What we do off duty should be our choice.... Here we are fighting to defend the Constitution and rights of the free world, but we don't have those rights ourselves."[6]

By being in the military, we give up certain freedoms. We cannot go to certain places; they are off limits. We cannot dress in certain ways. We are told how to cut our hair. Some tattoos are against the rules. If we are a member of a "ready" battalion or other unit, we may be restricted to a certain distance (time) from our home station.

Some Soldiers chafe under these restrictions, seeing them as an infringement on their personal freedoms. However, the rules have demonstrated through the years their worth in improving or maintaining combat effectiveness. Consequently, the Soldier and the unit benefit by the cohesiveness and sameness that ensues from these restrictions.

Familiarity between any commander or supervisor and a subordinate makes it almost impossible to avoid at least the appearance of favoritism. This difficulty exists whether the relationship is male to female or female to male. It may be impossible to avoid the perception by others of favoritism when "duty" or dangerous details are assigned. Favoritism causes jealousy and hostility and undermines discipline. Because of this concern, some businesses find sexual relationships hurtful to operations and prohibit those relationships.

Some marriages of an officer and enlisted Soldier that were in existence when the ruling was issued were "grandfathered." The reports of "no problem" with current marriages may be accurate. However, if both spouses are in the same unit, there probably will be a suspicion of favoritism.

The Uniform Code of Military Justice (UCMJ) governs the military. It "is a comprehensive federal statute that established essential procedures, policies, and penalties for the military justice system."[7] Article 134 is a "general" article and applies to anything prejudicial to good order and discipline not covered by other articles.[8] Is the article too general or nebulous to be of use? Are there some guidelines for relationships? Is it difficult to decide when a relationship might be prejudicial to good order and discipline? The difficulty diminishes or disappears if you keep foremost in your mind why we have an Army. We have an Army to fight our wars. Our Army has to be ready—always—to take to the battlefield. Using that as the baseline makes it relatively easy to decide if a relationship is or could be detrimental to good order and discipline.

If it would be detrimental to combat effectiveness, the relationship should be unacceptable in the Army. Using that criterion—is it detrimental to combat effectiveness? —would clarify the murkiness that surrounds this contentious issue.

GENDER INTEGRATION OF THE ARMY

Their maternal ancestors walked across the Great Plains on bare feet. Why the hell can't they serve in the military? Of course they can.[9]

—Major General John LeMoyne

Military tasks that used to be classified as one-man jobs are now reclassified as two-man jobs to make it easier for women to succeed.[10]

—Mona Charen, Reporter

Our Army depends on female Soldiers. They are more than "fillers." In the early '70s when the Army went all-volunteer, females helped the Army continue as a viable component of our military power. In 1980, 50 percent of the male Soldiers were Category IV. To offset this drop in quality, more women were permitted to serve.[11] Women comprise about 15 percent of today's Army. The roles have changed significantly from purely administrative, behind-the-desk jobs to caliber .50 machine gunners on vehicles. These female Soldiers are acquitting themselves well.

After retiring from the Army in 1971, I became the National Programs Coordinator for Outward Bound, an internationally acclaimed organization that focused on developing confidence and teamwork. Two years later, I established Discovery, Inc., a program exemplified by its slogan, "Personal Growth through Safe Adventure." Convinced that females were constrained by false societal restrictions, my staff and I worked diligently to overcome those inhibitions. We were not disappointed; young girls and women blossomed in the supportive "You can do it!" environment. We had females on the staff. At times, as many as half of the instructors were female.

There have been major studies to determine whether gender integration of the military is appropriate. The 1992 "Report to the President: Women in Combat" prepared by the Presidential Commission on the Assignment of Women in the Armed Forces proposed greater assimilation.

The 1997 Federal Advisory Committee on Gender-Integrated Training and Readiness Issues (the Kassebaum Committee)[12] and the 1999 Congressional Commission on Military Training and Gender-Related Issues strongly supported a gender-integrated military. Both stressed the importance of basic training but disagreed on gender integration during basic. Kassebaum vigorously opposed it;[13] the Congressional Committee recommended, "Entry level training may be gender-specific as necessary."[14]

Gender integration is a volatile subject that sometimes stimulates heated arguments. Unfortunately, many of those discussing this divisive subject have little or no first hand knowledge of the subject. (I, for one, must admit that I have no experience in working with female Soldiers. However, my two years with Outward Bound and 11 years with Discovery indicate that except in the areas of physical strength and stamina, females are as capable as men. There are, of course, some women who can outdo most men in these categories.)

Often those who discuss the subject use the term "combat" to mean any situation in which an individual is exposed to the possibility, no matter how remote, of being killed by the enemy. There is a world of difference between serving in a unit not involved in direct combat—closing with and killing the enemy—and the brutal conditions facing the Infantryman in the rifle squad. James Webb, a former Marine Infantryman and secretary of the navy, who, because of his service as a Marine "grunt" knows that difference, expressed it so well when he said, "I know nothing about air or naval warfare, but I know about being an Infantryman—and it is no job for women."[15] On the other hand, Secretary of Defense Les Aspin described the proposed changes in rules concerning women as "a range of new opportunities for women."[16]

Gender integration is the topic of numerous books and articles. Stephanie Gutmann provides an excellent discussion in her *The Kinder, Gentler Military: Can America's Gender-neutral Fighting Force Still Win Wars?* (2000). She concludes that the impact has been detrimental. Two earlier books that have similar conclusions, both written by Brian Mitchell, are *Weak Link: The Feminization of the American Military* (1989) and *Women in the Military: Flirting with Disaster* (1998). These authors, of course, could not consider the experiences of women in Desert Shield/Desert Storm, Operation Enduring Freedom (Afghanistan), and Operation Iraqi Freedom (Iraq).

Many pundits support the opposite position. They generally base their arguments on equality—anyone physically able and otherwise qualified should be allowed to serve anywhere.

One of the most influential groups lobbying to make the military forces gender-neutral is the Defense Advisory Committee on Women in the Services (DACOWITS). The Center for Military Readiness (CMR) strongly opposes DACOWITS describing it as "a tax-funded power base for civilian feminists and social engineers who want to transform the culture of the military."[17] DACOWITS wants to re-define the definition of "Direct Ground Combat" which now prohibits women from serving in certain units.[18] If successful, the CMR believes the change would have a deleterious effect on combat readiness.[19]

There is widespread, strong disagreement about how much gender integration is appropriate. The most often cited objection to expanding the roles of women is their physical ability.[20] Another is pregnancy. Pregnancies may cause a significant disruption in a unit preparing for deployment or already deployed. (Proponents of greater integration do not usually discuss pregnancy.) Less than 1 percent of the Army is pregnant at any one time. However, in some specialties the ratio can rise to 10 percent of the unit. This problem would be significantly diminished if all women would adhere to a birth control regimen as part of the requirement for deployment.[21] Pregnant women are not deployable.

Deployment of the heads of single-parent families is another problem. Since females comprise the major portion of single parents in the Army, the difficulty arises most often with females. However, there are many males who are the spouses left behind. They face the same difficulties faced by wives who are left behind. Requiring that single parents make arrangements for their children in the event the parents are deployed helps alleviate some of the detrimental effects.

Male-female relationships have been, are, and will continue to cause significant problems in integrated units. Managing these difficulties is a leader's responsibility.[22] The commander is responsible for everything his Soldiers do both on and off duty! However, just by recognizing that responsibility does not make it any easier to accomplish.

Do females want to be assigned to units currently closed to them? Majors Kim Field and John Nagl surveyed USMA female cadets concerning their assignment preferences. Field and Nagl are West Point graduates with high educational credentials and military experience. Field (female) was a Military police platoon leader in Desert Storm. Nagl was a tank platoon leader in the same conflict.

Of the 112 female cadets surveyed, 30 percent would choose a combat arms branch currently closed to them if given the opportunity. Four cadets selected Infantry with the remainder choosing armor and field artillery, "branches less associated with difficult field conditions, physically arduous tasks, and hand-to-hand fighting."[23] Of the approximately 400 female officers that the Army acquires each year, 133 would choose a military occupational specialty now closed to them. Of that number, only five would choose the Infantry.

Gender integration is expanding inexorably. In Iraq and Afghanistan, females man (certainly an interesting verb when used here) machine guns on convoy duty and perform other "direct, close combat" functions; they are exposed to as much as any male doing the same task. Command Sergeant Major Greg Birch, a former CSM of the 75th Ranger Regiment and a veteran of twenty-nine years of Special Operations Forces experience in peace and war, had this to say:

> I went on patrol in Baghdad this summer with an MP (military police) Company. My vehicle commander was a female corporal, who was one of the finest, most intuitive, tactically switched on leaders I have met in twenty-nine years of service. Don't count them out because of the 'male only' mindset.[24]

Currently (2006) the Army War College is studying "Women in Combat." While not yet completed, there are some thoughts that are emerging. Women are being killed or seriously wounded fairly often—at a rate seldom if ever mentioned several years ago when the push for gender integration became quite strong. Surprisingly to some, the forecast outcry over such a happening has not occurred; perhaps it is because the women are volunteers. Students in the 2006 class at the War College generally feel that if women want to sign up to fight in direct, close combat, they should be allowed to do so and then should be evaluated on their performance—just like the men. To date, there is every indication that both female officers and enlisted Soldiers have performed as well as or better than their male counterparts perhaps as a result of their having to "prove" themselves. Physical differences matter some but not as much in Iraq as in previous major conflicts. Restricting women from assignment to units that have a remote possibility of coming in direct contact with the enemy is impossible. There are no such units in Iraq. Modesty seems to have gone out the window. And something that should be evident to all—we cannot man the force without them![25]

"Lessons learned" in Iraq and Afghanistan are not necessarily applicable to all scenarios. As bloody and as physically and emotionally demanding as they are at times, they are not the same as the horrendous pressures experienced by Infantrymen in WWII, Korea, and Vietnam. However, the two conflicts in which we are now engaged certainly indicate that some restrictions placed on female assignments in the past may be inappropriate.

What are the proper roles for females? Should there be any restrictions? If so, how can they be determined? How can we establish what the correct balance is? A standards-based test permitting women to enter any branch whose standards—physical, mental, and psychological—they could meet could provide valuable insights.[26] The Army could establish and publish requirements for all the occupational specialties now closed to women. (These standards would be applied to men, also.) Standards required by armor, Infantry, certain artillery, and special operations forces now closed to women would not be lowered.

Standards-based requirements pose potential costs. They include disruptions in unit effectiveness associated with pregnancy, the temporary turmoil caused by policy changes, the belief that the military ethos will be degraded, and the diminishing of the vital cohesion in combat units if women are included.[27] These outcomes, if they occur, degrade combat effectiveness.[28]

A well-constructed and implemented test could help determine the validity of such concerns. The Army on its own volition should conduct a fair test before being forced to integrate completely at a time and in a manner not of the Army's choosing.[29] The test would include females serving in any specialty where they can meet physical and other requirements[30] and for which they volunteer. Because of the small number of women involved, the test would not impact significantly on combat readiness. (Special Operations Forces could be excluded from the test because of the importance and immediacy of their mission.)

Unfortunately, it will be extremely difficult if not impossible to develop an easily administered test that evaluates the capability, both physical and emotional, of an individual to withstand the stress of sustained Infantry direct combat. The test must not be affected by "political correctness" and the desire to appear "fair." Otherwise combat effectiveness may be diminished and increased casualties result. The current physical fitness standards for the physical training test are a case in point. They were determined in part by the desire to reward "equal points for equal effort" and avoid the "unfair" label by females. It is both "age normed" and "gender normed." Females have to complete fewer repetitions of an exercise than men to achieve a 100 percent rating in that event. Battlefield circumstances are not "normed."

Although only bloody, extended ground combat could validate any assessment, a test properly developed, conducted, and analyzed could do much to settle this contentious issue.

When considering any significant change in our Army, we should heed the caution expressed by then Secretary of Defense Dick Cheney on March 26, 1992:

> [I]t's important for us to remember that what we are asked to do here in the Department of Defense is to defend the nation. *The only reason we exist is to be prepared to fight and win wars* [emphasis added]. We're not a social welfare agency. We're not an agency that's operated on the basis of what makes sense for some member of Congress' concern back home in the district. This is a military organization. Decisions we make have to be taken based upon those kinds of considerations and only those kinds of considerations.[31]

Women are vital to a successful Army. As the ongoing study at the Army War College indicates, they are doing as well as the men if not better. We must make best use of this valuable resource. Deciding how that goal is to be accomplished will take insight based on firsthand experience, mental astuteness, an open mind, and tremendous moral courage.

Section X

TACTICS AND STRATEGY

ARE WE READY?

There is nothing so likely to produce peace as to be well prepared to meet the enemy. [1]

—George Washington

In his campaign for president, Governor George W. Bush criticized the Clinton Administration for its neglect of the military stating that it was overextended and understrength. Vice President Gore countered that our military was the best trained and equipped in the world. Both of their superficial appraisals were correct. There is no conventional force on the scene that can challenge our military. On the other hand, almost all nonpartisan, informed observers would say that our forces are over committed and stretched very thin. The asymmetric warfare waged by insurgents in Afghanistan and Iraq is a significant challenge to our capability. The Army has major problems, which need to be addressed immediately. The Army itself can correct some of these problems by internal changes; others will require congressional support.

Although Bush and Gore were criticized for "injecting" this issue into politics, there is no concern more important than national security. It deserves incisive examination by leaders who put their political agenda behind them and analyze the status of the military to determine what is best for America. In the words of Congressman Floyd D. Spence:

America faces a fundamental choice: either we accept our role as the sole global superpower and provide our military with the resources required to meet
this role, or we decline this responsibility and retreat
from our position as leader of the free world. [2]

Writing in the January 2001 issue of the *Armed Forces Journal
International*, Senator Pat Roberts (R-KS) and Senator Max Cleland (D-GA) began a series of dialogues with the goal of initiat-
ing "a serious debate in the U.S. Senate on the proper role of our
country in the post-Cold War world." They believed "that such a
process is absolutely necessary for us to garner the bipartisan con-
sensus on national security policy that our nation so badly needs,
but has been lacking since the fall of the Soviet empire."[3]

Vice President Dick Cheney said in January 2001:

Many Americans seem to think that simply because the communist Soviet Union no longer exists,
the world is as safe as Beaver Cleaver's neighbor-
hood. This, of course, ignores three facts: 1) Dozens of countries have nuclear weapons that could
take out millions of people with the turn of a key.
2) Leaders of several countries (e.g. North Korea,
Iraq, Iran, Libya, Lebanon and perhaps China and
Russia) would love to see the U.S. and its people
blown to pieces and, most importantly 3) The U.S.
has the greatest collection of human, economic,
natural and technological resources anywhere on
Earth, making it the greatest natural target for military aggression.[4]

General Charles C. Krulak, USMC Retired, former commandant, USMC, while praising the caliber of the individual Soldier,
airman, sailor, and Marine, had this to say:

There is a shortage of spare parts for almost all of our systems, a lack of flight hours for aircraft, a lack of steaming hours for our ships, a lack of tank miles for our rolling stock, a lack of training ammunition. All of this is causing combat readiness to decline. Not necessarily on the "tip of the spear" forces, but for all those that would follow and fight, the readiness levels are absolutely below what they were eight years ago.[5]

When the question is asked, "Are we ready?" an immediate follow-on question is, "Ready for what?"

In the fall of 1993, Les Aspin, then President Clinton's secretary of defense, said that the United States should:

Simultaneously be capable of meeting the following challenges: fighting a Persian Gulf War-sized regional conflict; participating in a similar conflict where U.S. allies are using their own considerable ground forces (say, in Korea); undertaking naval air action in America's own hemisphere or an operation comparable to that which ousted Panamanian dictator Manuel Antonio Noriega in 1989; carrying out a humanitarian relief operation the size of the Kurdish rescue; maintaining enough land and air forces for a 'rotation base' able to sustain the initial Desert Storm-sized deployment; maintaining a 'foundation block' consisting of everything from strategic nuclear forces for defending U.S. territory to research and development to procurement to operations and training.[6]

Secretary Aspin's list included a lot more than present mission requirements. Currently (2007), the United States is having great difficulty meeting the rotational requirements for Iraq and Afghanistan. It is highly doubtful that we could participate in a significant conflict in Korea and undertake "naval air action in America's own hemisphere or an operation comparable to that which ousted Panamanian dictator Manuel Antonio Noriega." (The United States did not hesitate to mount a significant humanitarian effort during the tsumani disaster in the Indian Ocean.)

The former Director of the CIA, George Tenet,[7] said that terrorism is the greatest threat that the United States faces, something that Aspin did not mention. The Afghanistan and Iraq conflicts underscore the accuracy of Tenet's statement.

During Desert Shield/Desert Storm in 1990–91, the United States committed over 530,000 people to the theater of operations.[8] The coalition forces added more than 224,000. The U.S. force structure in the Middle East contained seven Army divisions, four brigade-size forces, and two Marine divisions. About half of the total Army capability was committed. The navy, Marines, and air force committed from 25 to 100 percent of different categories of forces. The Army currently has ten divisions.[9] Consequently, the Army would be required to commit almost its total capability to fulfill one Desert Storm-sized requirement.

One may argue about the appropriateness of the requirements established by President Clinton. However, if we consider the current wars in Afghanistan and Iraq, the most recent flare-up in Korea (which soon became dormant), the deployments to Haiti, the Middle East, Bosnia, Kosovo, the continuing deployment to the Sinai and the many other commitments, the requirements do not seem so far-fetched.

General John Shalikashvilli, former chairman, Joint Chiefs of Staff, stated in 1994 that he believed the force structure was sufficient. He stressed, "Every little piece of the force has to be able to hit on all twelve cylinders."[10] Since he made that statement, the force structure has been further downsized. Simple, elementary school arithmetic makes it clear: the current Force structure is insufficient for the stated requirements! For whatever reason, the former Administration placed our security in jeopardy. President George W. Bush has done little to alleviate the disparity between requirements and force structure.

General Hugh Shelton, former chairman, Joint Chiefs of Staff, has said that we have insufficient forces to support our national strategy. He stated that the use of major resources including those needed for modernization or near-term readiness is not sustainable. He continued,

> I fully realize that today America has no peer competitor. However, we must remain alert to the possibility of peer competition in the future. There is also the potential for the emergence of a single power or combination of forces that could mount a focused campaign against U.S. interests. In our business, we need to keep in mind that this environment could develop a lot sooner than any of us might think.[11]

It should be obvious to any open-minded, thinking observer that our Army forces are insufficient to meet the continuing requirements for the conflicts in Afghanistan and Iraq. Unfortunately, the lengthy mobilizations of guard and reserve forces and the repetitive deployments of the active Army have not made it clear to the Administration (or it refuses to face facts) that the Army is stretched dangerously thin. When, and if it does, it will take months, if not years, to meet requirements. The current Administration, like previous ones, is placing our national security in jeopardy.

THE CLOCK IS TICKING

Be Prepared!

—Boy Scout Motto

It is a doctrine of war not to assume the enemy will not come, but rather to rely on one's readiness to meet him; not to presume that he will not attack, but rather to make one's self invincible.[12]

—Sun Tzu, Chinese Master Strategist

Let him who desires peace, prepare for war.[13]

—Vegetius, Roman Author

The Korean War started on June 25, 1950. When the North Korean Army attacked across the 38th parallel, the inadequately equipped and trained South Korean Army was rapidly thrown into headlong retreat. President Harry S. Truman quickly authorized the use of our military forces stationed in Japan. Task Force Smith, ground troops from the 24th Infantry Division, were the first to go but were insufficient to slow the advancing North Koreans.

The Eighth U.S. Army on occupation duty in Japan rushed other troops to Korea as rapidly as possible. These units, like the 24th Infantry Division, were short personnel, inadequately equipped, and insufficiently trained. Many Soldiers became casualties as they tried to stem the North Korean onslaught.

The Eighth Army was woefully unprepared for war. Budget cuts enacted by Secretary of Defense Louis Johnson had forced all the services to cut personnel, training, and equipment.

Author Uzal W. Ent, writing in the June 2000 *Military History*, described the lack of readiness. Eighth Army divisions had been cut from three regiments to two, regiments were short one of three battalions, and battalions were short one company. Artillery battalions were short a battery and one-third of their guns. Units were unable to train—fight—according to doctrine. In the entire Eighth Army there were twenty-one recoilless rifles of the 226 authorized. Radios, batteries, mortars, spare parts, grenades, and other ammunition were in short supply. Many of the 2.36 rockets were duds. The 24th Infantry Division, the first sent to Korea, was drastically under strength. Approximately 4,500 officers and men were stripped from other divisions and sent to the 24th. It was still almost 3,500 men short of its authorized strength.[14] The fighting troops were in the shortest supply. There were plenty of support troops but not enough riflemen.[15]

Considering only rifle companies, the division was operating at less than one regiment strength. Based on three regiments per division with three battalions per regiment with three companies per battalion, a full-strength division would have twenty-seven rifle companies. The understrength division consisting of two regiments of two battalions of two companies each would have a total of eight rifle companies. Eight companies are one short of the nine in the "standard" regiment. Considering that these companies themselves were short personnel, we see how woefully understrength a division could be.[16]

Of 18,000 jeeps in Japan, 10,000 were unserviceable. Only 4,471 two-and-a-half-ton trucks of 17,780 were serviceable. Some vehicles were towed onto the ships to be taken to Korea. In February 1950, an Eighth Army inspection found 90 percent of the 34th Infantry Regiment's weapons "unfit for training." The regiment went to Korea with these weapons.[17]

The unpreparedness was not just in the shortage of equipment and the numbers of men. The training and readiness for war was lamentable.[18] The Army had been civilianized. This unhappy result can be blamed in part on the Doolittle Board established after WWII to look into the "caste system" in the Army. Many of the complaints from the Soldiers who appeared before the Board or whose letters were reviewed by that body were justified. The Board could have recommended steps to improve the officer selection and qualification procedures but, instead, chose the "easier" way—civilianize the Army, make it more "democratic." Discipline became poor, or almost nonexistent particularly in service units.

Some blame can be placed on the Doolittle Board if one wants a scapegoat. However, while difficult, discipline could have been improved tremendously by the focused effort of the junior officers and noncommissioned officers; unfortunately many if not most of them were the problem. The war (WWII) was over. The world was at peace although an uneasy one. Why not sit back and take it easy? That is what had happened in the Eighth Army. The results were to be expected.[19] American forces in Japan unashamedly became accustomed to the sloth of occupation life.[20]

Despite the shortages in men, money, and materiel, training could have been focused on the tactics and techniques of the individual Soldier (TTIS), immediate action drills, and physical fitness. Combat readiness could have been achieved and maintained. Money and great training areas can contribute mightily. However, it requires little or no money and limited training areas to learn fire and maneuver, camouflage, map reading, marksmanship, use of supporting fires, scouting and patrolling and the myriad other skills necessary to be combat ready.

An effective physical training program requires absolutely no money. It only requires a readiness-driven leader. Despite the current emphasis placed on Indian clubs, dumbbells, and other equipment by the Army Physical Fitness School, calisthenics, road runs, and grass drills, when properly used, can do the job without unacceptable injuries. The training program of the Eighth Army Ranger Company in Korea focused on those activities and changed soft, inadequately trained Soldiers into the most physically fit condition of their lives. They were "tigers." There was no equipment available except pull-up bars; none was needed.

Retreating in front of the North Korean Army, Soldiers threw away canteens, helmets, and other pieces of equipment as they struggled to move through the rice paddies. They discarded weapons—anything and everything that hindered their withdrawal.[21] Soldiers were not fit. The soft life and little or no physical training had made them unfit for the rigors of the tough terrain and the 110-degree heat.[22]

The Soldiers of the Eighth Army suffered from what I consider almost criminal malfeasance on the parts of their leaders. The Soldiers were not disciplined—that characteristic that must be ingrained by rigorous adherence to the highest standard of performance over and over again until doing things right becomes second nature. Disciplined troops will react properly instantaneously; proper action will become second nature.

The Eighth Army, as individual Soldiers and collectively, was not prepared. The failure, as is almost always the case, was not the fault of the men. It was the fault of leadership. The American Soldier, when properly trained, equipped, and led, is the equal of or better than any other Soldier.

The "clock is always ticking." The Army's job is to kill the enemies of our country. We must always be prepared. That is every leader's primary responsibility.

OUR ENEMIES ARE WILLING TO ACCEPT TREMENDOUS CASUALTIES

You will kill ten of our men and we will kill one of yours, and in the end it will be you who tire of it.[23]

—Ho Chi Minh, North Vietnam Leader

Many third world nations are willing to accept tremendous casualties. Therefore, overcoming those countries will not come cheaply. The Chinese in Korea and the North Vietnamese Army (NVA) in Vietnam are examples. In interviews since the war, NVA commanders have said that they would accept extremely heavy casualties because they knew that the Americans would not stick with the war. U.S. Army Rangers inflicted casualties in the ratio of 50 to 1 (some estimates are higher) on the Somalian militia in Mogadishu during the October 3-4, 1993 battle.[24]

In some conflicts—Somalia is an example—the American people, as represented by our politicians, have been averse to any casualties. We cannot win against a determined enemy without the backbone to go through with the mission. Before we enter any conflict, we must decide if the expected results are worth the probable cost.

The important lesson is more political than military. The President must ensure that the people are informed and that they are behind his actions. I believe that the Congress should enforce the War Powers Act. However, the Congress was unwilling to confront the President in Vietnam and Somalia. We in the Army don't have any say.

Commanders can, however, be aware of the mindset of the enemy. We must recognize that the enemy commander may accept any number of casualties in order to gain a victory. We should "cooperate" with his desire by preparing to inflict the maximum casualties on him. Remember: Our job is to kill the enemies of our country! Never forget that. That is why we have the Army.

NEVER GO ADMINISTRATIVE

Then the Lord said to Gideon, 'By the three hundred men who lapped I will save you, and deliver the Midianites into your hand.' [25]

—The Holy Bible

Gideon had the task of selecting a small fighting force from the thousands who had assembled before him. In accordance with the Lord's guidance, Gideon watched as they passed by water. Those who kept their weapons in their right hand and continued walking as they "lapped" (put their hand to their mouth as they continued to walk) were chosen. These 300 were selected because they were always "on guard." They never went "administrative."

"Going administrative" in a combat zone is dangerous. Our military history is replete with examples of individuals and units "going administrative"—relaxing as if no danger existed. In *The Red Badge of Courage*, author Stephen Crane describes Union Soldiers exulting after stopping an assault by rebel forces. The Yanks congratulated each other and lay around relaxing until suddenly, the rebels mounted another assault, taking the Union Soldiers by surprise. [26]

In the debacle in Korea caused by the intervention of the Chinese Communist Forces on November 25-26, 1950, many units lost all tactical cohesion. In some units, men loaded onto whatever vehicle was available. They did not maintain tactical integrity. They failed to hold the high ground as they retreated. When the convoys were ambushed, a disaster was the result. [27] The Marines in the Northeast controlled the high ground as they withdrew. The results were decidedly different.[28]

The 2-7th Cavalry in the Ia Drang Valley in 1965 took a "walk in the sun" as it moved from LZ X-ray to LZ Albany.[29] The engagement with the NVA contributed to a disaster for the 2/7th.

In the summer of 1967, Company A, 2-502nd, had contact with the enemy in which a chopper was shot down. The company established a defensive position around the chopper. I landed and spoke with the commander, Captain Steven Arnold (Arnold was one of the most outstanding officers I have ever known. He retired as a lieutenant general.). After being brought up-to-date, I began to walk the perimeter. On the far side from where I had landed, I encountered several Soldiers standing, smoking, laughing, and talking about the recent action. I admonished them and ordered them to dig in behind the rise that bordered the perimeter in that location. I added that the "bad guys" most likely would mortar the company's position and might follow up with a counterattack. I continued around the perimeter until I returned to where I had left Captain Arnold. I told him what had transpired and suggested that he might want to check on the position I had just left.

When Arnold reached those men, the position came under a short mortar barrage. Three men were killed as they stood in the open. They had gone "administrative" as soon as I left them. Arnold was wounded slightly as were several others. If those Soldiers had been in a foxhole or prone behind the rise in the ground, they most likely would have escaped injury.

One of the best ways to impress upon American Soldiers the value of always being alert is to catch them unprepared while on a training exercise. Since our Soldiers have the tendency to relax and "go administrative," this is not hard to do. The astute commander will be alert for the opportunity and inflict a humiliating "defeat" on his Soldiers by subjecting them to an unexpected attack or artillery barrage.

American Soldiers have a tendency to go administrative as soon as they are no longer in contact with the enemy. I have seen it within minutes after a heavy contact is broken off. Deaths result. Preventing it is a significant challenge for junior leaders. If, in training, you can hit one of your units from an unexpected direction or with significant force (units and/or firepower) that inflicts casualties (simulated) and causes confusion, you may impress upon your Soldiers the requirement to be ready always. But nothing beats leader supervision.

OPERATIONS OTHER THAN WAR

It may not be war, but it sure as hell ain't peace.[30]

—Major General Steven Arnold

That there was little success in stabilizing Haiti and moving it forward should have been no surprise to anyone who remembered the nation building doctrine of the '60s. That the first President George Bush could say with a straight face that the troops he sent to Somalia in 1992 would be out by Inauguration Day 1993 is incredible to anyone who gave any thought to the political situation in that forsaken land. That the deadline for withdrawing U.S. troops from Bosnia was extended twice and became indefinite should elicit nothing but "I told you so" from those who were thinking seriously about the prospects for success when President Clinton decided to commit peacekeeping troops.

In the mid-sixties, General Harold K. Johnson, chief of staff, U.S. Army, proclaimed that stability operations or nation building was the third principle mission of the Army. It was coequal with the responsibility to deter or win a general or limited war.[31]

Today, stability operations and nation building are generally called peacekeeping or, in the military, Operations Other Than War (OOTW).

President George W. Bush, when campaigning, stated that he intended reducing our commitments. He has found that goal easier said than done. His mention of cutbacks caused international repercussions.

Former chairman of the Joint Chiefs of Staff, General Colin

Powell, expressed his views on the criteria for deciding to intervene with military force. "When a 'fire' starts that might require committing armed forces, we need to evaluate the circumstances. Relevant questions include: Is the political objective we seek to achieve important, clearly defined and understood? Have all other nonviolent policy means failed? Will military force achieve the objective? At what cost? Have the gains and risks been analyzed? How might the situation that we seek to alter, once it is altered by force, develop further and what might be the consequences?"

Powell concluded that whenever the United States had been successful in using military force, "The reason for our success is that in every instance we have carefully matched the use of military force to our political objectives."[32]

There are two important additional considerations: the Congress and the people must be well informed about the purpose of the mission. And, just as important, they must understand that no mission is without risk, understand what that risk may entail, and be willing to accept it.

Bringing stability and establishing a nation capable of managing its own destiny is a very long, drawn-out process. To bring about this transformation from anarchy can take years. Conceptually, U.S. combat power provides the secure environment to permit this metamorphosis. Civil Affairs units develop a native capacity to govern. U.S. police advisors train and monitor the establishment and operation of security/police forces and a justice system. Psychological operations units support the efforts of the budding native government and the U.S. to "win the hearts and minds" of the populace. Specially selected and trained U.S. forces assist in the development of all governmental functions. Ultimately, a freely elected ruling body, capable and supported by the people, would govern in a relatively enlightened and competent manner. The United States is trying to implement this concept in Iraq and Afghanistan. Trying to make a country over in our self-image may be misguided. Democracy, as we know it, may not be the best form of government. In our country, we started with a pre-ordained leader—George Washington—whom people revered, respected, and trusted. Few, if any, emerging countries are so fortunate.

Today's world is in turmoil. Attempts to bring tranquility to places like Haiti, Bosnia, Kosovo, Macedonia, Afghanistan, and Iraq, (I consider the latter two as "wars"—not operations "other than war") and elsewhere have not been successful. Centuries old ethnic and religious animosities have proved intransigent to the best intentions of the peacekeepers. The U.S. Army, one of the main participants in these operations, has been overcommitted. An Association of the United States Army (AUSA) Institute of Land Warfare Defense Report in 2001 described the impact:

> Since 1989 the Army has been cut by more than 34 percent while undergoing a 300 percent increase in mission rates. [It] has provided most of the forces used in the thirty-five major deployments in which it has participated since then. The average frequency of Army contingency deployments has increased from one every four years to one every fourteen weeks. During the same period that the Army lost a third of its force structure, it also lost 21 percent of its infrastructure and 37 percent of its budget authority. The Army currently has more than 140,000 Soldiers deployed or forward-stationed in 101 countries.[33]

Since that statement was made, the impact on the Army has been increased significantly by the operations in Afghanistan and Iraq.

Former chief of staff of the Army, General Eric K. Shinseki, stated, "War fighting is job number one." These OOTW have had a significant impact on this primary mission.[34]

OOTW may result in lower unit combat readiness status. For example, in 2001 the Army downgraded one of its ten active duty divisions because of a shortage of training and people caused by peacekeeping in the Balkans.[35]

A commitment of a battalion, say, to Kosovo could remove that battalion from its war-fighting mission for as much as eighteen months. Six months might be used for preparation and special training, six months for the deployment, and six months for re-honing war-fighting skills upon the return to the United States.

If the battalion was "combat ready" when alerted for the mission, why are six months needed to prepare for a mission that, it is hoped, is less difficult than "hot war"? To reduce personnel turnover the battalion may have replaced those who would become eligible for discharge or whose overseas tour is scheduled for termination during the deployment. These replacements may have come from sister battalions creating turmoil in those units.[36]

Units may undergo a change in basic mission. For example, some artillery units were assigned foot-patrolling missions in Iraq (a "hot war").

Significant changes in equipment may be required. Some units may leave their heavy combat vehicles behind and obtain HMMWVs (Humvees) in storage in the theater of operations.

The unit conducts special training including crowd control, checkpoints, vehicle search, rules of engagement, and orientation on the political groupings in the deployment area. The battalion may go to one of the National Training Centers for focused training against a live opposing force (OPFOR).

What happens to the combat skills during deployment? Because of terrain restrictions, peacekeepers may lose heavy weapons practice and the ability to conduct extensive field exercises. On the other hand, if deployed to Saudi Arabia, say, there may be a wonderful opportunity for tank gunnery and battalion size exercises.[37] In either area, junior leaders and their Soldiers can gain invaluable experience at the small unit level.[38] Positive leadership influences the impact on training and morale significantly, as always.

One commander of a deployed battalion had this to say:

> While on OOTW my battalion staff and I are
> working full blast planning and overseeing what

my troops are doing. Good training for us. The junior Soldiers—NCOs and Officers—have a great
opportunity to operate on their own. Seems like
that would be great for team building and leadership development.

The small units spend a lot of time patrolling,
preparing and running checkpoints, etc. Things
that they would do in combat. We hope that they
won't receive enemy fire but they might.

The difference between "peacekeeping" and combat may be
nebulous. Major General S. L. Arnold, the commanding general
of the 10th Mountain Division in Somalia said, "It may not be war,
but it sure as hell ain't peace."[39]

Units on peacekeeping missions must be combat ready and
mentally prepared for a change in focus. Major General David
Grange, commanding general, 1st Infantry Division, advised,
"Keep the total war mentality during OOTW."[40]

The potential danger is an incentive for alertness. As Colonel Tony Cuculo, an experienced brigade commander, expressed
it, "There are people who don't want you to [succeed]. They are
constantly at work, looking for ways to impede, slow, or stop you,
even kill you. Peacekeeping isn't peace, it is merely an absence
of fighting... Prepare for combat...it is your credibility and your
credibility will be tested."[41]

Upon return from deployment, all participants take leave. Soldiers need time to regenerate themselves physically and mentally
before reentering the grind and are not forced immediately into an
intensive training cycle.

Many who were assigned to the battalion pre-deployment
come due for discharge or reassignment. They are replaced, causing additional turbulence.

The heavy maintenance required for vehicles and other equipment left behind and that used on the deployment require several
weeks of effort.

The combat readiness achieved or maintained while deployed

and the number of squad, platoon, company, and battalion evaluation exercises the unit conducted during that training determine what is necessary to achieve combat readiness. The usual training distractions of post details, required subjects not related to the combat mission, and special duties (athletic teams, Soldiers Chorus, etc.) all impact negatively on returning the unit to a high level of combat readiness. As a result, several months transpire before the unit is combat ready.[42]

Some people believe that conducting OOTW the same way we operate during extended combat can significantly shorten this eighteen-month period. Deploying with personnel currently assigned and replacing Soldiers when vacancies occur because of ETS (expiration term of service) and other reasons minimizes personnel turbulence.

When the unit returns to the United States, it will have no more than normal personnel turbulence. By eliminating all non-mission activities, the unit's training program can focus on sharpening the go-to-war skills and can reach a combat-ready status in much less time than before. The battalion can perform effectively with a shorter train-up time. Leaders and Soldiers can and will do the job

Battalion Commander Lieutenant Colonel Rick Bassett remarked, "Our Soldiers want to Soldier, and our leaders want to lead, and in all cases, we want to excel whatever the challenge. Some say it's tough being in the Army today. I believe it's always been tough being in the Army. Defending a nation and its interests is not a game. As the saying goes, if it were easy, they would contract it out."[43]

Preparation for OOTW deserves as much emphasis as preparation for combat. They are as difficult and may evolve into combat. We must be ready. Our Army has performed and will continue to perform exceptionally well. America should be proud.

OPERATION BUSHMASTER

---

*All warfare is based on deception.... Offer the enemy
a bait to lure him.*[44]

  —Sun Tzu, Chinese Master Strategist and General

The wars in Korea, Vietnam, and the Middle East were against
what we sometimes disparagingly term "third world" nations.
They may be behind in technology and other modern characteristics but their military is far from backward or "slow." To defeat
them takes more than our superior technology. We have to be
innovative; we have to outsmart them.

We planned a new twist to our procedures in the 1-506 in
Vietnam. It was similar to what the 1st Brigade (Separate), 101st
Airborne Division had used during its first year in Vietnam. Brigadier General Willard Pearson, the brigade commander, describes
the stay-behind operational concept.

> Following a successful airmobile assault in an
> area heavily infested with guerrillas, the attacking
> unit counts enemy killed, collects their weapons,
> and then moves to a base area. The helicopters used
> for extraction bring in a stay-behind force, which
> immediately disappears into the jungle. Supplied
> with five days rations, this force moves at night
> and observes during the day. Since the Vietcong
> invariably return to a battle area, the stay-behind
> force is in an excellent ambush position. Reinforc-

ing units, if required, reenter to complete the destruction of the enemy.[45]

What we used in the 2-502nd was much smaller in scope and
employed only one company. No one was aware if the brigade
had done anything similar in the past. There was no "institutional
memory" as far as we knew.

The first example of our stay-behind concept occurred when
we had a company from another battalion under our operational
control. The company commander, a first lieutenant, was exceptionally sharp. We planned to insert him on a mission. After its
completion, the company minus one platoon would be extracted
as usual. Before we extracted him, he would prepare an ambush
position for that platoon. This position would be near the extraction Landing Zone (LZ). The platoon's members would get into
their holes and hunker down; no one would move or make any
noise. There was to be no smoking; we wanted no telltale smoke
or odor to give away the surprise we planned. We hoped that the
enemy, as it usually did, would return to the LZ to police up anything left behind by the Americans. When it did, the stay-behind
platoon would ambush them.

It worked like a charm. Shortly after dark, the enemy in platoon
size returned to the LZ. The hidden American platoon opened fire
and killed twelve to fifteen of the enemy. Colonel Larry Mowery,
the brigade commander, when he received the report, immediately ordered his Charlie Charlie to prepare for flight and invited
me to go with him. We flew over the platoon and radioed con-
gratulations to the company commander who had stayed with his
platoon. The resounding success was directly due to the company
commander. Colonel Mowery named this technique a "Bushmaster Operation."

I would use the "Bushmaster" technique again—this time
with one of my own companies. The opportunity occurred when
a company discovered a major guerrilla complex. It was lightly
defended so the company was able to occupy it without difficulty.
As the troopers explored the underground labyrinth, they found

vast stores of rice. Destruction or extraction of the rice would be a significant blow to the effectiveness of the guerrillas or main force operating in our area. We were ordered to destroy it and were given engineer support to prepare and carry out the demolition.

I briefed my company commander on the "Bushmaster" concept. I stressed the importance of secrecy to ensure surprise. The stay-behind platoon must be concealed in the defensive position before the company minus was extracted. The platoon members must be totally silent, could not smoke, and must remain hidden beginning before the company minus began its extraction until any enemy appeared. I talked to the Platoon Leader stressing this vital element. Without total secrecy, "Bushmaster" would fail.

At the completion of the mission, extracting the company minus went without a hitch. Within a few minutes, I heard the platoon leader's excited, almost panicky voice, reporting that he was under fire. I immediately called for artillery to "seal off" the area thinking that the platoon was under heavy attack. After much back and forth between the platoon leader and me, I learned that the enemy consisted of one rifleman! Fortunately for us, the enemy did not return in platoon size as in our previous Bushmaster Operation. He had not fallen into our trap. The platoon experienced several casualties—KIA and WIA—as it tried to recover its wounded without first suppressing the enemy's fire. Finally, however, the one lone Vietnamese withdrew and we extracted our beaten platoon.

The platoon leader had violated my specific instructions concerning concealment. Instead of getting into his foxhole before the extraction of the company minus he sat on the lip smoking a cigarette and talking to his troops. That one lone enemy had returned to the area almost immediately after the last chopper had departed with the company minus. Seeing the platoon leader and others he took them under fire hitting the first man at whom he fired. As other Troopers tried to rescue their comrade, they, in turn, became casualties.

The platoon leader had failed miserably. He failed because he had violated the single most important part of the plan. Because he and his platoon had not "hunkered down" and remained out of sight, that one lone enemy had spotted the platoon leader and other Soldiers and taken them under fire. Some of our Soldiers had been killed—needlessly, in my opinion. A lone enemy Soldier who deserved the enemy's equivalent of a Silver Star or Distinguished Service Cross (if there were such a thing) had beaten my platoon.

Trying something new, if based on sound principles, can pay dividends by surprising the enemy; it can help keep the initiative with our forces. It helps avoid falling into the trap of following set procedures and routines, almost always dangerous. The Bushmaster concept was sound. The second operation failed because of improper implementation. Soldiers died unnecessarily.

TERRORISM

Victory at all costs, victory in spite of terror, victory however long and hard the road may be; for without victory there is no survival.[46]

—Sir Winston Churchill

I will not forget the wound to our country and those who inflicted it. I will not yield, I will not rest, I will not relent in waging this struggle for freedom and security for the American people.[47]

—President George W. Bush

Terrorists have been at war with the United States for a long time although our government and its citizens have refused to recognize that fact. U.S. Navy Captain Dan Ouimette, executive officer (XO) of the Naval Air Station, Pensacola, Florida, described this war so well in an article in the *Pensacola Civitan* in February 2003.

The seizure of the American Embassy in Tehran in 1979 set the stage. President Carter's ill-fated attempt at rescue only emboldened the terrorists. The Great Satan could be humiliated. Terrorists began to kidnap and kill Americans throughout the Middle East.

In April of 1983, terrorists drove a large vehicle packed with high explosives into the U.S. Embassy compound in Beirut. The explosion killed sixty-three people.

Six short months later, a large truck heavily laden with over

2500 pounds of TNT smashed through the main gate of the U.S. Marine Headquarters in Beirut, killing 241 U.S. servicemen.

Two months later in December 1983, terrorists drove another truck loaded with explosives into the U.S. Embassy in Kuwait.

The following year, in September 1984, terrorists drove another van into the gates of the U.S. Embassy in Beirut.

In April 1985 terrorists exploded a bomb in a restaurant frequented by U.S. Soldiers in Madrid.

Then in August terrorists drove a Volkswagen loaded with explosives into the main gate of the U.S. Air Force Base at Rhein-Main, killing twenty-two.

Fifty-nine days later, terrorists hijacked the cruise ship, the Achille Lauro, and executed a wheelchair-bound American.

In April 1986 terrorists bombed TWA Flight 840, killing four.

Terrorists then bombed Pan Am Flight 103 over Lockerbie, Scotland, in 1988, killing 259.

Terrorists brought the fight to America in January 1993, killing two CIA agents as they entered CIA headquarters in Langley, Virginia.

The following month, February 1993, terrorists drove an explosive-packed van into the underground parking lot of the World Trade Center. The explosion killed six and injured over 1,000.

In November 1995, terrorists exploded a car bomb at a U.S. military complex in Riyadh, Saudi Arabia, killing seven service men and women.

A few months later in June of 1996, terrorists detonated another truck bomb only thirty-five yards from the U.S. military compound in Dhahran, Saudi Arabia, destroying the Khobar Towers, a U.S. Air Force barracks, killing nineteen and injuring over 500.

Next, terrorists simultaneously attacked two U.S embassies in Kenya and Tanzania killing 224. America responded with cruise missile attacks and then went back to sleep.

Changing tactics, terrorists attacked the USS Cole in Aden, Yemen, on October 12, 2000, killing seventeen U.S. Navy sailors.

Attacking a U.S Warship is an act of war, but we sent the FBI to investigate the crime and went back to sleep.[48]

The terrorist attacks on September 11, 2001, showed just how ill-prepared the United States is.[49] America is at war! We are under attack! The terrorists finally got our attention. Better late than never.

The FBI defines terrorism as "the unlawful use of force or violence against persons or property to intimidate or coerce a government, the civilian populace, or any segment thereof, in furtherance of political or social objectives."[50] The objective "is to provoke a reaction disproportionate to the act itself. The truest terror is the random sort, which carries the implication that anyone, anywhere, might find themselves the next target."[51] Terrorism causes fear in those hurt and others affected.[52] There is no clear delineation between who is and who is not a terrorist.[53] One man's terrorist may be another man's freedom fighter.[54]

Whether an act is terrorism depends neither on whether the cause is good or bad nor on whether those espousing it have the chance to express their demands democratically. A good cause may use terrorism in a bad way. For the most part, the African National Congress used mass demonstrations and industrial sabotage to advance its cause. However, the men who shot members of a white church congregation or planted a bomb outside a theater were terrorists.

Terrorism is a way the powerless wage war. It is low cost and high yield. Terrorists are devoted to their cause; they risk their liberty and life. Some enjoy violence for its own sake. Others may be advancing a general cause and themselves. They may be rationally pursuing a policy hoping that it will succeed. Any success breeds stronger devotion and more vigorous action. The PLO's actions in the Middle East made the PLO the dominant representative of the Palestinians. Terrorists helped drive the British from India, the Middle East, Cyprus, and Kenya.[55]

Can a state be responsible for terrorism? Our government has accused North Korea, Cuba, Iran, Libya, Iraq, Syria, and Sudan of supporting international terrorism. Indications are that prior to our intervention, Afghanistan had been supporting Osama bin Laden, the individual named as the mastermind behind the 9/11 attacks on the United States.

Can regular armies in regular warfare be guilty of terrorism? Under International Law, the Japanese "rape of Nanking" was a crime, the U.S. firebombing of Japan a legitimate act of war.

Extremists who take issue with some law or group are a growing source of violence. They attack abortion clinics, their staff, and clients. They attack scientists, laboratories, and businesses that use animals in research. Attacks at the Atlanta nightclub frequented by homosexuals may be another example of issue-specific violence or a random, irrational act of violence.[56]

Since the Berlin Wall came down, the control of nuclear weapons and fissionable material in Russia has been inadequate. Some weapons have disappeared or been lost through administrative error. The former Soviet Union has a large disaffected population that would not hesitate to sell weapons or materials.[57]

Preventing a rogue nation or terrorist from obtaining a nuclear weapon or the material and the know-how to construct a nuclear weapon is impossible. In February 2001, the London *Sunday Times* reported that Iraq had a nuclear stockpile.[58] This belief was a primary reason President George W. Bush gave for attacking that country. Iran is attempting to acquire weapons of mass destruction.[59] This effort is a source of contention between the United States and Russia; the latter has been supportive of Iran's effort.

Cyber terrorism is another threat. The Department of Defense is "invaded" 250,000 times each year. Other likely targets include communications, banks, financial markets, utilities, transportation, and other systems.[60]

Experts differ as to whether military intervention encourages terrorist counteraction.[61] Firm evidence that a government is responsible for the terrorism may justify retaliation. If the evidence is weak, retribution may be counterproductive.[62] The United States views terrorism as a matter of national security; it is an act of aggression and must be punished.[63] That conclusion has stimulated our reactions in Iraq and Afghanistan. However, our anger and shock must not cause us to lower ourselves to the same level as the terrorists. If we do, we become no better than they.

News about a terrorist assault feeds the terrorists' ego. Throughout the hostage crisis that occurred during President Carter's administration, Walter Cronkite closed each broadcast by stating the number of days the hostages had been incarcerated. This attention may have prolonged the crisis. However, terrorists today are not as dependent upon the media as they once were. Terrorists draw strength from their audience.[64] Some terrorist groups have the ability to stage and videotape their terrorism![65] The *Tupac Amaru*, the group that held hostages in Peru, had its own Web page.

Preventing terrorism is impossible. It may be inhibited. Strong, focused, national leadership must be determined to persevere. International cooperation is vital.[66] Hindering or mitigating terrorism requires tough measures that may include but not be limited to:

- Declaring a state of emergency and putting the nation on a war footing.

- Eliminating our dependence on Middle Eastern oil.

- Increasing exponentially the number of students studying Middle Eastern languages and cultures. Include China and North Korea.

- Instituting National Service.

- Increasing the Army significantly (perhaps 200,000) with emphasis on Infantry, military police, civil affairs, and psychological operations Soldiers.

- Controlling immigration. Secure our borders and our ports.

- Improving air travel security. Do not permit aircraft to land in the United States if they originated in countries whose security measures do not meet our standards.

- Making a major and continuing effort to regain and strengthen our ties with our former allies and to make new friends.

- Working to establish a worldwide counterterrorism program.

- Increasing efforts to control or disrupt financial transactions of terrorists and those who support terrorists. Freeze assets of countries that harbor or support terrorists.

- Increasing exponentially our HUMINT (human intelligence) capability.

- Making no deals with terrorists despite blackmail or threats.

- Imposing strong penalties on state sponsors of terrorism or those that provide a safe haven and support. (President George W. Bush said, "We will make no distinction between the terrorists who committed these acts and those who harbor them."[67])

- Establishing terrorism as an international crime so that a terrorist can be tried and punished by any nation that has legal custody.

- When appropriate, limiting all publicity about terrorism to brief general news coverage. (It would have been impossible and unwise to try to prevent media coverage of the 9/11 attacks.)

- Punishing those who create false alarms with the same severity as that applied to terrorists.[68]

- Developing International agreement as to what constitutes terrorism and cooperation in combating it.

One of the most important and difficult tasks that faces President George W. Bush is convincing the citizenry that we are threatened and that we need to sacrifice. In the first few days after the 9/11 attacks, the president could have asked just about anything from Americans and he would have received it. Unfortunately, about all that he did was tell us to go shopping at the mall. While he was saying this in a humorous vein to encourage us not to become immobilized by fear, he missed a marvelous opportunity to focus our attention on the risks and to call for some small sacrifices and actions on our part. He could have:

- Initiated a "Buy War Bonds" campaign.

- Called for or, at least, encouraged people to consider participating in some National Service program.

- Vitalized the Blue Star/Gold Star program that was so popular during WWII.

- Authorized a lapel pin for parents and spouses who have a family member serving in our Armed Forces

- Revitalized the USO.

- Encouraged schools, social clubs, and other organizations to invite veterans to speak to their members.

If terrorism is to be repressed, additional money, time, and significant restrictions are required. Obviously, there are countervailing influences. In our society individuals and groups that emphasize individual freedoms will resist restrictive measures although most people have accepted the minor inconvenience and delays of airport security checks. They are minimally intrusive and, unfortunately, far from 100 percent effective. (How did the hijackers breach security?) Laws enacted to control terrorism may impact unconstitutionally or unacceptably on our personal freedom. Is the price too high for the risk involved? Trade sanctions can harm the United States and its citizens. Our exporting companies can lose business. Corporations may be at a disadvantage when competing with companies that do not honor the trade sanctions. Our citizens may be forced to pay higher prices for goods.[69] For our military to protect itself its alert status must be maintained at or almost at its highest level in areas of possible threats. (That is almost everywhere in the world!) A relaxed, Sunday afternoon mindset invites attack.

We cannot prevent terrorism; we can only make it more difficult for the terrorist.

TRANSFORMATION

The Army "must restructure, reshape and transform its weapons, its equipment and itself from a heavy-weight Cold War champion to a lighter, more responsive expeditionary force. It must reinvent itself to meet an uncertain future of short-notice commitments that may occur anywhere around the globe.... [N]ever has it undertaken such a sweeping change as is called for in its new Transformation initiative."

—Gordon R. Sullivan, General, U.S. Army Retired, former Chief of Staff.[70]

The Army either becomes more mobile and deployable or it will lose its role as America's preeminent land warfare force. It must be strategically responsive and dominant at every level of conflict to provide the National Command Authority with appropriate options for peacekeeping, deterrence, and war-fighting.[71] To fulfill this mission, the Army is developing a flexible, lethal, and mobile force.[72] "Transformation" is the name the Army has given to this process.[73]

During Desert Shield, in 1990, the United States moved its 82nd Airborne Division to Saudi Arabia almost immediately and then waited anxiously as we took months to build up our forces. If Saddam Hussein had ordered his Army—particularly his armored divisions—to attack, the 82nd, having only a minimum of anti-armor capability, would have been in for an exceedingly rough time.[74]

In the past, our Army has had difficulty getting forces on the ground quickly with the requisite combat power.[75] It needed a "medium" combat force that is more mobile and deployable than the current "heavy" units with their Abrams tanks and Bradley Infantry vehicles and better armed with more staying power than the airborne and light Infantry units that enter combat lightly armed.[76]

Former chief of staff of the Army, General Eric K. Shinseki, directed that the Army transform itself into a force "that is deployable, agile, versatile, lethal, survivable, and sustainable."[77] The distinctions between "heavy" and "light" forces are being erased as technology permits.[78] The goal is for the Army to be able to put a combat-capable brigade anywhere in the world within ninety-six hours, a division on the ground within 120 hours, and five divisions within thirty days.[79] (This requirement presupposes that the forces exist and sufficient lift—primarily air—is available for this deployment.)

To meet this timetable, high-speed strategic air and sealift capable of entering an undeveloped area of operations[80] are necessary.[81] The Army must develop units with smaller support requirements.[82]

The Army looked to the air force for ideas on speed. Instead of relying on ever-heavier equipment that can survive a hit, the Army wanted a system similar to that of stealth aircraft.[83]

To transform itself, the Army began with the Interim Brigade Combat Team (IBCT).[84] This brigade was not an experimental force. As quickly as possible, interim brigades were readied for combat.[85] The initial Table of Organization and Equipment (T/O&E) for the brigade consisted of 389 officers and 3,112 enlisted Soldiers for a total of 3,501 Soldiers. It contained three Infantry battalions of 665 Soldiers each, equipped with several variants of the interim armored vehicle (IAV), an eight-wheeled (wheels, not tracks), lightly armored carrier built by General Dynamics. The Brigade also contained a Reconnaissance, Surveillance, and Target Acquisition Squadron of 414 Soldiers, and supporting artillery, engineer, antiarmor, intelligence, signal, and logistics support units. While the Infantry battalions' manpower strength is roughly equal to those in airborne and light Infantry brigades, the IAV provides far greater mobility and protection for the Soldiers. Additionally, the IBCT had over three times the reconnaissance capability of most other U.S. brigades. It was optimized for small-scale contingency operations, in cities or rough terrain, both of which make heavier armored vehicles difficult to employ.[86]

In developing the organization for the Interim Brigade, the guiding thought was that the most likely need would be for a force with Infantry as the centerpiece. For that reason, the Air-borne Infantry Battalion organization was the core. Although the light armored vehicle enables the unit to move about the battle-field rapidly, the Infantry is organized and equipped to fight dis-mounted.[87]

There are two core capabilities—high tactical and strategic mobility and the ability to achieve decisive combat action through dismounted Infantry assault. The brigade and all its equipment are transportable by C-130 aircraft.[88] (The Army is now seeking a "very heavy lift" vehicle to permit the Army to move heavier than originally anticipated vehicles about the battle area.)

A major hurdle was the development or selection "off the shelf" of an appropriate armored vehicle. The Army decided in March 2000 that the backbone of the new lighter, faster, more mobile force, would be a light, twenty-ton armored personnel car-rier that could be deployed in the workhorse C-130J. Converting to the light armored vehicle (LAV) is the Army's most significant armor program in thirty years. This important change was not de-layed in order to field the new IBCT by May 2003; instead the brigade initially used substitute vehicles.[89]

The light armored vehicle (LAV) provides the ground mobil-ity for the IBCT. There are two important variations: the Infantry carrier vehicle and the mobile gun systems. The carrier has eight configurations for use in scout, support, and command roles. It is a fast, easily maintainable vehicle that provides some protection for Infantry.[90] The vehicle has a maximum speed of sixty mph and a range of three hundred miles on a tank of gas.[91]

The other variety is a platform for a Mobile Gun System with a 105mm cannon, the same gun used on the original M-1 Abrams tanks. Although not a tank replacement, the LAV can provide direct fire support for the Infantry.[92]

Since the IBCT first came onto the scene, the Army has developed Heavy, Airborne, Light (Infantry), and Stryker Brigade Combat Teams. Sustainment and Maneuver Support and Aviation Support Brigade Teams followed. Transformation is an ongoing process designed to field the most combat-effective combat teams possible.

It takes more than superior technology to dominate the battlefield. Transformation requires new doctrine and flexible organizations to take advantage of key technological advancements.[93] Transformation needs the same emphasis on the development of high quality leaders that is placed on equipment and technology.[94] The U.S. Army Infantry School, Fort Benning, Georgia, continues to develop technically competent and innovative Infantrymen schooled in doctrine, organization, and operational concepts. The Interim Brigade allowed the Army to train Soldiers and develop leaders who will compose the Objective Force, what the Army wants to be long term.[95]

As always, the most important element on the battlefield is the individual Soldier. As it was with the Spartans at Thermopylae, the Roman legions, the Continental Army Soldiers who won our freedom, and all who have followed them, the leadership and the courage and the training status of the men being led make the difference. Soldiers are the ultimate weapons.[96]

WILL WE EVER LEARN? THE MOST IMPORTANT LESSON FROM VIETNAM

The war in Vietnam was not lost in the field, nor was it lost on the front pages of the New York Times or on the college campuses. It was lost in Washington, DC, even before Americans assumed sole responsibility for the fighting in 1965 and before they realized the country was at war; indeed, even before the first American units were deployed.[97]

—Major H. R. McMaster

Saigon fell in 1975. The President, the Congress, Secretary of Defense Robert McNamara, the military high command, the media, and practically everybody else have been blamed for the first war America ever lost. "One of the great tragedies of the Vietnam War is that although American armed forces defeated the North Vietnamese and Vietcong in every major battle, the United States still suffered the greatest defeat in its history.[98] What can we learn from it?

The antagonism—even hatred—that some Americans directed toward the military is a great tragedy. The military was castigated unjustly for fighting in Vietnam in accordance with the orders of the Commander in Chief. Some Americans have gone so far as to say the military as an institution or as individuals should have refused. Ridiculous! The military is a disciplined, capable instrument of national power that executes to the best of its ability the orders of the Commander in Chief. The high military command can be criticized, but the American GI is blameless. As always, he did his job.

Thirty years later, the media attention, much of which is still antagonistic, lacks the vitriol, the rancor, and the unbridled anger of so many years ago. While the arguments are the same, the criticism seems less strident. Perhaps the climate of hate that had been engendered by protests has been diminished by time. I hope so. We need to move ahead. The important task now is to insure that we don't make the same mistakes again.

Much has been written to explain what went wrong; I have about two dozen books in my library about Vietnam. As each book unfolds, the author paints an environment of impending doom. Not surprising since each author knew the outcome. Each enumerates the "lessons" as he sees them. They include a warning against involvement in a "land war" in Asia with a government willing to pay any price including unlimited casualties in order to be victorious; the failure to mobilize the National Guard; the unfairness of the draft; the failure to destroy the sanctuaries in Laos and Cambodia; the incremental application of air power; the selection of targets by the highest civilian authority; the bombing halts "to send signals," the arrogance of our military toward the South Vietnamese Army and, initially, toward the North Vietnamese Army and Vietcong guerrillas; and the belief that our technology was so superior that no third world country could successfully resist it are some of those "lessons." Those who remember Korea see many similarities. Kosovo provides us with some of the same. Will we never learn? As Pogo said, "I have seen the enemy and he is us."

In his book, *In Retrospect*, former Secretary of Defense Robert McNamara wrote, "There were eleven major causes for our disaster in Vietnam."[99] (Some people are so bitter toward him that they have refused to read his book. That is a mistake; he has something to say.) Chapter 11 is entitled "The Lessons of Vietnam." The "lessons" are straightforward. They apply to decisions made at the highest civilian level. Some indicate a violation of doctrine taught at the U.S. Army Special Warfare Center when I went through the special forces course in 1960. Many critics of the war will agree with those lessons. They are important. They are on target. That there is nothing startling about them does not diminish their significance. The problem with most lessons is that we never learn them, do not apply them, or forget them. In Vietnam, tragedy was the result.

Doctrine emphasizes the importance of political stability. It was never achieved in South Vietnam. McNamara stated, "Since the days of the Kennedy administration, we had regarded political stability as a fundamental prerequisite for our Vietnam strategy."[100] The instability in South Vietnam also troubled Johnson causing him to wonder if it made our efforts worthless. There never was any indication that stability was achievable. There never was an acceptable leader in sight.

The overriding preponderance of evidence that pointed to one conclusion—we can't win without stability in South Vietnam—should have convinced anyone who was open to conflicting opinions that we would not be successful. McNamara stated, "It is clear that disengagement was the course we should have chosen. We did not."[101] The question any thinking person might ask is "Why continue sinking deeper into the quagmire?"

Any significant enterprise, especially a war, requires the support of the citizenry to be successful. Dean Rusk wrote in *As I Saw It*, "At no time did we think that the American people would not support an effort to prevent Southeast Asia from going Communist."[102] That support was not forthcoming during the war.

"The first Great Truth is that in this country the government cannot succeed in pressing any long-term policy without the support of the people. And the second, a corollary to that truth, is that the people won't support a government they do not believe."[103] Currently, (2006) President George W. Bush has lost much of the original support for the wars in Afghanistan and Iraq because many citizens no longer believe in him and his administration.

I believe that President Johnson should have asked the Congress for a declaration of war at the time of the Tonkin Bay incident (1964). The declaration may not have been forthcoming but the debate would have been enlightening. Much later, in 1990–91, the question of fighting in the Gulf (Desert Storm) was debated in the Congress. The American public was informed. It heard both sides: the dire predictions of horrendous casualties, the possibility of an easy victory, the advantages and disadvantages of economic sanctions. Comparable debate has not occurred since 1991. Why did the president fail to call for this debate?

There is a corollary that may be more important. American citizens must keep themselves informed. When we fail we give our politicians *carte blanche* by default. "I don't know what to think"— the comment I hear so often—is no excuse. In fact, when we, the citizens, avoid our responsibility to become knowledgeable and involved, we become part of the problem and deserve part of the censure.

In *Dereliction of Duty*, Major H. R. McMaster castigates President Johnson, Secretary of Defense McNamara, and the Joint Chiefs of Staff. In this impressively researched examination, McMaster criticizes the decisions and heaps scorn and blame on all who made them. He describes in detail how the Joint Chiefs were virtually excluded from the decision-making process. He concludes that they should have resigned in protest. I agree.

McNamara concluded on March 6, 1965, that every possible effort should be made to commence negotiations to bring the war to an end.[104] He made one unpardonable error. When he became convinced of the futility of continuing, he should have gone to the mat with the president. Leaders, whether civilian or military, need intelligent, courageous assistants willing to stand up and say, "With all due respect, sir, you're wrong." Without candid advice, leaders court disaster.

McNamara wrote that while our involvement may have been misguided, it was based on the belief that what we were doing was right.

> Let me be simple and direct—I want to be clearly understood: the United States of America fought in Vietnam for eight years for what it believed to

be good and honest reasons. By such action, administrations of both parties sought to protect our
security, prevent the spread of totalitarian Commu-
nism, and promote individual freedom and political democracy. The Kennedy, Johnson, and Nixon
administrations made their decisions and by those
decisions demanded sacrifices and, yes, inflicted
terrible suffering in light of those goals and values.

Their hindsight was better than their foresight....
We both overestimated the effect of South Vietnam's loss on the security of the West and failed
to adhere to the fundamental principle that, in the
final analysis, if the South Vietnamese were to be
saved, they had to win the war themselves.... Exter-
nal military force cannot substitute for the political
order and stability that must be forged *by* a people
for themselves (McNamara's emphasis).... In the
end, we must confront the fate of those Americans who served in Vietnam and never returned....
That our effort in Vietnam proved unwise does not
make their sacrifice less noble. It endures for all to
see. Let us learn from their sacrifice and, by doing
so, validate and honor it.[105]

Dean Rusk wrote, "Whatever views they might hold about
the war, all Americans owe a great debt to those who carried the
battle. I myself would hope that none of our men and women of
Vietnam feel that they were engaged in a shameful enterprise.
They served at the behest of constitutional authority, on issues
perceived to involve war and peace and the survival of the human
race. They have nothing of which to be ashamed."[106]

We (the politicians, the military high command, and the citizenry) must learn from experience. The war is over. Stop blaming;
start healing, and learning. Rusk asked, "Why keep these sores of
Vietnam open? We must learn from our experience, but we must

also put the war behind us."[107] In the words of George Santayana, "Those who cannot remember the past are condemned to repeat it." The lessons are there. They do us no good unless we learn and apply them.

WORTH DYING FOR

We face a dilemma that armies have always faced within a democratic society. The values necessary to defend that society are often at odds with the values of the society itself. To be an effective servant of the people, the Army must concentrate not on the values of a liberal society, but on the hard values of the battlefield. We must recognize that the military community differs from the civilian community from which it springs. The civilian community exists to promote the quality of life. The military community exists to fight and if need be to die in defense of that quality of life. We must not apologize for those differences. The American people are served by Soldiers disciplined to obey the orders of their leaders, and hardened and conditioned to survive the rigors of the battlefield. We do neither our Soldiers nor the American people any favors if we ignore these realities.[108]

—General Walter T. Kerwin

When the Founding Fathers signed their names to the Declaration of Independence, they pledged their lives, their fortunes, and their sacred honor. That was no action to be taken lightly. They were committing treason and they knew it. The punishment for treason in England at the time was horrible. The traitor would be drawn, disemboweled, and quartered.

Major General Patrick Brady, Medal of Honor recipient for his service in Vietnam, published an article in the Columbus (GA) *Ledger-Enquirer* lamenting the "moral decline of America." He cited numerous examples to support his contention. He wondered if the young men who gave their lives willingly in Vietnam would do the same today.[109]

Dr. Robert E. Connely, a Decatur, GA chiropractor, expressed similar sentiments in an article in *The Atlanta Constitution* entitled "To Die For." The author, decrying the loss of morality in America today, wrote that he saw nothing worth dying for. He blamed our political leaders for this lack of inspiration![110]

Many of our political leaders, rock stars, athletic heroes, movie actors, and others on the national scene inspire nothing but disgust. They do not measure up to the standards of our Founding Fathers and others who have set the example for us.

I'm saddened by these articles and others similar to them that I read in the media. Is our youth so jaded, so lacking in patriotism that they are unwilling to defend what has been given to them? I don't think so.

I have spent a lot of time with the Rangers and other Soldiers at Fort Benning. I have seen them at "work" and "play," when they are training, and when they are socializing. I'm impressed. I see them as dedicated, serious professionals who understand well the hazards of their chosen profession. All indications are that they are as good as or better than those who came before them. Today's Soldiers are ready to stand up and be counted. They will perform in a way that will make all America proud.

We pray that they never will be called to do so, but if ordered to "stand and die" on some future battlefield they will acquit themselves like warriors. They and their buddies feel a responsibility for each other. They won't let each other down. They will do their duty. They will fight because of pride in themselves and in their unit. Private First Class Vernon L. Haught, a Soldier in Company F, 325th, 82nd Airborne Division, exemplified this pride during the Battle of the Bulge. When he heard that the Germans were on the way, he said, "This is the 82nd Airborne Division and this is as far as the bastards are going!"[111] Today's Soldiers are just as proud.

Lieutenant Colonel William Barret Travis, the commander at the Alamo, wrote in his last hours, "I am determined to sustain myself as long as possible & die like a Soldier who never forgets what is due to his own honor & that of his country.[112] Rangers in Mogadishu October 3–4, 1993, like Travis, stood their ground; they did not flinch.

Our Army is composed entirely of volunteers. Every Soldier who enlists today can expect to be deployed to either Afghanistan or Iraq. He knows that he will serve in a combat zone. TV news programs and other media have to have convinced him that he may be wounded or killed while serving. Yet he volunteered. That act is not something indicative of a person who believes that there is nothing worth dying for. I believe that if Major General Brady and Dr. Connerly, who wrote their articles before 9/11, were asked their opinions today, they would agree that they had been incorrect in their appraisal of our youth.

Our Soldiers are meeting the challenges of a battlefield that is both lethal and unforgiving. They know that their buddies depend on them. They know that they are fighting to protect the freedoms that were won by the expenditure of so much blood and treasure in the past. They know that they must persevere if their children are to enjoy those freedoms. Today's Soldiers know that there are some things worth dying for.

You Can't Defend a Position by Sitting on It!

I told Herren that as soon as enough of Tony Nadal's Alpha troops were on the ground to secure the landing zone, Bravo Company would be cut loose to search the lower slopes of the mountain…. If those enemy battalions were on the way, we needed to engage them as far off the landing zone as possible.[113]

—Lieutenant General Harold G. Moore

To defend an objective or a piece of terrain (an airfield, a landing zone), units must push out to gain control of the commanding terrain and prevent a surprise attack.

In the Ia Drang Valley battle at LZ (Landing Zone) X-ray in 1965, the battalion commander, Lieutenant Colonel Hal Moore, made a very wise and crucial decision when he ordered one of his companies to push up the ridgeline that jutted toward the LZ. Although the company was unable to advance far, it gave early warning to Moore and helped the battalion hold its position while other troops arrived.

I had a company standing operating procedure (SOP) in Korea dictating that a patrol would be pushed forward immediately after we took an objective. I hoped to avoid a surprise. When the president ordered troops to Lebanon, they were ordered to stay put at the airfield. Those troops suffered a disaster in a terrorist attack.

You cannot defend an airfield (or any other objective) by sitting on it.

To protect an objective, troops must control the commanding terrain nearby. Aggressive patrolling helps prevent surprise. This principle is one we teach in our service schools. It is often disregarded or violated. Disaster is often the result.

Section XI

THE GOAL

THE GREATEST COMPLIMENT

An Army fearful of its officers is never as good as one that trusts and confides in its leaders.[1]

—General Dwight D. Eisenhower

Units will follow only leaders who have earned their trust through demonstrations of honor and willingness to sacrifice for the good of their men.[2]

—James Fallows, American Journalist and Writer

"If I have to go to war again, I want to serve under you." There can be no greater compliment than that from a Soldier who says that to someone who was his commander in combat. Nothing can exceed that compliment because it says that the Soldier, if he has to risk his life again, wants the confidence that comes from serving under a leader whom the Soldier trusts. He trusts him because he has seen him in action. He knows that his commander is competent. He knows that his commander will do all in his power to "take care of the troops." He knows that his commander has the moral courage to stand up to higher commanders if the need arises.

How is this confidence developed? Probably the best way is to be successful in battle. That means more than just "winning." It means doing all the appropriate things to accomplish the mission with the least loss of life. It means living the Ranger and Soldier Creeds: "Leave no man behind." It means "leading from the front." It does not mean taking unnecessary risks. The commander who becomes a casualty is a handicap to his unit, not an asset. It means sharing the hardships. It means setting the example, the most important leadership principle. It means exemplifying all the leadership principles.

Developing that confidence does not have to wait until the unit serves in combat. It begins in training and magnifies the probability of combat success. Tough, realistic, battle-focused training with high standards is the best way to prepare your Soldiers. Training is the best place to begin if you are fortunate enough to have the opportunity to prepare your men before being committed.

When a Soldier says, "If I go to war again, I want to serve under you," he is saying "I trust you with my life. I know that you will protect it as if it were your own."

Nothing more needs to be said than that.

BIBLIOGRAPHY

BOOKS

Advanced First Aid & Emergency Care, Second Edition, American Red Cross, Doubleday & Co., 1981.

Appleman, Roy E., *South to the Naktong, North to the Yalu*, U.S. Army Center for Military History, Washington, 1961.

Baker, Senator Nancy Kassebaum, "Report of the Federal Committee on Gender-Integrated Training and Related Issues," 12/16/97.

Barber, Brace E., *Ranger School No Excuse Leadership*. Colorado Springs, CO: Patrol Leader Press, 2002.

Bowden, Mark. *Black Hawk Down*, New York: Atlantic Monthly Press, 1999.

Bugle Notes, USMA 1945.

Carruth, Gorton, & Ehrlich, Eugene, *The Giant Book of American Quotations*. New York: Portland House, 1988.

Case, John, *The Syndrome*. New York: Ballantine, 2001.

Chamberlain, Joshua Lawrence, *The Passing of the Armies*. Gettysburg, PA: Stan Clark Military Books, 1994.

Chambers, John Whiteclay II, *American Military History*. New York: Oxford University Press, 1999.

Crane, Stephen, *The Red Badge of Courage*. Mineola, NY: Dover Publications, 1990.

Dupuy, Colonel R. Ernest, *The Compact History of the United States Army*, New York: Hawthorn Books, 1961.

Fehrenbach, T. R., *This Kind of War*. Dulles, VA: Brassey's, 1998.

Fischer, David Hackett, *Washington's Crossing*. New York: Oxford University Press, 2004.

Fleming, Thomas, *Washington's Secret War*. New York: HarperCollins, 2005.

Franks, General Tommy, with McConnell, Malcolm, *American Soldier*. New York: Regan Books, 1994.

Freeman, Douglas Southall, *Washington*, an abridgment by Richard Harwell of the seven volume *George Washington*. New York: Charles Scribner's Sons, 1968, dust cover.

Gregg, Gary L. II, and Spalding, Matthew, editors, *Patriot Sage*. Wilmington, DE: ISI Books, 1999.

Handbook of First Aid and Emergency Care. New York: American Medical Association, Random House, 1980.

Hastings, Max, *The Korean War*. New York: Simon & Schuster, 1998.

Hifler, Joyce Sequiche, *A Cherokee Feast of Days*. Tulsa, OK: Council Oaks Books, 1992.

Holton, Bil, PhD, *Leadership Lessons of Ulysses S. Grant*. New York: Random House, 2000.

Holy Bible, The New King James Version. New York: Thomas Nelson Publishers, 1979.

Hqs, D/A, FM *21-20*, *Physical Training*, December 1957.

Hqs, D/A, FM *21-20*, *Physical Fitness Training*, 9/30/92.

Hqs, D/A, FM *22-100*, *Army Leadership*, August 1999.

Hqs, D/A, TC *25-20*, A *Leader's Guide to After-Action Reviews*, 9/30/93.

Keegan, John, *The Mask of Command*. New York: Penguin Books, 1987.

Ketchum, Richard M., *The Winter Soldiers*. Norwalk, CT: The Easton Press, 1973.

Lanning, Michael Lee, *Inside The LRRPS*. New York: Ballantine Books, 1988.

Laumer, Frank, *Dade's Last Command*. Gainesville, FL: University Press of Florida, 1995.

Le Storti, Anthony J., *When You're Asked to Do the Impossible*. Guilford, CT: Lyons Press, 2003.

Maihafer, Harry J., *The General and the Journalists*. Brassey's, Inc., 1998.

Marshall, BG S.L.A., *Men Against Fire*. Alexandria, VA: Byrd Enterprises, Inc., 1947.

Marshall, BG S.L.A., *The River and the Gauntlet*. New York: William Morrow & Company, 1953.

Marshall, BG S.L.A., *The Soldier's Load and the Mobility of a Nation*. Arlington, VA: The Marine Corps Association, 1980.

McAlister, George A., *Alamo: The Price of Freedom*. San Antonio, TX: Docutex, Inc., 1988.

McMaster, Major H.R., *Dereliction of Duty*. New York: Harper Collins, 1997.

McNamara, Robert S., *In Retrospect*. New York: Random House, 1995.

Moore, LTG Harold G., and Galloway, Joseph L., *We Were Soldiers Once ... And Young*. New York: Harper Perennial, 1992.

Montross, Lynn, *War Through the Ages*. New York: Harper & Row, 1944.

Nordyke, Phil, *All American All the Way*. St. Paul, MN: Zenith Press, 2005.

Ogburn, Charlton, Jr., *The Marauders*. New York: Harper & Brothers, 1959.

Pappas, George S., *To the Point*, Westport, CT: Praeger, 1993.

Perry, Mark, *Conceived in Liberty*. New York: Viking, 1997.

Peters, Ralph, *Beyond Baghdad: Postmodern War and Power*. Stackpole, Mechanicsburg, PA, 2003.

Peters. Ralph, *Beyond Terror*. Mechanicsburg, PA: Stackpole, 2002.

Presidential Commission on the Assignment of Women in the Armed Forces, The, "Report to the President: Women in Combat." Washington: Brassey's, 1992.

Pressfield, Steven, *The Gates of Fire*. New York: Doubleday, 1998.

Rusk, Dean, *As I Saw It*. New York: W. W. Norton & Co., 1990.

Schwarzkopf, GEN H. Norman, with Petre, Peter, *It Doesn't Take a Hero*. New York: Bantam Books, 1992.

Sears, Stephen W., *Gettysburg*. Boston: Houghton Mifflin Co., 2004.

Stanton, Colonel Martin N., *Somalia on Five Dollars a Day*, Novato, CA: Presidio, 2001.

Stanton, Shelby L., *Rangers at War: LRRPs in Vietnam*, New York: Ivy Books, 1992.

Stokesbury, James L., *A Short History of the Korean War*, New York: Quill William Morrow, 1988.

Summers, Colonel Harry G., Jr., *Vietnam Almanac*, New York: Facts on File Publications, 1985.

Sun Tzu: The Art of War, Translated by Griffith, Samuel B. London: Oxford University Press, 1963.

Sustaining the Transformation, MCRP 6-11D, U.S. Marine Corps, Washington, D.C., 1999.

Trulock, Alice Rains, *In the Hands of Providence*. Chapel Hill, NC: University of North Carolina Press, 1992.

Wallace, Willard M., *Soul of the Lion*. Gettysburg, PA: Stan Clark Military Books, 1960.

Wellman, Paul I., *Death in the Desert*. Lincoln, NE: University of Nebraska Press, 1935.

ANTHOLOGIES

Allen, William B., editor, *George Washington: A Collection*, Liberty Fund, as quoted in "The American Spectator."

Anderson, Stevens E., Ed., *The Great American Bathroom Book*, Vol. II, Compact Classics, Inc., Salt Lake City, UT, 1993.

Andersen, Stevens W., Ed., *The Great American Bathroom Book*, Vol. III, Compact Classics, Inc., Salt Lake City, UT, 1994.

Annals of America, The, Vol. 2, 1755–1783, Encylopaedia Britannica, Inc., Chicago, 1968.

Bennett, William J., Editor, *The Book of Virtues*, Simon & Schuster, NY, 1993.

Brown, H. Jackson, Jr., and Spizman, Robyn, ed., *A Hero in Every Heart*, Thomas Nelson Publishers, Nashville, TN, 1996.

Carruth, Gorton, & Ehrlich, Eugene, *The Giant Book of American Quotations*, Portland House, NY, 1988.

Celebrating Excellence, Inc., *Motivation Lombardi Style*, Celebrating Excellence, Inc., Lombard, IL, 1992.

Charlton, Charles, ed., *The Military Quotation Book*, St. Martin's Press, NY, 1990, p. 2.

Curtis, Bryan, ed., *Quotations from the Presidents of the United States*, Rutledge Hill Press, Nashville, TN, 2002.

Dupuy, Trevor Nevitt, ed., *Holidays: Days of Significance for All Americans*, first printing, Franklin Watts, Inc., NY, 1965.

Fall, Bernard, "The New Communist Army," Bernard Fall, ed., *Vietnam Witness*, Prager, NY, 1966.

Fitton, Robert A., *Leadership Quotations from the Military Tradition*, Westview Press, Boulder, CO, 1994.

James, William, "The Energies of Men," *Man and Society*, Vol. 7, Gateway to the Great Books, Encyclopedia Britannica, Inc., Chicago, 1963.

Johnson, Oliver A., *Ethics, Selections from Classical and Contemporary Writers*, Holt, Rinehart and Winston, NY, 1958.

Lloyd, BG (Ret.) Herbert J., ed., *The Reasons Why*, 7/1/92.

Malloy, Merritt, & Sorensen, Shauna, *The Quotable Quote Book*, Citadel Press, NY, 1990.

Patton, Robert A., Ed., *Leadership Quotations from the Military Tradition, Westview Press*, Boulder, 1990.

Shakespeare, William, *Julius Caesar, The Oxford Dictionary of Quotations*, Oxford University Press, London, 1955.

Shakespeare, William, *King Henry V, The Oxford Dictionary of Quotations*, Oxford University Press, London, 1955.

Tsouras, Peter G., *Warriors' Words*, Cassell Arms and Armour, London, 1992.

Vietnam 10 Years Later, Defense Information School. Ft. Benjamin Harrison, IN, 1983, p. 89.

Wickham, John A. Jr., General (Ret.), *On Leadership and the Profession of Arms*, Department of the Army Information Management Support Center, Washington, DC, 4/25/95.

PERIODICALS

Adams, Tony. 1998. "Soldiers: Military should stay out of personal relationships," *The Benning Leader*, p. 11.

"Army Announces FY '95 Proposed Budget." *The Bayonet*. 1994, p.1.

"Army Report: Research and Development: Enabling Transformation," *AUSA News*, Arlington, VA, Oct 2000, p.9.

"Army to continue to improve body armor," *Washington Update*, AUSA News, Arlington, VA, 2/06.

"Army Unveils Wheeled Armored Vehicles for Lewis Brigades," *Washington Update*, AUSA Institute of Land Warfare, Arlington, VA, Dec 2000, p. 1.

Arnold, S.L. 1993. "Somalia: An Operation Other Than War." *Military Review* p. 26.

AUSA News, "Shelton: Strategy, Structure Must Be in Balance," Feb 2001, p. 1.

"AUSA Transformation Panel Briefing," *AUSA News*, 10/26/00, p. 1.

Bartlett, Rep. Roscoe, (R-MD). 2001. "Q: Has the Military's Gender-Integrated Basic Training Been Successful? No: Gender-Integrated Basic Training Has Been Proved Deficient in All Respects," *Insight* p. 41.

Bennett, Doraine. 2004. "Task Force Soldier." *Infantry Bugler* p. 6-7.

Bennett, William J. 1998. "Does Honor Have a Future?" *Imprimis* p. 8.

Bowman, James. 1999. "The Oscar for Historical Accuracy Goes To ..." *Wall Street Journal* p. A18.

Brady, James. 1993. "Women in the Infantry?" *Atlanta Constitution* p. A21.

Brady, MG (Ret.) Patrick H. 1998. "United States Has Become a Land of Lost Ideals." *Ledger-Enquirer* p. A13.

Bush, President George W. 2001. "Bush's address to the nation." *Columbus Ledger* p. A4.

Campbell, Joseph. 2004. *Columbus Ledger-Enquirer* p. F1.

Charen, Mona. 2001. "Lowering Bar for Women Hurts Military," *Atlanta Constitution* p. A17.

Cheney, Dick, VP Elect. 2001. *Commentary.*

"CIA: Iran seeking high-tech weapons," *Atlanta Constitution*, 9/8/01, p. A9.

"Combating Terrorism, Preserving Freedom," *Cato Policy Report*, Nov./Dec. 96, p. 7.

Connerly, Robert E. 1995. "To Die For." *Atlanta Constitution.*

Cooper, COL Charles D., USAF Ret. 1991. *The Retired Officer Magazine* p. 4.

Cox, Matthew. 2001. "Tougher Training." *Army Times* p.14.

Dickey, SFC Connie E., "Fraternization Policy Gets DOD Approval," *The Bayonet* p. A1.

Dempsey, CPT James K. 1998. "Up Is Our Only Option: Improving Army Policies on Gender Integration," ARMY p. 12.

Dickey, SFC Connie E., and Gilmore, Gerry J. 1998: "New APFT standards to take affect (sic) Feb. 1." *The Bayonet* p. A-3.

Dupuy, Trevor N. 1991. "How the War was Won." *National Review* p. 30.

Ent, Uzal W. 2000. "War on a Shoestring." *Military History* p. 41-2.

Field, Kim, and Nagl, John. 2001. "Combat Roles for Women: A Modest Proposal," *Parameters* p. 74.

Galloucis, MAJ Michael S. 1996. "The Military and the Media." *Army* p. 14.

Garland, Albert. 1992. "Army needs to stop jerking Infantry around, *The Benning Patriot* p. 2.

Geewax, Marilyn. 2001. "Attack from Cyberspace." *Atlanta Constitution* p. C1.

Garland, Albert N. 1997. "Honor is most important Soldier value." *Benning Leader* p. 2.

Greenwood, Bryon E. 2000. "The Anatomy of Change: Why Armies Succeed or Fail at *Transformation*," Institute of Land Warfare, p. v.

Hall, Wayne M. 2000. "The Janus Paradox: The Army's Preparation for Conflicts of the 21st Century," Institute of Land Warfare p. v.

Haney, Eric L. 1997. "Violent Import Has Taken Root." *The Atlanta Constitution* p. A17.

Heral, Ethan. 1985. "Yasotay and the Mangoday of Genghis Khan." *Armed Forces Journal International* p.361.

Houston, COL James. 1997. "Wanted: International Treaty Against Terrorism." *Officer Review* p. 8.

Krulak, Charles C., General, USMC. 1998. "The Standard." *Officer Review* p. 3.

Maddox, Sergeant Michael. 2001. "Objective Force Needs High-Speed Strategic Lift." *Bayonet* p. A1.

Mahnaimi, Uzi, and Walker, Tom. 2001. "Defectors Say Iraq Tested Nuclear Bomb," *Sunday Times.*

"Making Sense of Killing," *Army*, November 2005, p. 64–67

McCain, John. 2004. "In Search of Courage." *Fast Company* p. 52.

"Media and the Tactical Commander," Center for Army Lessons Learned, Ft. Leavenworth, KS, December 1992

Moskos, Charles. 2001. "Peacekeeping Improves Combat Readiness." *Commentary.*

Murray, Williamson. 1999. "Military Culture Does Matter." *Strategic Review* p. 36.

Naylor, Sean D. 2003. "You're a Rifleman First." *Army Times* p. 14.

Nix, Dusty. 2000. "Top Brass." *Columbus Ledger* p. F1.

"Objective Force Is Needed for Relevancy," *AUSA News*, Apr 2001, p. 2.

Ouimette, Dan. 2003. *Pensacola Civitan.*

Pearson, Brigadier Willard. 2006. "Find 'em, Fix 'em, Finish 'em." *The Always First Brigade* p. 4.

Powell, Colin L. 92/93. "U. S. Forces: Challenges Ahead." *Foreign Affairs* p. 38.

Puckett, Ralph. 1992. "Are Women Physically, Mentally Ready for War?" *Benning Leader* p. 1.

Puckett, Ralph. 1997. "A Right to Fight?" *Columbus Ledger-Enquirer* p. F1.

Reingold, Jennifer, 2004. "Soldiering On." *Fast Company.*

Roberts, Sen. Pat (R-KS) and Cleland, Sen. Max (D-GA). 2001. "Realistic Restraint: Seven Principles for Shaping a New National Security Strategy." *Armed Forces Journal International* p. 12.

Scaborough, Rowan. 2001 "Pentagon Urged to Separate Sexes in Training." Washington *Times* National Weekly Edition p. 19.

Shalikashvilli, General John M. 1994. *TROA Magazine* p. 63.

Shelton, General Henry H. Shelton. 2001. "Professional Education: The Key to Transformation," *Parameters* p.16.

Shinseki, General Eric K., 2000. *Retired Officer* p. 52.

Spence, Cong. Floyd D. 2001. "Defense Challenges for the Twenty-First Century," *Officer Review* p. 6.

Sloan, Stephen. 1995. "Terrorism: National Security Policy and the Home Front," edited by Stephen Pelletiere, The Strategic Studies Institute of the U.S. Army War College.

Stevens, Sen. Ted. 2000. "The Army Must Transform." *AUSA News* p. 6.

"Strategic Responsiveness: New Paradigm for a Transformed Army," *Defense Report*, AUSA, Arlington, VA, Oct 2000, p. 1.

Summers, Harry. 1997. "Good Military Order and Discipline." *Washington Times* p. B1.

Summers, Harry. 1997. "Take One Fit Man." *Washington Times* p. A12.

Taylor, Karen. 2000. "The Bayonet," p. A-1.

"The Fallen," *Army Times*, 11/07/05, p. 29.

Tiboni, Frank. 20001. "Officials: No Delay in Fielding of First IBCT." *Army Times* p. 44.

Tonelson, Alan. 1993. "Superpower Without a Sword." *Foreign Affairs* p. 170.

Trainor, Bernard E. 2000. "The Still Forgotten War." *Boston Globe* p. A27.

"U.S. Army at the Dawn of the 21st Century: Overcommitted and Underresourced, The" Defense Report, AUSA *Institute of Land Warfare*, Jan 2001, p.1.

Wall Street Journal, 1/29/99, p. w11.

Wilkerson, Paul. 1995. "Terrorism: Motivations and Causes." Canadian Security Intelligence Service, Commentary No. 53.

Will, George. 1998. "Gap between civilian, military cultures necessary." *Columbus Ledger-Enquirer* p. F4.

Woodring, CDR Marcus E. 2001. "Build Trust with the Media." *Proceedings* p. 90.

Worrell, Ivan, Ed. 2006. *The Always First Brigade*. Vol. 8, No. 1, p.14.

LETTERS, NOTES, UNPUBLISHED MEMORANDA, ETC.

Eighth Army Ranger Company Rangers' comments to Company Commander, Ralph Puckett, on numerous occasions

Abrams, General Creighton, Guidance when forming the 1st Ranger Battalion, Fall 1973

Bassett, LTC Rick, response to questionnaire

Berry, Chaplain (MAJOR) Steve, notes to author

Birch, Command Sergeant Major Alfred G., *RSM Notes*, Note #3, undated

Bowman, Lieutenant Colonel (Ret.), Donald, note to author

Cole, COL Tom, Commander, Basic Combat Training Brigade, Ft. Benning, GA, *Interview*, 8/16/01

DA Form 705, June 1998

Hqs, 3/75th Rgr Bn, *Physical Training SOP*

Inscription on monument at Headquarters, Infantry Training Brigade, Ft. Benning, GA

Kearney, LTC Frank, "Impact of Leaders on Organizational Structure: A 75th Ranger Regiment Case Study," 4/7/97

LaCamera, Colonel Paul J., "Regimental Commander's Policy Statement #6, Hqs, 75th Rgr Rgt

LaCamera, Mrs. Paul, note to author

Leuer, MG Kenneth, memo to author

Maher, MG John, Commanding General, 25th Infantry Division (Light), letter to the author, 4/6/97

McGee, COL John H., Letter, Subject: Training Report of the Eighth Army Ranger Company, 1 October 1950, to Commanding General, Eighth United States Army Korea

Nixon, James C., COL, IN, and Birch, Alfred G., CSM, USA "Memo for All Rangers," 6/11/04

Odom, COL (Ret.) Ronald G., Letter to Association of Graduates, 2003

Pasquarette, LTC James, response to questionnaire

Pickering, Command Sergeant Major Jimmy R., "Welcome Letter and NCO Standards," Hqs, 11th Inf Rgt, 2/19/03

Ranger Creed

Robert Rogers Standing Order No. 2

"The Leadership Experience," Duke University Leadership Development Initiative brochure, NC, 4/27/05, p.10

Titus, Captain Kevin, Chemical Officer, 75th Ranger Regiment, memo to author

WD AGO Form 639, 1/11/51

Whitehead, Leslie D., quoted in 75th Ranger Regiment 20 February 1993 "Dining In" brochure

Lienhard, John H. "The Engines of Our Ingenuity: No. 997, Gene Bullard," University of Houston

SPEECHES

Anderson, Colonel Dorian, Commander, Ranger Training Brigade, quoted by Chaplain Tom Wheatley

"Army Transformation," Transformation Brief—short version, 10/17/00, slide 7 R, USAIC

Cucolo, Colonel Tony, "Chaos and Ambiguity: Leadership in the SASO Environment," Briefing to 75th Ranger Regiment Mangoday Panel, 4/17/01

Eisenhower, GEN Dwight D., Address in London, 12 June 45, quoted in Fitton, Robert A., *Leadership Quotations from the Military Tradition*, Westview Press, Boulder, CO, 1994, p. 234

Grange, MG David, Speaking to 75th Ranger Regiment officers, 2002

Johnson, Harold K., "The Role of the United States Army," Address, Portland, OR, Military Government Association Convention, 5/29/63

Keen, Colonel Ken, Commanders Conference, 10/12/99

Kernan, General William F. "Buck", Briefing 75th Ranger Regiment at 10th Anniversary of Panama Invasion

Shinseki, GEN Eric K., Chief of Staff of the Army, testimony before Congress, 9/27/00

ELECTRONIC SOURCES

Antonia, LTC (Ret.) Keith, e-mail to author, 10/28/02

AP Report, SIRO Intelligence Briefing, 9/05/01

Beck, Stephen, *The Battle of Agincourt*, Internet, updated 7/15/01

Birch, CSM Greg. E-mail to author, 8/04/04

Blocker, Lieutenant Colonel Marlon D., Commander, 1-11th Infantry, E-mail to author 1/24/06

Dao, James, "Army Says Unit Is Unprepared for War Duty," *New York Times*, 3/29/01, Internet

Economist Home Page, "Reacting to Terrorism," The Economist Newspaper Limited, 1996

Good Quotations by Famous People, Collected by Dr. Gabriel Robbins, University of Virginia

Hess, Pamela, "CIA: China, Iran, Terrorism, Pose Worst Threats" UPI, 2/7/01 (UPI) Internet

Hooker, Richard, "Sparta," Internet, updated 6/06/99

Metcalf, Geoff, "How to Choose a Commander in Chief," WorldNet Daily. com, 2000

Offley, Ed, "Outside Experts Uncertain of Success for Army Transformation Effort," *Stars and Stripes Omnimedia*, 12/19/00, p.1

quotationspage.com/quotes/Mark-Twain/31

Rosenthal, A.M., "Invitation to Murder," NY Times Web site, Jul 1996

Stine, Jason, CATD, TIS, Ft. Benning, GA, E-mail, 9/29/01

Stone, Colonel Frank, CATD, TIS, Ft. Benning, GA, E-mail, 9/29/01

Terrorism Resource Center, TRC@Terrorism.com

"What Is Terrorism?" *The Economist*, 1996, Web site

Wikipedia Encyclopedia On Line

www.murphys-laws.com

www.quoteland.com

The Quotations Page, Theoprastus from Diogenes Laerties, "Lives of Eminent Philosophers," Yahoo Quotations Page

ENDNOTES

INTRODUCTION

1   Marshal, BG S. L. A., *Men Against Fire*, Byrd Enterprises, Inc., Alexandria, VA 1947, p. 10

2   *Sun Tzu: The Art of War*, Translated by Griffith, Samuel B., Oxford University Press, London, 1963, p. 55

SECTION I: HONORARY COLONEL OF THE REGIMENT

1   Heral, Ethan, "Yasotay and the Mangoday of Genghis Khan," *Armed Forces Journal International*, January 1985, p.361

SECTION II: LEADERSHIP

1   Field Marshall Viscount Slim, *Unofficial History*, 1957, as quoted in Tsouras, Peter G., *Warriors' Words*, Cassell Arms and Armour, London, 1992, p.319

2   Keegan, John, *The Mask of Command*, Penguin Books, NY, 1987, p. 58

3   Keegan, p. 58

4   Keegan, p. 76–77

5   Keegan, p. 113

6   Keegan, p. 208

7   Keegan, p. 210

8   Keegan, p. 236

9   Odom, Colonel (Ret.) Ronald G., in letter to Association of Graduates, 2003

10 Hqs, D/A, FM 22-100, *Army Leadership*, August 1999, p. 6–31

11 Fuller, J.F.C., as Quoted by Holton, Bil, PhD, *Leadership Lessons of Ulysses S. Grant*, Random House, NY, 2000, p. 140

12   Curtis, Bryan, ed., *Quotations from the Presidents of the United States*, Rutledge Hill Press, Nashville, TN, 2002, p. 151

13   Hqs, D/A, *FM 22-100, Army Leadership*, August 1999, p. 2–6.

14   Eisenhower, General Dwight D., Address in London, 6/12/45, quoted in Fitton, Robert A., Leadership *Quotations from the Military Tradition*, Westview Press, Boulder, CO, 1994, p. 234

15   Hqs, D/A, *FM 22-100, Army Leadership*, August 1999, p. B-2

16   Worrell, Ivan, Ed., *The Always First Brigade*, Vol. 8, No. 1, Sweetwater, TN, January 2006, p.14

17   Holton, Bil, PhD, *Leadership Lessons of Ulysses S. Grant*, Random House, NY, 2000, p. 50

18   Maihafer, Harry J., *The General and the Journalists*, Brassey's, Inc., 1998, p. 209

19   Bryant, Coach Bear, quoted in Fitton, Robert A., *Leadership Quotations from the Military Tradition*, Westview Press, Boulder, CO, 1994, p. 148

20   Mangan, James T., Quoted in *The Great American Bathroom Book*, Vol. III, Andersen, Stevens W., Ed., Compact Classics, Inc., Salt Lake City, UT, 1994, p. 442

21   FM 22-100, *Army Leadership*, August 1999, p. 2–5

22   General George S. Patton, Jr., *War As I Knew It*, 1947, as quoted in Tsouras, Peter G., *Warriors' Words*, Cassell Arms and Armour, London, 1992, p. 443

23   Murray, Williamson, "Military Culture Does Matter," *Strategic Review*, Spring 1999, p. 36

24   Holton, Bil, PhD, p. 88

25   Naylor, Sean D., "You're A Rifleman First," *Army Times*, 10/20/03, p. 14

26   Naylor, Ibid, p. 14

27   Naylor, Ibid, p. 14

28   Hqs, D/A, *FM 22-100, Army Leadership*, August 1999, p. 5-4

29   Garland, Albert, "Army needs to stop jerking Infantry around, *The Benning Patriot*, 6/26/92, Columbus, GA, p. 2

30   Xenophon (c. 431 BC—c. 352 BC) rallying the few surviving officers of the Ten Thousand to action, after most of the officers were murdered under truce by the Persians in 401 BC, in *The March up Country (Anabasis)*, c. 370 BC—c. 365 BC, tr. Rouse as quoted in Tsouras, Peter G., *Warriors' Words*, Cassell Arms and Armour, London, 1992, p. 166

31 The Duke of Marlborough, quoted in Churchill, *Marlborough*, 1933, as quoted in Tsouras, Peter G., *Warriors' Words*, Cassell Arms and Armour, London, 1992, p. 167

32 Hqs, D/A, FM *22-100*, *Army Leadership*, August 1999, p. 1–6

33 Hqs, D/A, FM *22-100*, *Army Leadership*, August 1999, Foreword

34 Birch, Command Sergeant Major Alfred G., *RSM Notes*, Note #3, undated

35 "Memo for All Rangers," 11 June 2004, Colonel James C. Nixon, and Command Sergeant Major Alfred G. Birch

36 Tsouras, p. 169

37 Pickering, Command Sergeant Major Jimmy R., "Welcome Letter and NCO Standards," Hqs, 11th Infantry Regiment, 2/19/03

Section III: Command and Staff

1 www.murphys-laws.com

2 Carruth, Gorton, & Ehrlich, Eugene, *The Giant Book of American Quotations*, Portland House, NY, 1988, p. 85

3 Hqs, D/A, FM *22-100*, *Army Leadership*, August 1999, p. 5-3

4 Summers, Colonel Harry G., Jr., *Vietnam Almanac*, Facts on File Publications, NY, 1985, p. 141

5 Holton, Bil, PhD, *Leadership Lessons of Ulysses S. Grant*, Gramercy Books, NY, 1995, p. 83

6 Blocker, Lieutenant Colonel Marlon D., Commander, First to 11th Infantry, E-mail to author 1/24/06

7 Blocker, Lieutenant Colonel Marlon D., Commander, First to 11th Infantry, E-mail to author 1/24/06

8 Bowman, Lieutenant Colonel (Ret.), Donald, in note to author

9 Bowman, Lieutenant Colonel (Ret.), Donald, in note to author

10 Fitton, p. 258

11 Keen, Colonel Ken, Commanders Conference, 10/12/99

12 Downing, General Wayne A., quoted in "Regimental Commander's Policy Statement #6, LaCamera, Colonel Paul J., Hqs, 75th Rgr Rgt

13 Downing, General Wayne A., quoted in "Regimental Commander's Policy Statement #6, LaCamera, Colonel Paul J., Hqs, 75th Rgr Rgt

14 Leuer, MG Kenneth, in memo to author

15 Fitton, p. 284

16 Hqs, D/A, *FM 22-100, Army Leadership*, August, 1999, p. 2–28

17 Hqs, D/A, *FM 22-100, Army Leadership*, August, 1999, p. 6–20

18 Fitton, p. 49

19 Anderson, Colonel Dorian, Commander, Ranger Training Brigade, to Chaplain Tom Wheatley

20 Charlton, Charles, ed., *The Military Quotation Book*, St. Martin's Press, NY, 1990, p. 2

21 Berry, Chaplain (Major) Steve, Notes provided to author

22 Le Storti, Anthony J., *When You're Asked to Do the Impossible*, Lyons Press, Guilford, CT, 2003

23 Hqs, D/A, *FM 22-100, Army Leadership*, August 1999, p. 6–15

24 Curtis, Bryan, ed., p. 294

25 Hqs, D/A, *FM 22-100, Army Leadership*, August 1999, p. C-12

26 Fitton, p. 281

27 Franks, General Tommy, with McConnell, Malcolm, *American Soldier*, Regan Books, NY, 1994, p. 249

28 Moore, Lieutenant General Harold G., and Galloway, Joseph L., p. 30-1

29 Moore, Lieutenant General Harold G., and Galloway, Joseph L., p. 51

Section IV: Warriors

1 Hqs, D/A, FM 22-100, *Army Leadership*, August 1999, p. 2– 21

2 Nordyke, Phil, *All American All the Way*, Zenith Press, St. Paul, MN, 2005, p. 627

3 Murray, Williamson, "Military Culture Does Matter," *Strategic Review*, Spring 1999, p. 36

4 Hqs, D/A, *FM 22-100, Army Leadership*, August 1999, p. 3– 6

5 Abrams, General Creighton, "Guidance when forming the First Ranger Battalion," Fall 1973

6 Wellman, Paul I., <u>Death in the Desert</u>, University of Nebraska Press, Lincoln, NE, 1935, p. x

7 Hqs, D/A, <u>FM 22-100, Army Leadership</u>, August 1999, p. 2– 21

8 Wellman, Paul I., p. 196

9 Wellman, Paul I., p. 201

10 Wellman, Paul I., p. 204

11 Wellman, Paul I., p. 202

12 Wellman, Paul I., p. 196

13 Wellman, Paul I., p. x

14 Hqs, D/A, FM 22-100, Army Leadership, August 1999, p. 2–21

15 Shakespeare, William, King Henry V, The Oxford Dictionary of Quotations, Oxford University Press, Oxford, London, 1955, p.445

16 Beck, Stephen, The Battle of Agincourt, Internet, updated 7/15/01

17 Beck, Ibid.

18 Beck, Ibid.

19 FM 22-100, p. 3–7

20 Beck, Op. Cit.

21 Montross, Lynn, War Through the Ages, Harper & Row, NY, 1944, p. 183–184

22 Beck, Op. Cit.

23 Hooker, Richard, "Sparta," Internet, Updated 6/6/99

24 Herodotus, The Histories, as Quoted in The Gates of Fire, by Pressfield, Steven, Doubleday, NY, 1998, Historical Note

25 Wikipedia, Thermopylae

26 Hooker, Op. Cit.

27 Hqs, D/A, FM 22-100, Army Leadership, August, 1999, p. 2–21

28 Ranger Creed

29 Bowden, Mark. Black Hawk Down, Atlantic Monthly Press, NY, 1999, p. 333

30 Hqs, D/A, FM 22-100, Army Leadership, August 1999, p. 2–21

31 FM 22-100, p. 2–21

32 Bowman, James, "The Oscar for Historical Accuracy Goes to..." Wall Street Journal, 3/19/99, p. A18

33 Hqs, D/A, FM 22-100, Army Leadership, August, 1999, p. 2-2

34 Chamberlain, p. 20

Section V: Training: Individual Training

1 Fitton, Robert A., ed., Leadership Quotations from the Military Tradition, Westview Press, Boulder, CO., 1994, p. 238

2 Hqs, D/A, TC 25-20, A Leader's Guide to After-Action Reviews, 9/30/93, p. 5-1

3 Hqs, D/A, FM 22-100, Army Leadership, August 1999, p. 5–26

4   Hqs, D/A, *TC 25-20*, *A Leader's Guide to After-Action Reviews*, 9/30/93, p. 1–3

5   Fitton, p. 185

6   Fitton, p. 241

7   Bowman, Lieutenant Colonel (Ret.) Donald, in a note to the author

8   TC 25-20, p. 5-3

9   Hqs, D/A, *TC 25-20*, *A Leader's Guide to After-Action Reviews*, 9/30/93, p. 5-3

10 Fitton, p. 240

11 Fitton, p. 303

12 Hqs, D/A, *FM 22-100*, *Army Leadership*, August 1999, p. 1–6

13 Krulak, Charles C., General, USMC, "The Standard," *Officer Review*, November 1998, p. 3

14 Summers, Harry, "Take one fit man," *Washington Times*, 7/10/97, p. A12

15 Wickham, John A. Jr., General (Ret.), Ibid. p. 2

16 Johnson, Oliver A., *Ethics*, *Selections from Classical and Contemporary Writers*, Holt, Rinehart and Winston, NY, 1958, p. 1

17 Summers, Harry, "Good military order and discipline," *Washington Times*, 6/15/97, p. B1

18 *Wall Street Journal*, 1/29/99, p. w11

19 Aitken, Major R.I., Quoted in *Leadership Quotations from the Military Tradition*, Fitton, Robert. A., Ed., Westview Press, Boulder, 1990, p. 163

20 Will, George, "Gap between civilian, military cultures necessary," *Columbus Ledger-Enquirer*, 11/22/98, p. F4

21 Fitton, p. 304

22 FM 22-100, p. 2–3

23 "The Leadership Experience," Duke University Leadership Development Initiative brochure, NC, 4/27/05, p.10

24 Hqs, D/A, *FM 22-100*, *Army Leadership* August 1999, p. 2-2

25 Bennett, William J., "Does Honor Have a Future?" *Imprimis*, Hillsdale College, December 1998, p. 8

26 Garland, Albert N., "Honor is most important Soldier value," *Benning Leader*, 2/21/97, p. 2

27 Wickham, John A. Jr., General (Ret.), "On Leadership and the Profession of Arms," Department of the Army Information Management Support Center, Washington, DC, 4/25/95, p. 52

28 Tsouras, Peter G., *Warriors' Words*, Cassell Arms and Armour, London, 1992, p. 34

29 *The Battalion Commander's Handbook,*" as quoted in *FM 2-100 Army Leadership*, Department of the Army, Oct 1998, p. 6–12

30 Hqs, D/A, *FM 22-100, Army Leadership*, August 1999, p. 2–22

31 Fitton, p. 302–3. This quote was taken from General MacArthur's address to the Corps of Cadets, USMA, 1962

32 Comment made by Initial Briefer at USAF Academy for spring 2002 Falcon Heritage Forum

33 Hqs, D/A, *FM 22-100, Army Leadership*, August 1999, p. B-1

34 Perry, Mark, *Conceived in Liberty*, Viking, NY, 1997, p. 273

35 Perry, p. 274

36 Perry, p. 274

37 Perry, p. 388–389

38 Perry, p. 390

39 Perry, p. 390

40 Perry, p. 272

41 Perry, p. 164

42 Perry, p. 174

43 Perry, p. 175

44 Perry, p. 282

45 Wallace, Willard M., *Soul of the Lion*. Stan Clark Military Books, Gettysburg, PA, 1960, p. 149–50

46 Wallace, p. 189

47 Chamberlain, Joshua Lawrence, *The Passing of the Armies*, Stan Clark Military Books, Gettysburg, 1994, p. 270

48 Chamberlain, p. 261

49 Bowman, Lieutenant Colonel (Ret.) Donald C., Note to author

50 Trulock, Alice Rains, *In the Hands of Providence*, University of North Carolina Press, Chapel Hill, NC, 1992, p. 174

51 Perry, p. 282

52 Trulock, p. 52

53 Trulock, p. 42–46

54 Lieutenant General Arthur S. Collins, Jr., *Common Sense Training*, 1978, as quoted in Tsouras, Peter G., *Warriors' Words*, Cassell Arms and Armour, London, 1992, p. 444

55 Bennett, Doraine, "Task Force Soldier," *Infantry Bugler*, Spring 2004, p. 6–7

56 Naylor, Sean D., "You're a Rifleman First," *Army Times*, 10/20/03, p. 14

57 Baker, Senator Nancy Kassebaum, "Report of the Federal Committee on Gender-Integrated Training and Related Issues," 12/16/97, p. 2

58 Baker, p. 8

59 Baker, p. 4

60 Baker, p. 5

61 Basic Trainees' Comments to author

62 Cox, Matthew, "Tougher Training," *Army Times*, 4/16/01, p.14

63 Baker, p. 13

64 Baker, p. 5

65 Baker, p. 7

66 Baker, p. 6

67 Baker, p. 9

68 Baker, p. 15

69 Cole, Colonel Tom, Commander, Basic Combat Training Brigade, Ft. Benning, GA, *Interview*, 8/16/01

70 Baker, p. 17

71 DA Form 705, June 1998

72 Dickey, SFC Connie E., and Gilmore, Gerry J., "New APFT standards to take affect (sic) Feb. 1," *The Bayonet*, 12/11/98, p. A-3

73 Bartlett, Rep. Roscoe, (R-MD), "Q: Has the military's gender-integrated basic training been successful? No: Gender-integrated basic training has been proved deficient in all respects," *Insight*, 8/20/01, p. 41

74 Baker, p. 15

75 Scarborough, Rowan, "Pentagon urged to separate sexes in training," Washington *Times* National Weekly Edition, 8/13/01–8/19/01, p. 19

76 Inscription on monument at Headquarters, Infantry Training Brigade, Ft. Benning, Georgia

77 Tsouras, Peter G., *Warriors' Words*, Cassell, London, 1994, p. 442

78 Tsouras, p. 440

79 Fehrenbach, T. R., *This Kind of War*, Brassey's, Dulles, VA, 1998, p. 453

80 Fehrenbach, p. 456

81 Fehrenbach, p. xi

82 Lloyd, BG (Ret.) Herbert J., ed., *The Reasons Why*, 7/1/92, p. 51

83 Marshall, BG S. L. A., *The River and the Gauntlet*, William Morrow & Company, NY, 1953, p. 1

84 Fall, Bernard, "The New Communist Army," Bernard Fall, ed., *Vietnam Witness*, Prager, NY, 1966, p. 253

85 Wellman, Paul I., *Death in the Desert*, University of Nebraska Press, Lincoln, NE, 1987, p. 204–205

86 General J. Lawton Collins, as quoted in FM 22-100, p. 1-1

87 *Motivation Lombardi Style*, p. 2

88 Carruth, Gordon, & Ehrlich, Eugene, *The Giant Book of American Quotations*, Portland House, NY, 1988, p. 204

89 Sears, Stephen W., *Gettysburg*, Houghton Mifflin Co., Boston, 2004, p. 397

90 Moore, Lieutenant General Harold G., and Galloway, Joseph L., p. 78–88

91 Moore, Lieutenant General Harold G., and Galloway, Joseph L., p. 151

92 Moore, Lieutenant General Harold G., and Galloway, Joseph L., p. 155

93 Moore, Lieutenant General Harold G., and Galloway, Joseph L., p. 168

94 Charlton, p. 92

SECTION V: TRAINING: UNIT

95 The Emperor Maurice, *The Strategikon*, c. AD 600, as quoted in Tsouras, Peter G., *Warriors' Words*, Cassell Arms and Armour, London, 1992, p. 481

96 Major General Frederick Baron von Steuben, *Revolutionary War Drill Manual*, 1794, as quoted in Tsouras, Peter G., *Warriors' Words*, Cassell Arms and Armour, London, 1992, p. 481

97 *Advanced First Aid & Emergency Care*, Second Edition, American Red Cross, Doubleday & Co., Mar. 1981, p. 59

98 Hqs, D/A, FM 22-100, *Army Leadership*, August 1999, p. A-4

99 FM 22-100, p. 1–13

100 McGee, Colonel John H., Letter, Subject: Training Report of the Eighth Army Ranger Company, 1 October 1950, sent to Commanding General, Eighth United States Army Korea

101 Titus, Captain Kevin, Chemical Officer, 75th Ranger Regiment, provided much of the material for this essay.

102 Montross, *War Through the Ages*, Harper & Row, NY, 1944, p.702

103 Montross, p.702

104 Robert Rogers Standing Order No. 2 for his Rangers

105 Dupuy, Colonel R Ernest, *The Compact History of the United States Army*, NY, 1961, p. 78

106 Laumer, Frank, *Dade's Last Command*, University Press of Florida, Gainesville, FL, 1995, p. 177

107 Pappas, George S., *To the Point*, Westport, CT, 1993, p. 228–229

108 *Bugle Notes*, USMA 1945, p 63–64

109 Field Marshall Earl Wavell, unpublished, *Recollections*, 1946, as quoted in Tsouras, Peter G., *Warriors' Words*, Cassell Arms and Armour, London, 1992, p. 350

110 Marshall, Brigadier General S. L. A., *The River and the Gauntlet*, William Morrow & Co., NY, 1953, title page

111 WD AGO Form 639, Item 21, dtd 11 Jan 51

112 Moore, Lieutenant General Harold G., and Galloway, Joseph L., p. 426

113 Moore, Lieutenant General Harold G., & Galloway, Joseph L., *We Were Soldiers Once … and Young*, Harper Perennial, 1992, p. 106

114 General Matthew B. Ridgway, *Soldiers*, 1956, as quoted in Tsouras, Peter G., *Warriors' Words*, Cassell Arms and Armour, London, 1992, p. 444

115 Hqs, D/A, *FM 22-100, Army Leadership*, August 1999, p. 1–13

116 Hqs, D/A, *FM 22-100, Army Leadership*, August 1999, p. 3-2

117 Fitton, Robert A., ed., Leadership Quotations from the Military Tradition, Westview Press, Boulder, CO., 1994, p. 71

118 Weatherhead, Leslie D., quoted in BG (Ret.) Herbert J., ed., *The Reasons Why*, 7/1/92, p. 64

119 WD AGO FORM 639, 1 July 47, Par. 21, 11 Jan 51

120 Moore, Lieutenant General Harold G., and Galloway, Joseph L., p. 230

121 Stanton, Shelby L., *Rangers at War: LRRPs in Vietnam*, Ivy Books, NY, 1992, p. ix

122 Lanning, Michael Lee, *Inside The LRRPS*, Ballantine Books, NY, 1988, p. 161

123 Lanning, p. 161

124 Lanning, p. 170

125 Lanning, p. 185

126 *Annals of America, The*, Vol. 2, 1755–1783, Encylopaedia Britannica, Inc., Chicago, 1968, p. 334

127 Fischer, David Hackett, *Washington's Crossing*, Oxford University Press, NY, 2004, p. 109

128 Stanton. Colonel Martin N., *Somalia on Five Dollars a Day*, Presidio, Novato, CA, 2001, p. 235

129 Bowman, Lieutenant Colonel (Ret.) Don, in note to author

130 *Motivation Lombardi Style*, p. 25

131 *A Hero in Every Heart*, edited by Brown, H. Jackson, Jr., and Spizman, Robyn, Thomas Nelson Publishers, Nashville, TN, p. 83

132 Case, John, *The Syndrome*, Ballantine, NY, 2001, p. 244–245

133 *Sustaining the Transformation*, MCRP 6-11D, U.S. Marine Corps, Washington, D.C., 1999, p. 21

134 The Emperor Maurice, *The Strategikon*, c. AD 600, as quoted in Tsouras, Peter G., *Warriors' Words*, Cassell Arms and Armour, London, 1992, p. 438

135 Anonymous America Soldier, quoted in Cowing, *Dear Folks at Home*, 1919, as quoted in Tsouras, Peter G., *Warriors' Words*, Cassell Arms and Armour, London, 1992, p. 443

136 Trainor, Bernard E., "The Still Forgotten War," *Boston Globe*, 6/29/00, p. A27

137 Hastings, Max, *The Korean War*, Simon & Schuster, NY, 1998, p. 334

138 Fehrenbach, p. xi

139 Hqs, D/A, *FM 22-100, Army Leadership*, August 1999, p. 6–25

140 Tsouras, p. 453

141 Antonia, Lieutenant Colonel (Ret.) Keith, E-mail to author, 10/28/02

SECTION VI: TAKING CARE OF SOLDIERS

1   Quoteland.com, www.quoteland.com

2   The Quotations Page, Theoprastus from Diogenes Laerties, "Lives of Eminent Philosophers, www.quotationspage.com

3   Patton, Lieutenant General George S., *War As I Knew It*, 1947, as quoted in Tsouras, Peter G., *Warriors' Words*, Cassell Arms and Armor, London, 1992, p. 172

4   "Army to continue to improve body armor," Washington Update, AUSA *News*, Arlington, Virginia, 2/06

5   Marshall, Brigadier General S. L. A., *The Soldier's Load and the Mobility of a Nation*, The Marine Corps Association, Arlington, Virginia, 1980, p. 71

6   Marshall, Brigadier General S. L. A., *The Soldier's Load and the Mobility of a Nation*, The Marine Corps Association, Arlington, Virginia, 1980, p. iii

7   Marshall, Brigadier General S. L. A., *The Soldier's Load and the Mobility of a Nation*, The Marine Corps Association, Arlington, Virginia, 1980, p. 5

8   Fitton, p. 68

9   Holton, Bil, PhD, p. 142

10 CSM David E. Wright, as quoted in FM 22-100, Army Leadership, Hqs, D/A, August 1999, p. 5-2

11 Bowman, Lieutenant Colonel Donald C., written suggestion on draft manuscript.

12 Barber, Brace E., *Ranger School No Excuse Leadership*, Patrol Leader Press, Colorado Springs, CO, 2002, p. 41

13 Carruth, Gorton, & Ehrlich, Eugene, *The Giant Book of American Quotations*, Portland House, NY, 1988, p. 30

14 Fitton, p. 162

15 Hqs, D/A, FM 22-100, *Army Leadership*, August 1999, p. 5–16

16 Wikipedia Encyclopedia On Line

17 FM 22-100, p. 5–16

18 Peters, Ralph, *Beyond Terror*, Stackpole, Mechanicsburg, Pennsylvania, 2002, p. 205

19 Juvenal, Quoted in *The Great Bathroom Book*, Vol. II, Anderson, Stevens E., Ed., Compact Classics, Inc., Salt Lake City, UT, 1993, p. 503

20 FM 22-100, p. 5–38

21 Birch, CSM Greg, E-mail to author, dated 8/4/04

22 Tsouras, Peter G., *Warriors' Words*, Cassell Arms and Armour, London, 1992, p. 440

23 FM 22-100, p. 5–14

24 Holton, p. 41

25 Morshead, Lieutenant General Sir Leslie, quoted by Tsouras, Peter G., *Warriors' Words*, Arms and Armor Press, New York, 1994, p. 327

26 *Motivation Lombardi Style*, p. 6

27 Taylor, General Maxwell D., quoted by Tsouras, Peter G., *Warriors' Words*, Arms and Armor Press, New York, 1994, p. 225

28 FM 22-100, p. 5–13

SECTION VII: PERSONAL DEVELOPMENT

1   *Motivation Lombardi Style*, Curtis Management Group, Indianapolis, IN, Published by Celebrating Excellence, Inc., Lombard Lloyd, IL, 1992, dust cover

2   *Motivation Lombardi Style*, p. 33

3   BG (Ret.) Herbert J., ed., *The Reasons Why*, 7/1/92, p. 16

4   Hifler, Joyce Sequiche, *A Cherokee Feast of Days*, Council Oaks Books, Tulsa, OK, 1992, p. 68

5   Bennett, William J., Editor, *The Book of Virtues*, Simon & Schuster, NY, 1993, p. 101

6   Fitton, p. 38

7   General Mathew B. Ridgway, 'Leadership,' *Military Review*, 10/1966, as quoted in Tsouras, Peter G., *Warriors' Words*, Cassell Arms and Armour, London, 1992, p.116

8   Hqs, D/A, *FM 22-100, Army Leadership*, August 1999, p. B-2

9   quotationspage.com/quotes/Mark-Twain/31

10 Field Marshall Viscount Slim, *Courage and Other Broadcasts*, 1957, as quoted in Tsouras, Peter G., *Warriors' Words*, Cassell Arms and Armour, London, 1992, p. 268

11 Reingold, Jennifer, "Soldiering On," *Fast Company*, Sep 2004, p.72

12 James, William, "The Energies of Men," *Man and Society*, Vol. 7, Gateway to the great Books, Encyclopedia Britannica, Inc, Chicago, 1963, p. 162

13 Shakespeare, "Julius Caesar," *The Oxford Dictionary of Quotes*, London, 1955, p. 449

14 Chamberlain, p. 20

15 Chamberlain, p. 19

16 Ogburn, Charlton, Jr., *The Marauders*, Harper & Brothers,. NY, 1959, p 286–287

17 Bowman, James, "The Oscar for Historical Accuracy Goes To ..." *Wall Street Journal*, 3/19/99, p. A18

18 Flavious Vegetius Renatus, *Military Institutions of the Romans*, c. AD 378, as quoted in Tsouras, Peter G., *Warriors' Words*, Cassell Arms and Armour, London, 1992, p. 50

19 McCain, John, "In Search of Courage," *Fast Company*, September 2004, p. 52

20 McCain, p. 47

21 Sequichie Comingdeer, as quoted in *A Cherokee Feast of Days*, by Hifler, Joyce Sequichie, Council Oaks Books, Tulsa, OK, 1992, p. 11

22 Bennett, William J. *The Book of Virtues*, Simon & Schuster, NY, 1993, p. 441

23 McCain, p. 52

24 Bowman, Lieutenant Colonel (Ret.) Don, in note to author

25 Curtis, Bryan, ed., *Quotations from the Presidents of the United States*, Rutledge Hill Press, Nashville, TN, 2002, p.143

26 CSA William G. Bainbridge, as quoted in *FM 22-100, Army Leadership*, Hqs, D/A, August 1999, p. 5–11

27 Curtis, Bryan, ed., p. 173

28 Curtis, Bryan, ed., p. 201

29 Good Quotations by Famous People, Collected by Dr. Gabriel Robbins, University of Virginia, Taken from the Web

30 The Quotation Page, www.quotationspage.com

31 Brigadier General S. L. A. Marshall, *Men Against Fire*, 1947, as quoted in Tsouras, Peter G., *Warriors' Words*, Cassell Arms and Armour, London, 1994, p. 445

32 Hqs, D/A, *FM 21-20*, Physical Fitness Training, 9/30/1992, p. iii

33 Stokesbury, James L., *A Short History of the Korean War*, Quill William Morrow, NY, 1988, p. 103

34 Appleman, Roy E., *South to the Naktong, North to the Yalu*, U.S. Army Center for Military History, Washington, 1961, p. 109

35 Appleman, p. 717

36 Hqs, D/A, *FM 21-20*, Physical Fitness Training, 9/30/92, p. 1–3

37 Hqs, 3-75th Rgr Bn, *Physical Training SOP*, p.3

38 FM 21-20, *Physical Training*, D/A Dec, 1957, p. 3

39 Campbell, Joseph, *Columbus Ledger-Enquirer*, 7/4/04, p. F1

40 Fitton, p. 273

41 Hqs, D/A, *FM 22-100, Army Leadership*, p. 3–9

42 Hqs, D/A, *FM 22-100, Army Leadership*, p. 3–6

43 Lloyd, Brigadier General Herbert J., *The Reasons Why*, a compilation of quotes from a myriad sources, p. 99

44 Abrams, General Creighton, "Guidance when forming the First Ranger Battalion, Fall 1973

45 Hqs, D/A, *FM 22-100, Army Leadership*, August 1999, p. B-2

46 Schein, Edgar H., *Organizational Culture and Leadership*, Jossey Bass, San Francisco, 1985, p. 319 as quoted by Frank Kearney in the "Impact of Leaders on Organizational Structure: A 75th Ranger Regiment Case Study," 4/7/97

47 Schein, p. 313 as quoted in Kearney, LTC Francis H. Kearney III, "The Impact of Leaders on Organizational Culture: A 75th Ranger Regiment Case Study," 1997, p. 1

48 Allen, William B., editor, *George Washington: A Collection*, Liberty Fund, as quoted in "The American Spectator"

49 Collins, General J. Lawton, quoted in Hqs, D/A, *FM 22-100, Army Leadership*, August, 1999, p. 2–8

50 McDonald, Forrest, "Today's Indispensable Man," in *Patriot Sage*, Gregg, Gary L. II, and Spalding, Matthew, editors, ISI Books, Wilmington, DE, 1999, p. 24

51 Barilleaux, Ryan J., "Foreign Policy and the First Commander in Chief," in *Patriot Sage*, Gregg , Gary L. II, and Spalding, Matthew, editors, ISI Books, Wilmington, DE, 1999, p. 162

52 Gregg, Gary L., and Spalding, Matthew, "Introduction," in *Patriot Sage*, Gregg , Gary L. II, and Spalding, Matthew, editors, ISI Books, Wilmington, DE, 1999, p. 2

53 Gregg, Gary L., and Spalding, Matthew, p. 2

54 Freeman, Douglas Southall, *Washington*, an abridgment by Richard Harwell of the seven volume *George Washington*, Charles Scribner's Sons, NY, 1968, dust cover

55 Patton, Robert A., Ed., *Leadership Quotations from the Military Tradition*, Westview Press, Boulder, 1990, p. 130

56 Nix, Dusty, "Top Brass," Columbus Ledger, 10/15/00, p. F1

SECTION VIII: HOME FRONT

1 Malloy, Merritt, & Sorensen, Shauna, *The Quotable Quote Book*, Citadel Press, NY, 1990, p. 195

2 Milton, "On His Blindness," as quoted in *The Oxford Dictionary of Quotations*, Oxford University Press, Oxford, London, 1955, p. 351

3 LaCamera, Mrs. Paul, in note to author

4 Fleming, Thomas, *Washington's Secret War*, HarperCollins, NY, 2005, p. 185

5 Peters, Ralph, *Beyond Baghdad: Postmodern War and Power*, Stackpole Books, Mechanicsburg, PA, 2003, p. xxiii

6   Quoted by Major Michael S. Galloucis, "The Military and the Media," *Army*, Aug 1996, p. 14

7   Napoleon, ed. Herold, *The Mind of Napoleon*, 1955, as quoted by Tsouras, Peter G., *Warriors' Words*, Cassell Arms and Armour, London, 1992, p. 51

8   Holmes, Oliver Wendell, Jr., as quoted by Colonel Charles D. Cooper, USAF Ret., *The Retired Officer Magazine*, Mar 1991, p. 4

9   Powell, General Colin, CJCS, Message to Operation DESERT SHIELD Commanders, 1990, quoted in "Media and the Tactical Commander," Center for Army Lessons Learned. Ft. Leavenworth, KS, December 1992, p. 1

10 Schwarzkopf, General Norman, Message to OPERATION DESERT SHIELD Commanders, 1990, quoted in "Media and the Tactical Commander," Center for Army Lessons Learned, Ft. Leavenworth, KS, December 1992, p. 1

11 Johnson, Dr. Douglas, Professor, U.S. Army War College, in note to author

12 Vuono, General Carl E., Former Army Chief of Staff, 1990, quoted in *Media and the Tactical Commander*, Center for Army Lessons Learned. Ft. Leavenworth, Kansas, December 1992, p. 17

13 Nix, p. F1

14 Sidle, MG (Ret.) Winant, "Public Affairs Open Lines Important," *Vietnam 10 Years Later*, Defense Information School. Ft. Benjamin Harrison, IN, 1983, p. 89

15 Woodring, CDR Marcus E., "Build Trust with the Media," *Proceedings*, December, 2001, p. 90

16 Woodring, p. 90

17 Woodring, p. 91

18 Words spoken by the mayor of Trois Ponts, Belgium, at ceremony honoring 50Eighth PIR veterans in 2001

19 Ketchum, Richard M., *The Winter Soldiers*, The Easton Press, Norwalk, CT, 1973, p. 331

20 Schwarzkopf, General H. Norman, with Petre, Peter, *It Doesn't Take a Hero*, Bantam Books, NY, 1992, p. 102

21 Rothenberg, Gunther E., "Veterans' Day," in Dupuy, Trevor Nevitt, ed., "Holidays: Days of Significance for All Americans," first printing, Franklin Watts, Inc., NY, 1965, p. 128

Section IX: Race and Gender

1 Cockfield, J. H., "All Blood Runs Red," Legacy: A Supplement to American Heritage, February/March 1995, p. 7–15, as quoted in "The Engines of our Ingenuity: No. 997, Gene Bullard," by John H. Lienhard at the University of Houston

2 "The Fallen," Army Times, 11/07/05, p. 29

3 Chambers, John Whiteclay II, American Military History, Oxford University Press, NY, 1999, p. 9

4 Dickey, SFC Connie E., "Fraternization policy gets DOD approval," The Bayonet, Ft. Benning, GA, 3/5/99, p. A1

5 Taylor, Karen, The Bayonet, 8/25/00, p. A1

6 Adams, Tony, "Soldiers: Military Should Stay out of Personal Relationships," The Benning Leader, Columbus, GA, 8/7/98, p. 11

7 Chambers, John Whiteclay II, American Military History, Oxford University Press, NY, 1999, p. 355

8 Chambers, John Whiteclay II, American Military History, Oxford University Press, NY, 1999, p. 357

9 Nix, Dusty, "Top Brass," Columbus Ledger-Enquirer 10/15/00, p. F1

10 Charen, Mona, "Lowering Bar for Women Hurts Military," Atlanta Constitution, 7/28/01, p. a17

11 Dempsey, Captain James K., "Up Is Our Only Option: Improving Army Policies on Gender Integration," ARMY, Nov 1998, p. 12

12 Final Report, Federal Advisory Committee Gender Integrated Training and Related Issues, (Kassebaum Committee), 12/16/97, Condensed Version, p. 3

13 Kassebaum Committee, Kassebaum Baker Report Recommendations, p. 3

14 "Women in Combat," The Presidential Commission on the Assignment of Women in the Armed Forces," Brassey's, Washington, 1992, p. 9

15 Brady, James, "Women in the Infantry?" Atlanta Constitution, 5/15/93, p. A21

16 Brady, p. A21

17 CMR Notes, April 2001, p. 1

18 CMR Notes, May–June 2001, p. 2

19 CMR Notes, May–June 2001, p.5

20 Puckett, Ralph, "Are Women Physically, Mentally Ready for War?" Benning Leader, 11/6/92, p. 1

21 Field and Nagl, p. 82

22   Field and Nagl, p. 82

23   Field and Nagl, p. 81

24   Birch, Command Sergeant Major Gregory, in written memorandum to author

25   Johnson, Dr. Douglas, in written notes to the author

26   Puckett, Ralph, "A Right to Fight?" *Columbus Ledger-Enquirer*, 11/9/97, p. F1

27   Field and Nagl, p. 81

28   Field and Nagl, p. 81–84

29   Puckett, Ralph, "A Right to Fight?" *Columbus Ledger-Enquirer*, 11/9/97, p. F1

30   Field and Nagl, p. 85

31   The Presidential Commission on the Assignment of Women in the Armed Forces, "Report to the President: Women in Combat," Brassey's, Washington, 1992, p. 43

Section X: Tactics and Strategy

1   Tsouras, Peter G., *Warriors' Words*, Cassell Arms and Armour, London, 1992, p. 332

2   Spence, Cong. Floyd D., "Defense Challenges for the Twenty-First Century," *Officer Review*, July 2001, p. 6

3   Roberts, Sen. Pat (R-KS) and Cleland, Sen. Max (D-GA) "Realistic Restraint: Seven Principles for Shaping a New National Security Strategy," Armed Forces Journal International, January 2001, p. 12

4   Cheney, Dick, VP Elect, Commentary, 1/7/01

5   Metcalf, Geoff, "How to Choose a Commander in Chief," WorldNetDaily. com, 2000

6   Tonelson, Alan, "Superpower without a Sword," (Foreign Affairs), Summer 1993, p. 170

7   Hess, Pamela, "CIA: China, Iran, Terrorism, pose worst threats" UPI, 2/7/01 (UPI) Internet

8   Dupuy, Trevor N., "How the War Was Won," *National Review*, April 1, 1991, p. 30

9   "Army Announces FY '95 Proposed Budget," *The Bayonet*, 2/25/94, p. 1

10   Shalikashvili, General John M., *TROA Magazine*, December 1994, p. 63

11   "Shelton: Strategy, Structure Must Be in Balance," *AUSA News*, Feb 2001, p. 1

12 Sun Tzu, *The Art of War*, c. 500 BC, tr. Griffith, as quoted in Tsouras, Peter G., *Warriors' Words*, Cassell Arms and Armour, London, 1992, p. 353

13 Charlton, Charles, ed., *The Military Quotation Book*, St. Martin's Press, NY, 1990, p. 21

14 Ent, Uzal W., "War on a Shoestring," *Military History*, June 2000, p. 41–42

15 Stokesbury, James L., *A Short History of the Korean War*, William Morrow, NY, 1990, p. 41

16 Bowman, Lieutenant Colonel (Ret.) Don, in note to author. I am indebted to him for this astute observation

17 Ent, Uzal W., "War on a Shoestring," *Military History*, June 2000, p. 41–42

18 Hastings, Max, *The Korean War*, Simon & Schuster, NY, 1987, p. 58

19 Fehrenbach, p. 23

20 Hastings, Max, *The Korean War*, Simon & Schuster, NY, 1987, p. 69

21 Fehrenbach, p. 87

22 Stokesbury, James L., *A Short History of the Korean War*, William Morrow, NY, 1990, p. 21

23 Charlton, p. 4

24 Bowden, Mark, "Black Hawk Down," Atlantic Monthly Press, 1999, p.333

25 *Holy Bible*, The New King James Version, Thomas Nelson Publishers, NY, 1979, p. 251–252

26 Crane, Stephen, *The Red Badge of Courage*, Dover Publications, Mineola, NY, 1990, p. 27–28

27 Marshall, BG S. L. A., *The River and the Gauntlet*, William Morrow & Co., NY, 1953, p. 290

28 Stokesbury, James L., *A Short History of the Korean War*, William Morrow, NY, 1988, p. 106–109

29 Moore, Lieutenant General Harold G., and Galloway, Joseph, p. 255

30 Arnold, Major General S. L., "Somalia: An Operation Other Than War," *Military Review*, December 1993, p. 26

31 Johnson, Harold K., "The Role of the United States Army," Address, Portland, OR, Military Government Association Convention, 5/29/63

32 Powell, Colin L., "U. S. Forces: Challenges Ahead," *Foreign Affairs*, Winter 92/93, p. 38

33 Defense Report, "The U.S. Army at the Dawn of the 21st Century: Over-committed and Underresourced," AUSA Institute of Land Warfare, Jan 2001, p.1.

34 Shinseki, General Eric K., Chief of Staff of the Army, in testimony before Congress, 9/27/00

35 Dao, James, "Army Says Unit Is Unprepared for War Duty," *New York Times*, 3/29/01, Internet

36 Bassett, Lieutenant Colonel Rick, Response to Questionnaire

37 Pasquarette, Lieutenant Colonel James, Response to Questionnaire

38 Moskos, Charles, "Peacekeeping Improves Combat Readiness," *Commentary*, 4/26/01, Internet

39 Arnold, S. L., p. 26

40 Grange, MG David, Speaking to 75th Ranger Regiment officers, in 2002

41 Cucolo, Colonel Tony, "Chaos and Ambiguity: Leadership in the SASO Environment," Briefing to 75th Rgr Rgt Mangoday Panel, 4/17/01

42 Pasquarette, Lieutenant Colonel James, response to questionnaire

43 Bassett, Lieutenant Colonel Rick, response to questionnaire

44 Sun Tzu, p. 66

45 Pearson, Brigadier Willard, "Find 'em, Fix 'em, Finish 'em," *The Always First Brigade*, January 2006, p. 4

46 Churchill, Sir Winston S., 13 May 1940, in the House of Commons, as quoted in Tsouras, Peter G., *Warriors' Words*, Cassell Arms and Armour, London, 1992, p. 455

47 Curtis, p. 327

48 Ouimette, Dan, Pensacola *Civitan*, 2/19/03

49 AP Report, SIRO Intelligence Briefing, 9/5/01

50 Terrorism Resource Center, TRC@Terrorism.com

51 Economist Home Page, "Reacting to Terrorism," The Economist Newspaper Limited, 1996

52 Terrorism Resource Center, TRC@Terrorism.com

53 "What Is Terrorism?" *The Economist*, 1996, Web site

54 Terrorism Resource Center

55 *The Economist*, 1996, Web site

56 "What Is Terrorism?" *The Economist*, 1996, Web site

57 Deutch, John M., DCI, Testimony before the Permanent Subcommittee on Investigations of the Senate Committee on Government Affairs, 3/20/96, Terrorism Resource Center, TRC@Terrorism.com

58 Mahnaimi, Uzi, and Walker, Tom, "Defectors Say Iraq Tested Nuclear Bomb," *Sunday Times*, London, 2/25/01

59 "CIA: Iran Seeking High-Tech Weapons," *Atlanta Constitution*, 9/8/01, p. A9

60 Geewax, Marilyn, "Attack from Cyberspace," *Atlanta Constitution*, 8/12/01, p. C1

61 "Combating Terrorism, Preserving Freedom," *Cato Policy Report*, Nov./Dec. 1996, p. 7

62 "Reacting to Terrorism," The Economist Home Page, 1996

63 Rosenthal, A. M., "Invitation to Murder," NY Times Web site, July 1996

64 Haney, Eric L., "Violent Import Has Taken Root," *The Atlanta Constitution*, 1/24/97, p. A17

65 Sloan, Stephen, "Terrorism: National Security Policy and the Home Front," edited by Stephen Pelletiere, published by The Strategic Studies Institute of the U.S. Army War College, May 1995

66 Wilkerson, Paul, "Terrorism: Motivations and Causes," Canadian Security Intelligence Service, Commentary No. 53, January 1995

67 Bush, President George W., "Bush's Address to the Nation," *Columbus Ledger*, 9/12/01, p. A4

68 Houston, Colonel James, "Wanted: International Treaty Against Terrorism," *Officer Review*, May 1997, p. 8

69 "Reacting to Terrorism," The Economist Home Page, 1996

70 Greenwood, Bryon E., "The Anatomy of Change: Why Armies Succeed or Fail at *Transformation*," Institute of Land Warfare, *AUSA News*, Arlington, Virginia, Sep 2000, p. v

71 "Army Report: Research and Development: Enabling Transformation," *AUSA News*, Arlington, Virginia, Oct 2000, p. 9

72 Stevens, Sen. Ted, "The Army Must Transform," *AUSA News*, Nov. 2000, p. 6

73 Hall, Wayne M., "The Paradox: The Army's Preparation for Conflicts of the 21st Century," Institute of Land Warfare, Arlington, Virginia, Oct. 2000, p. v

74 "Objective Force Is Needed for Relevancy," *AUSA News*, Apr 2001, p. 2

75 "AUSA Transformation Panel Briefing," *AUSA News*, 10/26/00, p. 1

76 Offley, Ed, "Outside Experts Uncertain of Success for Army Transformation Effort," *Stars and Stripes Omnimedia*, 12/19/00, p. 1

77 Shinseki, General Eric K., *Retired Officer*, Jan. 2000, p. 52

78 Shinseki, p. 53

79 Shinseki, p. 53

80 Maddox, Sergeant Michael, "Objective Force Needs High-Speed Strategic Lift," *Bayonet*, 8/3/01, p. A1

81 Maddox, p. A1

82 Stevens, Sen. Ted, "The Army Must Transform," *AUSA News*, Nov. 2000, p. 6

83 "Objective Force Is Needed for Relevancy," *AUSA News*, Apr 2001, p. 2

84 Hall, Wayne M., "The Janus Paradox: The Army's Preparation for Conflicts of the 21st Century," Institute of Land Warfare, Arlington, Virginia, Oct. 2000, p. v

85 "Army Transformation," Transformation Brief—Short Version, 10/17/00, p. 5, USAIC

86 Stine, Jason, CATD, TIS, Ft. Benning, Georgia, E-mail, 9/29/01

87 Stone, Colonel Frank, CATD, TIS, Ft. Benning, Georgia, E-mail, 9/29/01

88 "Army Transformation," Transformation Brief—Short Version, 10/17/00, Slide 7 R, USAIC

89 Tiboni, Frank, "Officials: No Delay in Fielding of First IBCT," *Army Times*, 9/24/01, p. 44

90 "Army Unveils Wheeled Armored Vehicles for Lewis Brigades," *Washington Update*, AUSA Institute of Land Warfare, Arlington, Virginia, Dec 2000, p. 1

91 "Army Unveils Wheeled Armored Vehicles for Lewis Brigades," *Washington Update*, AUSA Institute of Land Warfare, Arlington, Virginia, Dec 2000, p. 1

92 "Army Unveils Wheeled Armored Vehicles for Lewis Brigades," p. 1

93 Shelton, General Henry H. Shelton, "Professional Education: The Key to Transformation," *Parameters*, Autumn 2001, p. 16

94 Shelton, p. 16

95 "Strategic Responsiveness: New Paradigm for a Transformed Army," *Defense Report*, AUSA News, Arlington, Virginia, Oct 2000, p. 1

96 Maddox, Sergeant Michael, p. A1

97 McMaster, Major H. R., *Dereliction of Duty*, Harper Collins, New York, 1997, p. 333–334

98 Summers, Colonel Harry G., Jr., *Vietnam War Almanac*, Facts on File Publications, New York, 1985, p. 1

99 McNamara, Robert S., *In Retrospect*, Random House, New York, 1995, p. 321

100 McNamara, p. 154

101 McNamara, p. 164

102 Rusk, Dean, *As I Saw It*, W. W. Norton & Co., New York, 1990, p. 434

103 Goulding, Phil, "A Lesson from Vietnam 'The Truth Is Not Enough'" *Vietnam 10 years later*, Defense Information School. Ft. Benjamin Harrison, Indiana, 1983, p. 30

104 McNamara, p. 181

105 McNamara, p. 333

106 Rusk, Dean, p. 493

107 Rusk, Dean, p. 493

108 Fitton, p. 302

109 Brady, Major General (Ret.) Patrick H., "United States has become a land of lost ideals," *Ledger-Enquirer, Columbus*, Georgia, 5/22/98, p. A13

110 Connerly, Robert E., "To Die For," *Atlanta Constitution*, 10/11/95

111 Nordyke, Phil, *All American All the Way*, Zenith Press, St. Paul, Minnesota, 2005, p. 627

112 McAlister, George A., *Alamo: The Price of Freedom*, Docutex, Inc., San Antonio, Texas, 1988, p. 161

113 Moore, Lieutenant General Harold G., and Galloway, Joseph L., p. 73

SECTION XI: THE GOAL

1 Eisenhower, General Dwight D., quoted by Fitton, Robert A. ed., *Leadership Quotations from the Military Tradition*, Westview Press, 1994, p. 293

2 Fallows, James, quoted by Fitton, Robert A. ed., *Leadership Quotations from the Military Tradition*, Westview Press, 1994, p. 294

INDEX

10th Special Forces Group, 4, 21–22, 67, 166–167, 206, 237
25th Infantry Division, 32
"40 & 9," 36–37, 126
65th Regimental Combat Team, 52–54, 209
75th Ranger Regiment, 3, 5, 12, 24, 31–32, 43, 59–60, 63–64, 68, 86–87, 105–106, 130–131, 140, 150, 165, 172, 181, 188, 236–237, 254, 258, 281
   junior leaders and, 32
   Physical Training SOP, 236
   See also specific topics
101st Airborne Division, 24, 27, 32, 68, 71–72, 79–80, 135, 307
502nd Infantry, 16–20
507th Ordnance Maintenance Company, 36

A
Abrams, Creighton, 23, 86, 244–245
Abshire, David M., 202
Academie Francaise, 225
Adams, Henry, 140
Adams, John, 247
Afghanistan, 78, 135
after action reviews (AARs), 9, 22, 105–108, 135, 232
Agincourt, Battle of, 92
Alexander the Great, 15–16
Allen, William B., 247

Ammerman, Jim, 67–68
Anderson, Dorian, 67
Antonia, Keith, 188–190
Apaches, 88–89
Aristotle, 220
Armed Forces Journal International, 288
Army, 136, 147
Army Combat Action Badge (CAB), 40
Army Leadership (FM 22-100), 42, 76, 85, 91, 105, 109, 152
   Army school system, 208–209
   courage, 223
   junior leaders, 163–164
   mentoring, 202–203
   punishment, 205–206
   training, 187
Army War College, 74, 281
Arnold, Steven L., 167–168, 299, 301, 305
artillery, 143–144
As I Saw It (Rusk), 324, 326–327
Aspin, Les, 279, 289
Athenian Warrior Creed, 218
atrocities, Army values and, 109–116

B
Bainbridge, William G., 231
Baker, Russell, 112
Barber, Brace E., 200
Barr, Roseanne, 253

Basic Combat Training (BCT), 125–129, 220

Basic Combat Training Brigade (BCTB), 37

Basic Officer Leadership Course II (BOLC II), 56–57

Bassett, Rick, 306

being there, 16–20

Ben Franklin in Paris, 267

Bennett, William J., 113

Bennis, Warren: *Training and Development Journal*, 106

Berry, Steve, 68–70

"Big Four," 63–64

Birch, Greg, 43, 172, 208, 236, 281

Blair, Clay: *Ridgway's Paratroopers*, 161

Bowman, Don, 179–180, 255

Bowman, James, 100, 229, 229–230

Boyd, Dick, 18

Bradley, Omar N., 20, 51, 226

Brady, Patrick, 329

Branch Immaterial Course, 75–76

Bryant, Bear, 28

Bugle Notes, 157

Bullard, Eugene, 273

Bush, Doug, 227

Bush, George W., 287, 290, 301, 311, 316, 324

C

Campbell, Dave, 18

Campbell, Joseph, 239

Camus, Albert, 221

Carter, Jimmy, 315

casualties, 149–151
    leave no man behind, 170–172
    "manhandling" of, 151

chain of command, 152–153

Chamberlain, Joshua Lawrence, 101, 117–124, 227–228

chaplains, 67–70, 242

character, 100–101

chemical warfare, 154–156

Cheney, Dick, 283, 288

Churchill, Winston, 311

Clanton, Wilbert, 273–274

Clark, Bob, 32

Clarke, Bruce C., 62

Clausewitz, Carl von, 110, 113

Cleland, Max, 288

Cohen, William, 126, 275

Collins, Arthur S., Jr., 125

Collins, J. Lawton, 247

Collins, Rip, 146

commitment, 23–25

Connely, Robert E., 329

Connett, Bud, 68, 145–146

cooks, 210–211

cooperation, 71–72

courage, 223–230

Courtney, Tom, 19, 145–146

Crane, Stephen: *Red Badge of Courage*, 298

Creed of the Noncommissioned Officer, 218

Cronin, Barney, 177–178

Cronkite, Walter, 315

Cuculo, Tony, 305

Cummings, Barney, 161

Cummings, William Thomas, 67

D

Dade, Francis L., 157–159

d'Albert, Charles, 91

Danford, Dan, 146

Dawson, Frank, 4

Defense Advisory Committee on Women in the Services (DACOWITS), 187, 279

Dereliction of Duty (McMaster), 325

Desert Shield/Desert Storm, 290, 318

Dickey, Connie E., 275

Dien Bien Phu, 52

disasters, 160–164

discipline, 33, 138–139

Discovery, Inc., 32, 59–60, 277–278

Doolittle Board, 294
Downing, Wayne A., 60

E
Edison, Thomas Alva, 232
Eighth Army, 292–295
Eighth Army Ranger Company, 4,
    32, 63–64, 82, 107–108, 144,
    153, 158, 161, 170, 178, 188,
    227, 273, 294
  leader rotations and, 162
Eisenhower, Dwight D., 26, 77, 197,
    335
Ent, Uzal W., 293
ethics, 110–116
excellence, 244–246
Expert Field Medic Badge (EFMB),
    39–40
Expert Infantryman Badge (EIB),
    39–40
experts, 73–74

F
Fallows, James, 335
Family Readiness Group, 254
feet, care of, 200–201
Fehrenbach, T. R., 185
  This Kind of War, 131–132
Field, Kim, 280
Fischer, David Hackett, 176
fitness, physical, 57
FM 21-20. See Physical Training (FM
    21-20)
*FM 22-100. See Army Leadership (FM
    22-100)*
FM 100-1, 109
Fogelman, Ronald, 110
Franklin, Benjamin, 200
Franks, Tommy, 78
fraternization, 275–276
Freeman, Douglas Southall: *George
    Washington*, 247–248
fundamentals, attention to, 9–10,
    181–183

G
gender
  integration, 277–283
  norming and, 128, 282–283
  pregnancy and, 279–280
  single-parent families and, 280
  standards-based requirements and,
    282
Geneva Conventions, 112, 115–116
George Washington (Freeman),
    247–248
Gettysburg, 118, 121
Gideon, 298
Global War on Terrorism (GWOT),
    23, 33–34
Gordon, Gary, 172
Gordon, John B., 122
Gore, Al, 287
Graham, Billy, 147
Grange, David, 305
Grant, Ulysses S., 16, 20, 28
Gray, Jim, 7–8
Greece, 21–22
Green, Luke, 6
Gutmann, Stephanie: *The Kinder,
    Gentler Military*, 279

H
Harding, Warren G., 231
Haught, Vernon L., 86, 329–330
Hay, John, 173
Henry V, 90–93
Herodotus, 94
Herrick, Henry, 142–143
Hitler, Adolf, 16
Ho Chi Min, 296
Holmes, Oliver Wendell, Jr., 260
Holton, Bil, 35, 55, 197, 199, 210
Holy Bible, 298
honesty, 247–249
Honorary Colonel, 1, 3–12, 105, 181,
    188, 258

I
"I Am the Infantry," 218
impact on others, 212–213
Infantry Officer Basic Course
     (IOBC), 227
"In Flanders Fields" (McCrae), 268
In Retrospect (McNamara), 323–326
Institute of Land Warfare Defense
     Report, 303
insubordination, 51–54
integrity, 57
     See also honesty
Interim Brigade Combat Team
     (IBCT), 319–321
Iraq, 224

J
James, William, 225
Jenkins, Sean, 107–108
Johnson, Douglas, 261
Johnson, Harold K., 301
Johnson, Jim, 106
Johnson, Lyndon B., 324–325
Joint Readiness Training Center
     (JRTC), 8
Jones, June, 182
Judy, Bill, 171, 178
Juvenal, 205

K
Kassebaum Committee, 126–127,
     128, 278
Kearney, Frank, 106
Keegan, John: *Mask of Command*, 16
Keen, Ken, 11, 59, 106–107, 258
Kelly, Frank, 268
Kernan, William F. "Buck," 31
Kerwin, Walter T., 327
Killer Angels, 118, 121
Kinder, Gentler Military, The
     (Gutmann), 279
Korean War, 133–134, 144, 184–185,
     234–235, 292–295, 298–300
Koster, Sam, 115

Kramer, Jerry, 212
Krulak, Charles, 109, 288–289
Kupau, Dick, 146

L
LaCamera, Paul, 5, 11, 60, 237,
     258
Lasley, Paul, 155
Leader's Guide to After Action Reviews
     (TC 25-20), 105
LeMoyne, John, 27, 248
Le Storti, Anthony J., 71
Leszczynski, William J., Jr., 3–4, 11,
     150
Levin, Carl, 224
Lewis, Francis, 67, 115
light armored vehicle (LAV), 320
listening, 197–199
Lombardi, Vince, 138, 181, 217
Long Range Reconnaissance Patrols
     (LRRPs), 173–175

M
MacArthur, Douglas, 52, 107, 114,
     117, 130
Maher, John, 142
mail, 241–242
Malone, "Bud," 167, 207
Malone, Dandridge M. "Mike," 109
Mangan, James T., 29
Mangodays, 6
marksmanship, 176–180
Marlborough, Duke of, 42
Marshall, S. L. A., 43, 134, 145, 165,
     234
     The River and the Gauntlet, 160
     A Soldier's Load, 195
Mask of Command (Keegan), 16
Matheson, Salve, 18, 206
Maurice, Emperor, 149, 184, 208
Mayor, Trois Ponts, Belgium, 265
McCain, John, 136, 229
McChrystal, Stanley, 5, 7, 11, 63,
     165–166, 237

McCrae, John: "In Flanders Fields," 268
McGee, John H., 153
McMaster, H. R.: *Dereliction of Duty*, 325
McNamara, Robert: *In Retrospect*, 323–326
MEDEVAC, 150
"Media and the Tactical Commander," 261
media relations, 260–264
medication, 81–82
medics, 150–151, 242–243
Mendez, Louis G., 227
mentoring, 202–204
Merrill's Marauders, 163
Merrill's Marauders (Ogburn), 228–229
Michaelis, John, 184–185
Military History, 293
Milton, John, 254
misfits, 205–207
Mission Essential Task List (METL), 62, 139
mistakes, 231–233
Mitchell, Brian
  Weak Link, 279
  Women in the Military, 279
Mobile Gun System, 321
Mogadishu, 135
Moniac, David, 158
Montross, Lynn, 154
Moore, Harold G. "Hal," 81, 134–135, 143, 149–150, 172, 331
Morshead, Leslie, 210
motivation, soldiers and, 35–41
Mowery, Larry, 308
Murphy, James J., 68
Murphy's War Laws, 47–50
My Lai, 115

N
Nagl, John, 280
Nana, Chief, 85–87, 88–89

Napoleon, 260
nation building, 302–303
Nemetz, Donald A., 17–18
Newman, Aubrey "Red," 59
New York Times, 112
Nix, Dusty, 262
Nixon, Craig, 5–6, 11, 43, 258
North Vietnamese Army (NVA), 81, 134–135, 296
Nuclear Biological Chemical NCO, 155
Null, Jack, 75–76

O
Odom, Ronald G., 17–19
Ogburn, Charlton: *Merrill's Marauders*, 228–229
Operation Appreciation, 185
Operations Other Than War (OOTW), 301–306
organizational culture, 245
Ouimette, Dan, 311
Outward Bound, 277

P
Patton, George S., Jr., 31, 188, 195, 228
Pearson, Willard, 27, 307–308
Peers, William, 173
Peters, Ralph, 205, 257
Petramalo, Thomas, 17
physical fitness, 234–238
Physical Training (FM 21-20), 235–236, 237, 239–240
Piazza, Phil, 7–8
Pickering, Jimmy, 43–44
"Planning Document for the Leaders and Operational Stress Panels," 240
Platoon, 111–112
Pollock, David L., 171
Powell, Colin, 260–261, 301–302
public, education of, 257–259

public affairs officers (PAOs), 262, 264

Puckett, Jeannie, 253–254

Putnam, Israel, 176

R

race, 273–274

Ranger Creed, 97–99

Ranger Indoctrination Program (RIP), 86–87

Ranger Physical Assessment Test (RPAT), 236–237

Ranger School, 4, 38, 140–141, 200, 209, 237

readiness, 287–295

Reagan, Ronald, 75

Red Badge of Courage (Crane), 298

reluctance to kill, 145–147

"Report to the President: Women in Combat," 278

rest, importance of, 7–8, 241

Ridgway, Matthew, 19–20, 51–52, 163, 223, 248

Ridgway's Paratroopers (Blair), 161

Ritchie, R. Stephen, 111

River and the Gauntlet, The (Marshall), 160

Roberts, Pat, 288

Rogers, Robert, 157

Roosevelt, Eleanor, 229

Roosevelt, Franklin D., 231–232

Roosevelt, Theodore, 21, 231, 247

Rotary Club, 257–258

Rumsfeld, Donald, 224

Rusk, Dean: *As I Saw It*, 324, 326–327

S

safety, 9, 59–61

Santayana, George, 327

Savage, Ernie, 142–143, 163

Saving Private Ryan, 203

scheduling, 193–194

Schoomaker, Peter J., 35–36, 126

Schwarzkopf, Norman, 261

Schweikert, Kent, 24

Sears, Stephen W., 142

Sequichie Comingdeer, 229

Sergeant York, 178

Shakespeare, William, 90, 226

Shalikashvilli, John, 290

Shelton, Hugh, 291

Sherman, W. T., 28

Shinseki, Eric K., 42, 224, 303, 319

Shugart, Randy, 172

Slim, Viscount, 223–224

small unit leaders, 4–5

Soldier's Creed, 36, 85, 218–219

Soldier's Load (Marshall), 195

Soljeim, Tom, 68

Southey, Robert, 65

Spartans, 94–96

Spears, James L., 17

Spence, Floyd D., 287–288

stamina, 237

Stanton, Martin, 179

Stanton, Shelby L., 173

Starr, Bart, 217

stay-behind operational concept ("Bushmaster"), 307–310

Steuben, Baron von, 149

Stockdale, James Bond, 239

stress, reducing, 239–243

Sullivan, Gordon R., 318

Sumner, Gordon, 171

Sun Tzu, 292, 307

supporting fires, 142–144

T

Tactical Operations Center (TOC), 77–80

Talleyrand, 247

Task Force Ranger, 97–99

Task Force Soldier, 35–36, 39

Taylor, Maxwell D., 212, 221

Tenet, George, 290

terrorism, 311–317

cyberterrorism, 314–315

definition of, 313
mitigation of, 315–317
Theophrastus, 193
Thermopylae, Battle of, 94–95
This Kind of War (Fehrenbach),
    131–132
Thucydides, 184
Tower, John B., 209
Townsend, Steve, 106
training
    Basic, 125–129
    battle-focused, 130–132
    gender and, 126–129, 282–283
    goals, 55–56
    higher levels of, 10–11
    principles, 56–58
    tough, 184–187
    veterans and, 188–190
Training and Development Journal
    (Bennis), 106
Trainor, Bernard E., 184
transformation, 318–321
Travis, William Barret, 330
Truman, Harry, 52, 273, 292
Twain, Mark, 223

U
unexpected, the, 165–169
Uniform Code of Military Justice
    (UCMJ), 276
unit pride, 39

V
values, Army, 117–124
Vegetius, 292
veterans, honoring, 265–269
Vietnam War, 134–135, 142–143,
    149–150, 177, 307–308
    lessons learned, 322–327

Votel, Joe, 11, 130–131
Vuono, Carl E., 261

W
Wallace, William, 36
Walls, Billy G., 171
Wall Street Journal, 110–111
Warrior Ethos, 85–87, 96, 126
Washington, George, 247–249,
    265–267, 287
Waters, Allen, 273–274
Wavell, Earl, 160
Weak Link (Mitchell), 279
Weatherhead, Leslie D., 170
Webb, James, 278–279
weight carried by Soldiers, 195–196
Wellman, Paul, 88
Wheatley, Tom, 68
Whitehead, Alfred North, 220
Whitney, Courtney, 27
Wickham, John A., Jr., 110, 113
Will, George, 112
Wilson, Woodrow, 267
wives, Army, 24–25, 253–256
Wolfe, Tom, 244
women. *See* gender
"Women in Combat" (Army War
    College), 281
Women in the Military (Mitchell), 279
Woodring, Marcus E., 263
Woodyard, John D., 213
World War I, 267–268
Wright, David E., 198

X
Xenophon, 42

Z
"Zero Defects" mentality, 33

ABOUT THE AUTHOR

Colonel Ralph Puckett was an inaugural inductee into the United States Army Ranger Hall of Fame in 1992 for extraordinary valor and distinguished service as a Ranger qualified leader. He formed, trained, and commanded the Eighth Army Ranger Company in Korea as a second and, later, first lieutenant. He earned the Distinguished Service Cross for his actions on November 25-26, 1950.

Following the Korean War, Puckett served over two years in the U.S. Army Infantry School Ranger Department. As the first Ranger Advisor in the U.S. Army Mission to Colombia, he planned and established the Colombian Army Escuela de Lanceros (Ranger School). Later, he commanded "B" and "C" teams in the 10th Special Forces Group in Germany.

He was awarded a second Distinguished Service Cross in the Republic of Vietnam. Puckett's other decorations and awards include two Silver Stars, three Legions of Merit, two Bronze Stars, the Commendation Medal, ten Air Medals, and five Purple Hearts. In 2001, he was awarded the United States Special Operations Command Medal for his outstanding contributions to Special Operations.

Puckett is a qualified Master Parachutist and Glider Trooper. He has also earned the coveted U.S. Army Ranger Tab and the Lancero Badge from Colombia.

He is a 1949 graduate of the United States Military Academy and has a Master's Degree in Personnel Administration from George Washington University.

Retiring in 1971, he became the National Programs Coordinator of Outward Bound, Inc. He subsequently established Discovery, Inc., a leadership and teamwork development program that focused on "Personal Growth through Safe Adventure."

Still very active in military affairs, he has seved as the Honorary Colonel of the 75th Ranger Regiment for 12 years and as an Honorary Instructor at The Infantry School. Other honors include induction into the USAF Gathering of Eagles, appointment as an Ambassador of Goodwill by the Western Hemisphere Institute for Security Cooperation, selection as a Distinguished Graduate of the United States Military Academy, and selection as the Infantry's Doughboy Award recipient.

He lives in Columbus, GA with his wife, the former Jean Martin. They have two daughters, a son, and six grandchildren.

CPSIA information can be obtained at www.ICGtesting.com
Printed in the USA
LVOW060901281011

252499LV00002B/5/A